Tyrone Power

International Film Stars
Series Editor: Homer B. Pettey and R. Barton Palmer

This series is devoted to the artistic and commercial influence of performers who shaped major genres and movements in international film history. Books in the series will:

- Reveal performative features that defined signature cinematic styles
- Demonstrate how the global market relied upon performers' generic contributions
- Analyse specific film productions as case studies that transformed cinema acting
- Construct models for redefining international star studies that emphasise materialist approaches
- Provide accounts of stars' influences in the international cinema marketplace

Titles available:

Close-Up: Great Cinematic Performances Volume 1: America
edited by Murray Pomerance and Kyle Stevens

Close-Up: Great Cinematic Performances Volume 2: International
edited by Murray Pomerance and Kyle Stevens

Chinese Stardom in Participatory Cyberculture
by Dorothy Wai Sim Lau

Geraldine Chaplin: The Gift of Film Performance
by Steven Rybin

Tyrone Power: Gender, Genre and Image in Classical Hollywood Cinema
by Gillian Kelly

www.euppublishing.com/series/ifs

Tyrone Power

Gender, Genre and Image in Classical Hollywood Cinema

Gillian Kelly

EDINBURGH
University Press

Edinburgh University Press is one of the leading university presses in the UK. We publish academic books and journals in our selected subject areas across the humanities and social sciences, combining cutt ing-edge scholarship with high editorial and production values to produce academic works of lasting importance. For more information visit our website: edinburghuniversitypress.com

Edinburgh University Press Ltd
TheT un – Holyrood Road
12(2f) Jackson's Entry
Edinburgh EH8 8PJ

First published in hardback by Edinburgh University Press 2021

Typeset in 12/14 Arno and Myriad by
IDSUK (Dataconnection) Ltd

A CIP record for this book is available from the British Library
ISBN 978 1 4744 5294 6 (hardback)
ISBN 978 1 4744 5295 3 (paperback)
ISBN 978 1 4744 5296 0 (webready PDF)
ISBN 978 1 4744 5297 7 (epub)

Contents

Figures

Acknowledgements

Firstly, thank you to everyone at Edinburgh University Press for their enthusiasm and encouragement throughout this project, especially Gillian Leslie, Richard Strachan, Fiona Conn and Bekah Dey. To the series editors Homer B. Pettey and R. Barton Palmer for their kind words, and for including my book in this exciting series on international stars. Thanks also to Belinda Cunnison for copyediting the manuscript.

Many thanks to Jenny Reburn, Christine Geraghty, Oline Eaton, Hollie Price, Lucy Bolton, Lies Lanckman and Ryan Shand for invaluable feedback and comments.

Thanks to my best friend, Allison. To my family: Mum, Steven, Barry, Emma and Robyn, I love you all more than words can say.

This book is dedicated to the memory of Gran, Auntie Mae and Uncle Alan, forever remembered and missed.

Introduction

Star power

> I believe in one kind of immortality. People live in the people they leave behind. There are probably people who have passed away who have influenced you. So long as that influence remains, they are alive in you. Just because we happen to 'shuffle off this mortal coil' and leave some worm food behind, we are not dead, so long as someone remains on earth on whose life we have left some mark. (Power 1946)

This quotation comes from the 1946 *Screenland* article 'This is what I believe', allegedly written by actor Tyrone Power (1914–58). Set out in subsections revealing the actor's thoughts on life, death, immortality and religion, it presents something more contemplative than the light fare one tends to associate with film fan magazines. However, given that Power had just returned to Hollywood after active duty in the Marine Corps during World War II, these subjects take on a particularly dark and sombre tone at the pen, or typewriter, of Power. His concerns with leaving a mark and living in those left behind are apt themes with which to begin a book that aims to bring much-needed scholarly attention to the performance skills and star image of Power, who is a largely overlooked but extremely important star of Hollywood's studio era. Reappraising his career from various angles, mainly gender, genre and image, given Power's prominent good looks and the type of star he personified, there is a specific focus on the social construction of beauty, specifically male beauty, throughout. An oddly neglected concept in star studies, it is one that is crucial to discussions on Power, since it affected his on- and off-screen image at all stages of his career.

Although Power died aged just forty-four, his film career spanned three separate decades from the 1930s to the 1950s. Thus, aside from Chapter 7, which explores Power's off-screen image, each chapter focuses on a specific genre that he worked in. Mostly examining his progression, or lack thereof, chronologically within each genre, this study takes into account industrial developments, such as the evolution of Hollywood's sound era and the studio and star systems in which Power was a key player, while also focusing on the actor's career trajectory. A particularly noteworthy aspect of this genre approach is that, while Power appeared in some genres within a limited timeframe – for example, he made musicals only in the 1930s – his work in other genres spanned much longer time periods. Most obviously, his first and last films, made twenty-five years apart, were both dramas. Thus, while this book explores the advancement of Power's screen persona, it also places him within the historical and industrial timeframes in which he worked, helping to demonstrate how stardom and the industry itself functioned at specific periods. Consequently, each genre chapter helps cement ideas around Power's screen persona and its development, while granting a close reading of Power's performance skills and star image.

Power's evolution from pretty boy 'pin-up' in the 1930s to more mature action-adventurer near the close of his career allowed his star image to progress naturally as he entered early middle age, although he would never surpass it due to his premature death. Yet as will be discussed, Power was only permitted to display his diverse acting range after leaving his home studio, for example in Columbia's *The Long Gray Line* (John Ford, 1955) where he came his closest to character acting. Certainly, given Power's reported frustration at Twentieth Century-Fox limiting him to lightweight roles (Power 2014: 125), one of the studio's strangest decisions was to have him remake his early comedy *Love is News* (Tay Garnett, 1937) as *That Wonderful Urge* (Robert B. Sinclair, 1948) over a decade later, which seemed a regressive step for Power's career and image.

While a select few of his films, such as *Jesse James* (Henry King, 1939), *The Mark of Zorro* (Rouben Mamoulian, 1940) and *Nightmare Alley* (Edmund Goulding, 1947), have received some, albeit limited, attention within the academy, this book both expands on these studies by exploring Power's performance within them, while also paying attention to his more neglected work. Although Power has posthumously been best remembered as a swashbuckler (Finler 1984; Solomon 1988; Stephens 1995; Mayer and McDonnell 2007), he actually had very few roles of this kind. He has thus been misremembered and his important work in drama, comedy and war films have been overlooked and underexplored. Thus the six individual genre chapters forming the book's core, alongside the chapter on his extra-filmic image, work together to present an overview of how Power's image was constructed and developed both on- and off-screen throughout his career, and where the two personas interconnect or diverge. Accordingly, this book not only explores a neglected but significant star of Hollywood's studio era, but adds to the increasing body of scholarly work on individual stars whose previous omission within academic studies underestimates their major contributions to the success of their home studios, the Hollywood film industry and American culture of the mid-twentieth century overall.

Approaches

The approaches taken throughout the book are critical, theoretical and historical and include a discussion of all of Power's cinematic work. However, while some films are discussed at length, others receive less attention for reasons that will become apparent. Additionally, the final chapter, before a brief conclusion, explores a range of extra-filmic material concerning Power's off-screen persona, including magazine cover images, articles and reviews of his stage performances. Used collectively, these sources aid in producing a better understanding of Power's on-screen trajectory and how his off-screen image was presented to the public across his career.

This book's focus on Power's stardom, its alliance with his appearance and the construction of his persona in the range of genres discussed in the following chapters, places this work within the key areas of film and performance studies. As a film star, and one who was very much the focus of the camera's gaze, as well as the gaze of both his (usually) female co-stars and audiences throughout his career, Power was very much marketed as a star we are repeatedly invited to look at. In Power's films, female characters are often used as a surrogate for audiences, their desiring gaze helping draw attention to Power's appeal as much as lighting, framing and costume, and working to elicit a response from viewers. This is particularly true of his early career when he was being established as a male 'pin-up' in romantic comedies, dramas and musicals, but is also true of his later years when his manlier frame and mature handsomeness were highlighted to appeal to an audience that was ageing with him. Thus, visual and textual analysis are used to explore how Power's star persona and screen image shifted across his career. Furthermore, detailed textual analysis reveals how he was presented to spectators in relation to lighting, camera angle, costume, interaction with co-stars and so forth, the predominant focus being on a visual approach because of the continued emphasis placed on his beauty.

The on-screen analysis chapters also engage with performance studies in their account of how Power embodied a diverse range of characters and discussion of notable scenes in intricate detail concerning Power's bodily and vocal portrayals, which 'combine with other filmic elements to create character and spectacle' (McDonald 2019: 49). There are also discussions of tropes and themes that developed, changed or remained stable across his career, with possible explanations (an altering film industry, World War II, his inevitable ageing, or his move from contract star to independent actor).

This book is part of a welcome new wave of scholarly studies on overlooked film stars, to which my previous monograph on Power's contemporary Robert Taylor contributed (Kelly 2019). Since it is predominantly concerned with the construction and development of the individual star image of Hollywood actor Tyrone Power, it belongs first and foremost to the film studies subcategory of star studies. However, it is by no means limited to this subject area and research was conducted across a wealth of other disciplines, not least anthropology, sociology, philosophy, history and fine art, as well as theology, English, gender studies and theatre. This multi-disciplinary approach largely focuses on, first, the concept of beauty and its position as a social construction. Within the perimeters of this study, this principally involves exploring male beauty, which remains a neglected area across most disciplines except, arguably, fine art. Second, studies of masculinity and the male body are engaged with throughout in order to determine ways in which Power's body was presented to audiences and what this reveals about the specific construction of his star image, and of contemporary American masculinity more generally.

Socio-historical and industrial contexts must also be explored when engaging with the construction and progression of any star image and the performer's filmic output, since neither occurs in a vacuum. Thus Power's image and work are placed within their industrial, cultural and historical frameworks, as well as their social and ideological stimuli, allowing for broader concepts beyond his career to be explored. In Power's case, the industrial context is the Hollywood film industry of the early 1930s to the late 1950s, with a strong focus on Twentieth Century-Fox, since this was Power's home studio for most of his career. This period, known as Hollywood's classical era, brings up further industrial concerns regarding the studio and star systems, as well as filmmaking within the confines of the Production Code and later technological advancements such as

CinemaScope, a process developed by Twentieth Century-Fox in the 1950s and adopted by other studios in an attempt to fight the widespread popularity of television and entice audiences back into movie theatres.

Stars and films that were popular in certain time periods tell us much about producers' values and audiences' taste, as well as contemporaneous social change. While individual star images have often been considered in relation to specific types of films or eras (for example, Gene Kelly and the musical or James Stewart and the Western), with Jennifer Barnes recently exploring Laurence Olivier as a 'Shakespearean star' (2017), very few studies explore the whole of a star's career. I would argue that to understand a star persona and the important contribution an individual performer has made to cinema it is necessary to consider the whole of their career. The fact that Power began and ended his career in dramas brings the book full circle, allowing us to see how his body of work, as well as his corporeal body, changed over time, thus taking into account his physical appearance, the development of his performance skills and the types of roles he was given at specific time periods.

The findings are drawn from extensive viewing of all of Power's films and the examination of ephemeral material. Since the mid-1990s there have been great changes in how research is conducted, requiring researchers to develop academic digital literary skills to find, evaluate and write about material from digital platforms. We may also consider whether online files offer the same value as their three-dimensional counterparts, a point particularly pertinent when thinking about fan magazines and other historical ephemera, such as postcards and cigarette cards. Indeed, a digital file of a fan magazine gives us the same information and imagery as a physical copy, but the printed version has its own history and personal owner(s). Virtual documents can be interpreted only as images, whereas physical copies have a more immediate presence – we can touch them, smell them and see the rusty staples and yellowing pages of surviving copies of what was, essentially, throwaway material. We may own a physical copy where we cannot truly 'own' a digital one, even if we download it; therefore, we tend to put more value on something we can hold. Physical documents have individual journeys of ownership and a unique corporeal presence, whereas a digital copy can be viewed and downloaded by hundreds, if not thousands, of people while the original remains physically unchanged. This film ephemera, alongside the film texts themselves, are the non-written evidence used by film historians and the key focus of Chapter 7, which explores Power's presence within fan magazines across his career. Yet digital resources have added richness and diversity to research, allowing today's academics to invest less time than was traditionally the case, since digital files can be accessed from anywhere in the world without the need for travelling, looking up paper versions of index cards, searching shelves for books and documents, and so forth. It also means that we can conduct research from a fixed physical space, with less at stake in terms of time and monetary expense (travelling, accommodation, and so on) if a source, file or archive does not yield what was hoped. However, not everything is digitalised, especially in the case of more obscure stars or films, and we do still search catalogues and archives; therefore, these two journeys will continue to cross throughout the research period.

Likewise, with the advent of VHS in the 1970s, DVD in the 1990s and Blu-ray shortly afterwards, the primary source of interest here, the film itself, has become, in the words of Mark Parker and Deborah Parker, the 'attainable' text, now accessible for a wide audience to own and watch freely in their own homes as and when desired. Thus, the DVD 'embodies a bold experiment in not only the delivery of film but also its history', and is of particular use to those wishing to document film history (Parker and Parker 2011: viii–ix). Additionally, the ability to pause, rewind and replay scenes and individual moments is a vital tool for star studies scholars to examine subtle changes in performers' facial expressions, bodily gestures and vocal intonations, which are easily missed in a single viewing and were undoubtedly underappreciated by historical audiences seeing a film once in a darkened cinema surrounded by other people.

As discussed throughout the book, it is these fleeting but magical flashes, referred to by Murray Pomerance as 'virtuoso moments' (2019), that Power excelled in and that undeniably display his underappreciated acting skills, which have long been overlooked in favour of the visual spectacle of his breath-taking appearance on-screen. Although Power was unarguably a rare beauty, he was also an extremely talented actor. Detailed textual analysis of how he delivered his lines with impeccable pauses, momentary flashes of his eyes and minuscule bodily gestures highlight his performance skills which have been overshadowed by the overall visual spectacle of his presence on-screen. I suggest that his 'tall, dark, and strikingly handsome' persona is one reason for his being falsely remembered, as Joel W. Finler refers to him, as 'a likeable star of limited talent [but] not . . . a great actor' (1984: 84).

(Male) beauty

Being not only a top leading man of the era, but one repeatedly referred to as both beautiful and handsome, as well as in somewhat more derogatory terms like 'pretty boy', 'heartthrob' and 'sex symbol' by the press, undermined Power's status as a skilled performer. My primary concern here, however, is the social construction of male beauty, since this is the label most often applied to Power, and a concept that is greatly under-scrutinised in academia, particularly in film and star studies. The lack of scholarly writings on beauty may seem unusual given that Hollywood stars are often considered to be beautiful, but for the most part it continues to be female stars who are discussed in this way, and there remains a discomfort around using traditionally 'feminine' terms like 'beautiful' to describe male stars. Power, however, juxtaposes these two ideals since he was both beautiful and 'manly', as his work in male-driven genres such as war films and Westerns, and physical fights in his action-adventure films, clearly demonstrate.

The complex and changing idea of beauty is explored from its origins with the ancient Greek philosophers, such as Aristotle, who attempted to give the concept a concrete definition, through several centuries of deliberation and, finally, to the use of the term in academia today, predominantly within the discipline of fine art. In 1950, Eric Newton highlighted the multidimensional nature of the term by proposing to write a book about 'the meaning of a word', that word being 'beauty'. Newton begins, however, by suggesting that 'except within the vaguest limits, beauty cannot be described', nor does he feel it can provide the basis of a science since 'it cannot be measured in either quantity or quality' (1950: 9). Nonetheless, he concludes by suggesting that the definition of beauty 'is that aspect of phenomena which, when perceived by the senses ... has the power to evoke responses drawn from [an] accumulated experience' (1950: 204). Written during Power's lifetime, this idea can be applied to watching a film, particularly for historical audiences together in a theatre. Film unquestionably aims to evoke the senses, primarily of sight but also of sound, in order to incite a response from viewers. Thus, for example, the brightly lit close-ups of Power's beautiful face as he makes love to Norma Shearer in *Marie Antoinette* (W. S. Van Dyke, 1938) are designed to provoke a (collective) response from audiences watching these images being projected on a giant screen in a darkened theatre – particularly female viewers whom the film was predominantly aimed at.

Similarly, Doreen Bolger Burke notes that during art's Aesthetic movement in the US between the 1870s and 1880s, American artists strived 'not so much for truth to nature as for beauty', the painter's 'idealizing' tools, such as line, colour and shape, being carefully used to arrange compositions showing the 'distinction between the painted surface and the reality it represented' (1987: 329). The same could be said of Hollywood studios (the artists) and their presentation of stars (the subjects) to audiences, particularly since stars' faces were 'painted' with make-up (including the men), carefully lit and arranged in on-screen compositions and publicity stills that highlighted their beauty. Burke's conclusion that the Aesthetic movement was typically American in both its integration into the nation's mainstream culture and its capacity to 'retain some measure of its own originality, integrity and identity as the legacy of its principles strengths and enriches the fabric of our daily lives' (1987: 336) could again be applied to the Hollywood film industry and the impact it had, and still has, on our lives, from the impressive *mise en scène* of a Technicolor MGM musical to the stark black and white publicity stills of glamorous stars by George Hurrell.

Since there is a distinct lack of writing about male beauty, particularly within film studies, it is necessary to turn to the world of fine art, where studies on the concept of beauty have only recently been taken seriously. Discussing the relationship between art and beauty, Elizabeth Prettejohn poses several important questions: 'how have artists responded to speculations on the beautiful? Which works of art have been called beautiful, and why? What are we saying about these works when we call them beautiful, rather than finding them useful or informative?' (2005: 9). These questions are equally relevant to the frequent emphasis on the beauty of film performers over their abilities as believable performers or 'good' actors, although this is another loaded term, since what do we deem as a 'good' performance? In Power's case, as is true for many female stars such as Elizabeth Taylor, his physical beauty outweighs most discussions on his performance; with contemporary critics often focusing on his appearance over his talent (Finler 1984: 84; Stephens 1995: 293). Consequently, it appears as if beauty and usefulness/ skill are separate entities, thus, just as a beautiful piece of art cannot also be a useful one, a beautiful actor is rarely seen as also being a skilled one. Critical acclaim is more readily given to performers portraying plain or 'ugly' characters who are often depicted as more genuine and requiring additional acting skills, especially if the performers themselves are beautiful. This was certainly the case for Joan Fontaine in *Suspicion* (Alfred Hitchcock, 1941), Grace Kelly in *The Country Girl* (George Seaton, 1954) and Vivien Leigh in

A Streetcar Named Desire (Elia Kazan, 1951), who were made to look less attractive and won Academy Awards for their performances. Correspondingly, during the many interviews Power's eldest daughter, Romina Power, conducted for her book about her father, Power's beauty was the most dominant focus of both male and female interviewees' answers, mentioned as often as his friendliness and likeability and much more than his films or acting ability (Power 2014). Romina herself begins the book by saying she kept glossy photographs of her parents in her nightstand at school, noting that 'they were beautiful. Perfect' (2014: 1). She adds that, although her classmates would pause to look at both parents (her mother was Mexican actress Linda Christian), 'they dwelled longer on my father, always commenting on his good looks. Dreamy-eyed' (2014: 2).

According to Prettejohn, many critics, curators and artists within the field of fine arts have recently drawn 'a new attention to beauty as a significant issue of both contemporary life and contemporary art' (2005: 10). This is an idea I wish to transfer to film studies in order to re-evaluate stars like Power, whose acting skills and important contribution to the medium continue to be overlooked as a direct result of this focus on their looks. However, this is a complex argument, since it is often because of their striking appearance that performers achieve cinematic stardom. Prettejohn suggests that the love of beauty 'has seemed at best an evasion or escape from the problems of social reality, at worst a way of shoring up the status of the rich and powerful' (2005: 9); but the concept of beauty as a social construction, and what beauty means in any given historical timeframe or geographic location, varies greatly. Being just over a century old, cinema is a relatively new medium in comparison to fine art and has always been portrayed as an art form for the masses. Popular cinema, in particular Hollywood, has often been dismissively viewed as being for the lower classes, not fine art's 'rich and powerful' target audience. As Prettejohn advises, 'speculation about beauty cannot and should not be separated from the concrete practices of making, studying, and enjoying particular works of art' (2005: 10–11). This book applies the same principle to filmmaking, exploring ways in which studios manipulated star personas and dictated to audiences how they should view certain stars, using Power as a dominant case study.

Stardom

As with any scholarly account of a star, this book is indebted to the pioneering work of Edgar Morin (1961) and Richard Dyer (1979), whose initial writings on stars as the focus of serious academic work provide a foundation for academics to engage with film stardom within the academy. Christine Gledhill, Paul McDonald, Christine Geraghty, Martin Shingler and Ginette Vincendeau are just a few names to whose work I am also indebted. While undertaking the initial stages of my doctoral research at the University of Glasgow, which led to the completion of my first monograph on Robert Taylor, the field of star studies was a moribund area of film studies. However, with the release of the Star Decades: American Culture/American Cinema and the BFI Star Studies book series, alongside several conferences and symposiums dedicated exclusively to the scholarly study of stars, the last decade has seen star studies re-emerge as a highly respectable and exciting area of the discipline, with much important work still being done.

Stardom, and the notion of becoming a star, particularly within different historical time periods, is not a stable concept. Performers can become stars for different reasons, and stardom can be sustained, disappear, or, occasionally, re-emerge; thus, it is always in flux. Although today we may think of Frank Sinatra as an Oscar-winning actor and the singer dubbed 'The Voice of the Century', during his marriage to Ava Gardner he could win neither a movie role nor a concert booking. Similarly, Katharine Hepburn, now viewed as one of the greatest actresses of all time and the recipient of the most Oscars for Best Actress, was once deemed 'box office poison' before reviving her career with *The Philadelphia Story* (George Cukor, 1940) when she bought the rights to the stage play. Along with the likes of Taylor and Clark Gable, Power was one of the first generation of sound-era heartthrobs created to embody the romance and excitement of his silent-era predecessors, such as Rudolph Valentino and Douglas Fairbanks, for ever-expanding audiences. He even reprised some of their most famous roles in *Blood and Sand* (Rouben Mamoulian, 1941) and *The Mark of Zorro* respectively. Additionally, Fairbanks's final screen role was a brief cameo playing himself at a fictional film premiere in the Eddie Cantor vehicle *Ali Baba Goes to Town* (David Butler, 1937), which also featured Power in a similar 'role' as himself. Made by Twentieth Century-Fox, the construction of this scene meant that the newly formed studio could generate publicity for its top leading man, even though the footage was taken from an actual premiere and inserted into the film. Furthermore, it set Power up as a new star and inheritor of his predecessor's stardom without provoking obvious rivalry since the two are neither co-stars nor have a leading role.

In relation to same generation performers with a similar audience appeal, like Gable and (less so) Taylor, Power sometimes played working-class characters (such as journalists), but other times he portrayed nobility (including a prince and several counts). Like Taylor, he was presented very much as a star to be looked at, particularly early in his career, with framing and bright lighting inviting us to gaze at his face through a series of lingering shots, a convention that will be discussed in relevant chapters. Filling in for the audience, female characters repeatedly stare at him, even if he does not return their gaze, and they often instigate a kiss, as if they cannot resist his masculine allure. Equally, though, his characters are often involved in physical fights and, despite his large frame, Power's displays of athleticism in films like *The Mark of Zorro* and *Blood and Sand* demonstrate that audiences were also being invited to view his masculine, active body as he fences, uses a sword or circles the bullring. This physicality aided Power when he moved into more male-driven genres, such as Westerns and war films, in addition to his natural ageing when the roles he played in his early twenties were no longer as feasible. Despite being used to demonstrate his physical skills, however, these films also repeatedly display his body in extremely tight-fitting costumes (justified by the plot), which help draw attention to not only his broad frame, but also his crotch and buttocks, thus adding a sense of dangerous eroticism to Power's persona. Particularly noteworthy are his costumes in *The Mark of Zorro* and his lack of costume in *Son of Fury: The Story of Benjamin Blake* (John Cromwell, 1942), both discussed in Chapter 6.

While no academic accounts of Power currently exist, scholarly monographs on male stars more generally also remain sparse, although the last few years have seen an increase in publications, including my own on Taylor (Kelly 2019) and some books within the BFI Film Stars series. Particularly pertinent to this work are John Mercer's *Rock Hudson* (2015) and Paul McDonald's *George Clooney* (2019), examining successive stars who began their careers as 'pin-ups' who were predominantly known for their good looks before becoming more respected as actors as they matured. Additionally, two monographs on Montgomery Clift, a star born slightly after Power but who also died young at the age of forty-five, have recently been published (Lawrence 2010; Girelli 2014). Other scholarly studies of male stars, although different types from Power, include Gill Plain's examination of John Mills (2006), Karen McNally on Sinatra (2008), and Sarah Thomas's books on Peter Lorre (2012) and James Mason (2018). The other male stars within the BFI series are Indian star

Amitabh Bachchan (Singh 2017), black actor Denzel Washington (Baron 2015), Asian star Tony Leung Chiu-Wai (Gallagher 2016) and American actor Mickey Rourke (Walsh 2014) who, ironically, became known for his 'ugliness'. Moreover, *Lasting Screen Stars: Images that Fade and Personas That Endure* (Bolton and Wright 2016), a collection of essays covering an eclectic range of stars whose images have either endured over time or have faded and become somewhat forgotten, has helped bring stardom back into focus within the discipline. It includes Lies Lanckman's chapter on Power's *Marie Antoinette* co-star Norma Shearer; Lisa Bode's study of Valentino, Power's most obvious predecessor regarding looks and appeal to female audiences, and my own chapter on Robert Taylor. Likewise, *Revisiting Star Studies* (Yu and Austin 2017) deals with new ways of engaging with stardom and reassesses this somewhat neglected subject area.

Genre theory

By focusing on Power's work within one genre at a time, this book details the progression of his star image and performance skills within the confines of each genre in question. Although a much-discussed term in film scholarship, with a vast number of books and articles dedicated to it, it is also one that invites debate as to what genre really is. According to Jeanine Basinger, a primary problem with genre studies is not only understanding a list of traits demonstrated by a particular type of film, but recognising what these traits stand for and how viewers receive and use them (1986: 41). Basinger suggests that an elementary study of genre commences with the basic observation that numerous films appear to have similar plots, characters, settings and events, but that it is 'this very awareness that makes genre what it is' (1986: 15). While Jacques Derrida suggests that every text falls under one or several genres, and that therefore there is no 'genreless text' (1980: 55), Celestino Deleyto proposes genres are not actually groups of films, but instead 'abstract systems formed by elements taken from many films', thus 'the generic bag contains conventions, structures, narrative patterns, but no films' (2009: 12–13). Likewise, Thomas Schatz suggests that genres can be studied like languages, 'as sign systems' that follow Ferdinand de Saussure's distinction between *langue* and *parole*. Therefore, a film genre 'would work like a system and individual genre films would be specific manifestations of those rules' (1981: 19).

Rick Altman is one of the most influential writers on the topic and, according to Robert Burgoyne, Altman's *Film/Genre* (1999) demonstrates a comprehensive theory that highlights the fact that genre approaches tend to focus on one of two paradigms when classifying films: either emphasising 'the syntax, the narrative and formal patterning' of a specific group of texts or classifying them according to their 'semantic meanings, the more general traits, settings, and characteristics of the film' (2008: 6). Steve Neale, another key theorist whose *Hollywood and Genre* (2000) heavily influenced Deleyto, attempted to shift emphasis away from texts and onto 'the systems of communication and expectation within which they operate' (Deleyto 2009: 5) – in other words, not only situating genres within film texts themselves but considering the industry that produced and marketed them and the audiences that consumed them. Consequently, Deleyto suggests that, given the elements of other genres interwoven throughout Howard Hawks's *Rio Bravo* (1959), not least romantic comedy, it can be argued that it is not just a Western; however, it has and continues to be marketed as such by the industry that made it, and is thus primarily consumed by audiences (2009: 5). Deleyto declares that Neale and Altman's efforts to expand genre theory beyond the texts themselves is a welcome move in film studies, and although components such as promotional material, trade press descriptions of films and contemporary reviews prove 'invaluable to understanding the workings of film genre', there remains 'room for consideration of the ways in which the texts themselves function generically' (2009: 5–6).

Discussing the complex nature of genre, Deleyto remarks that epics, comedies, musicals or Westerns are not mutually exclusive 'since they represent categories defined from different perspectives and can therefore all coincide in a single text' (2009: 11). However, Deleyto declares, this 'does not invalidate the generic system or its analytical usefulness', but instead reveals the fact that many film critics presume they are dealing with a set of static terms even though genres are constantly changing, as is the case with other complex systems. This is not only because of their 'intrinsic evolution' but relates to the specific interests of those creating them: the studios, directors, producers or critics themselves (2009, 11; Altman 1999: 117–22). A similar point can be made for subgenres, with several arguments emerging over the decades as to whether the likes of melodrama or *film noir* are genres in themselves, subgenres or merely styles of filmmaking.

Basinger calls the evolution of a genre a rather complex notion since there is a need for genres to change in order to remain popular, while also remaining the same, to a certain degree, to still be a genre. To be considered a genre, according to Basinger, 'a story with a list of familiar characteristics is repeated often enough for an audience to recognize it, expect it, want it, and fill in all the missing details' (1986: 122). If we consider the evolution of the Western, for example, one of the earliest forms of cinematic genre, from *The Great Train Robbery* (Edwin S. Porter, 1903) to *Stagecoach* (John Ford, 1939) in the early sound era, to *The Magnificent Seven* (John Sturges, 1960) in the post-studio era and, finally, to its 2016 remake by Antoine Fuqua, we see both patterns and developments across more than a century. Certain characteristics, including setting, plot, narrative, characterisation and costume, highlight to us that we are watching a Western, whether it is in black and white or colour, with sound or without. Indeed, although Fuqua's film may have had a bigger budget, a longer running time, more violence and coarse language and a black cowboy (Denzel Washington) as the posse leader, this twenty-first century Western is essentially not too far removed from its earlier counterparts. Indeed, more diversity exists between the Westerns Power made across his career than between these films. For example, *Rawhide* (Henry Hathaway, 1951) is not a 'typical' Western, since it is more psychological and takes place in one setting, but it is a Western just as much as *Jesse James*.

Burgoyne explores the issues he encountered when attempting to classify historical films, suggesting that most American films taking the past as their subject can be classified into one of five 'variant groups: the war film, the biographical film, the epic, the metahistorical film, and the topical film' (2008: 3). Collectively, these categories 'form a constellation of popular, mainstream films distinguished by their focus on the historical past' (2008: 3–4). Just as he notes that some readers may argue that the epic, war film and biopic are distinct genres in themselves, I am aware that my classification of Power's immense body of work into the confines of six distinct genres may provoke debate. However, if I used the same system as Burgoyne, I would run into several problems. Although I could have categorised several of Power's films as biopics, some are based on historical figures (Jesse James, Marie Antoinette), while others recount contemporaneous lives (Martin Maher, depicted in *The Long Gray Line*, outlived Power, while Eddy Duchin died only five years before *The Eddy Duchin Story* [George Sidney, 1956] was released). Additionally, all but one of Power's war films were made during World War II; the only one set in the 'past' being *American Guerrilla in the Philippines* (Fritz Lang): filmed in 1950 with the action taking place in 1942, it is therefore set in the very recent past. Perhaps surprisingly, *The Mark of Zorro*, most commonly categorised as an action-adventure film – as it is classified in this book – has an entry in *The BFI Companion to the Western*, with contributor Tise Vahimagi suggesting that it 'gallops between genres' (1993: 285), thus again proving problematic.

Accordingly, I had to make some executive decisions when deciding how to categorise Power's vast body of work in order to have a concise, and manageable, number of chapters. As discussed, even a film like *Jesse James*, which at first glance seems an obvious Western, could be categorised as a biopic, historical film or drama, perhaps even a tragedy, crime or adventure film. One film that seems to deny any genre classification is *The Long Gray Line* which, since it is based on Maher's memoirs, could be called a biopic. However, the first section of the film contains several elements of comedy, while the remainder leans more heavily towards drama; there are also aspects of tragedy, as well as a prominent war theme, and some sources even classify it as a sports film. Consequently, some overlapping of genres between chapters may occur, or readers may feel that certain films I have included under one genre may have fitted better under another, perhaps a genre not even included in the book. For example, *Nightmare Alley* is classified as a drama despite often being referred to as Power's only *film noir* (Stephens 1995: 293). Over the past few decades, there has been much debate over whether *film noir* is a genre or a style of filmmaking (Silver and Ward, 1980: 1); furthermore, since it was not a term used by filmmakers at the time of production, I feel confident in calling *Nightmare Alley* a drama. Moreover, if it were indeed Power's only *film noir*, then I would have had to dedicate a full chapter to one film, which I did not wish to do. Equally, studios designed their releases to appeal to as wide an audience as possible, therefore *In Old Chicago* (Henry King, 1938), for example, was marketed in trailers and publicity material as a combination disaster movie, factually based historical film, drama, romance and musical. Consequently, the six genres under which I have categorised Power's screen work are drama, comedy, musical, Western, war and action-adventure.

Power struggles

In her book *Searching for My Father, Tyrone Power* (2014), Romina Power includes, in full, the article from which the quotation that opens this chapter is taken. Perhaps it was a way of showing the profound effect his words had on her, or her wish to share her father's rather poignant thoughts on weighty topics with her readers. Born in October 1951, Romina had recently turned seven when her father died in November 1958 after collapsing on the set of *Solomon and Sheba* (King Vidor, 1959). Power's youngest daughter, Taryn, was only five years old at the time and his son, Tyrone Power Jr, was born in January 1959, two months after Power's sudden death. Having very few memories of him, given her age at the time of his death, Romina embarked on a decades' long journey of research for her book. This predominantly involved interviewing those who knew him in hopes of uncovering the real man (if such a task can ever truly be successful). Despite commencing research in the 1970s, her book was not published in English until 2014, thus coinciding with the centenary of her father's birth and becoming the first book on Power to be released in thirty-five years. Furthermore, despite the extensive work that obviously went into creating the book, it remains a tremendously difficult text to acquire. Printed in an extremely limited run, it is sold directly from the publisher who does not ship outside of the US.

Although Power died in 1958 while his career was still active, it is worth noting here that all three previous writings on him were released in 1979. These consisted of a filmography, *The Films of Tyrone Power* by Dennis Belafonte, and two biographies, *The Last Idol: Tyrone Power* by Fred Lawrence Guiles and *The Secret Life of Tyrone Power* by Hector Arce. The latter, in particular, has been highly criticised by those who knew Power as being essentially a fabricated account of the actor's life, filled with inaccuracies and unfounded rumours (Power 2014). Indeed, despite (or perhaps as a result of) these books being released simultaneously, these 'biographies' tell frequently conflicting versions of Power's life. As a scholarly text, this book is not interested in unearthing the 'real' Power as the previous authors proposed to do (whether or not they succeeded is up for debate); but these publications highlight the fact that over the past forty years there has been, and remains, a lack of attention to, and writings on, Power in general, let alone within academia.

In her epilogue, Romina states that her father 'did not love Hollywood and Hollywood has chosen to forget him', before concluding that there are people 'scattered throughout the world who still do remember him and love him', to whom she dedicates her book (2014: 321). Conducting interviews with Power's friends, colleagues and relatives, reproducing letters he wrote and received, and examining other documentation assisted in Romina's attempts to 'find' her father, the man rather than the film star. Perhaps this book does the opposite, since it examines Power's constructed star image and screen performances from an academic viewpoint. However, I suggest that these two books can be used together to give a more complete overview of Power's life and career, as well as his important, but long overlooked, place in cinema history and popular culture. Indeed, these books share the mutual aim of helping people remember, or discover, Power and his significant body of cinematic work so that he does not become, or remain, forgotten.

'Lost' or forgotten stars are a key area of interest of mine, and are a concept discussed extensively in my work on Taylor (2016, 2019). As Taylor and Power embodied extremely similar star images, many of the overarching themes I apply to Taylor can also be employed when discussing Power, and my paper 'Paradoxical Star Power: Robert Taylor and Tyrone Power as Male Pin-Ups and (Ageing) Respected Actors', presented at the *Surface and Substance: Reflections on the Male Star* symposium at the University of St Andrews (2016), compared the two. Both began their careers as male pin-ups in the 1930s, with star images predominantly aimed at female audiences, before moving into more male-driven genres as they began to mature and as America entered World War II; this resulted in their receiving newfound respect as actors when they returned to Hollywood in the post-war years. While their experiences with their home studios – Taylor at MGM (Metro-Goldwyn-Mayer) and Power at Twentieth Century-Fox – often parallel each other, sometimes their experiences were much more diverse. Taylor appears to have enjoyed working within the studio system much more than Power, who apparently vocalised his abhorrence of his treatment by Twentieth Century-Fox on more than one occasion (Power 2014: 79, 125, 263). Despite, or perhaps because of, their working for rival studios, Taylor is the actor who can most readily be compared to Power in terms of looks, audience appeal and the roles they were given at specific time periods, far more so than any of Power's contemporaries at Twentieth Century-Fox, such as Don Ameche, John Payne or, later, Gregory Peck. Nevertheless, fan magazines regularly pitted the actors against each other, calling Power 'Twentieth Century-Fox's answer to Robert Taylor', even though the start of Power's career preceded Taylor's, or warning Taylor to 'watch out Bob', since Power may steal his roles. Yet since the studios heavily censored what fan magazines could print at this time, these publications would have been 'in on' the constructed competition created between these performers with similar star images and audience appeal (see Slide 2010; Kelly 2019). The only possible competition between the two, before both actors became independent agents in the 1950s, was Power's being loaned to MGM to star opposite Norma Shearer in *Marie Antoinette*, allegedly at Shearer's request after the newly widowed actress saw him performing on-screen and saw great appeal in him (Lambert 1990: 251). Power's role as Count Axel de Fersen was almost a carbon copy of Taylor's performance as Armand Duval opposite Greta Garbo in *Camille* (George Cukor, 1936). Furthermore, since Shearer and Garbo were MGM's most valuable female stars at this time, both men were required to do little more than make attentive love to their leading ladies, wear historical costumes well and look beautiful in highly lit close-ups. In fact, Twentieth Century-Fox studio head Darryl F. Zanuck was said to be so enraged with how Power was presented on-screen that he vowed never to loan the actor out again, which he never did, and Power worked solely for the studio until his contract expired almost two decades later, in 1954.

A *Screenland* article from 1937 declared that Taylor's female fans were not too worried about his rumoured romances with Garbo and Ginger Rogers because 'Power came along' (Evans 1937: 21). Yet during this time, Power was also partaking in a string of publicised romances, most notably with actresses Janet Gaynor, Loretta Young and Sonja Henie. In 1939 both actors married, much to the dismay of their home studios who wished their top romantic leads to stay persistent bachelors in order to generate publicity and ticket sales from adoring female fans. While Taylor wed actress Barbara Stanwyck, Power tied the knot with his *Suez* (Allan Dwan, 1938) co-star Annabella. The French actress later told Romina Power, 'I got very bad press – I already had a daughter, I was older than he, I had already been married, etc, etc. I became the monster undermining the career of the "poor young Adonis"!' (2014: 62). Her statement not only reflects how the studio and public felt about the union but indicates how Power's looks were fittingly equated to those of Greek mythology's god of beauty and desire. Zanuck tried to break up their romance by sending Annabella to England to make several films, but when she refused the studio ceased to promote her and her US career never really took off. After the pair divorced in 1948, she returned to France where she made a few more films throughout the 1950s. She never remarried and died of a heart attack in 1996, at the age of 89.

Although Power arrived in Hollywood two years earlier than Taylor, his first four films between 1932 and 1935 awarded him rather unspec-tacular bit parts and he returned to the stage in the interim. In two of these films, *Flirtation Walk* (Frank Borzage, 1934) and *Northern Frontier* (Sam Newfield, 1935), he plays an uncredited West Point cadet and Mountie respectively, has no dialogue and is seen on-screen only fleetingly. In his film debut, *Tom Brown of Culver* (William Wyler, 1932), and in *Girls' Dormitory* (Irving Cummings, 1936), he has slightly more screen time and a few lines of dialogue, although his entrance in the latter does not occur until seven minutes before the film's conclusion. Power slightly moved up the rankings with his subsequent film, *Ladies in Love* (Edward H. Griffith, 1936), although the female leads, Loretta Young, Janet Gaynor and Constance Bennett, were the film's stars, with three actors playing their love interests limited to more minor roles (Power, Don Ameche and Paul Lukas, respectively). Up to and including *Ladies in Love*, the actor had been billed as 'Tyrone Power Jr' to distinguish him from his famous father, the English theatre and film actor Tyrone Power (1869–1931). Subsequently, demonstrating the fact that his son's fame eclipsed his own, the older Power has henceforth been known as 'Tyrone Power Sr' with his son becoming, and remaining, *the* Tyrone Power (with his own son now known as Tyrone Power Jr).

Both Taylor's and Power's star-making roles came around the same time, with *Magnificent Obsession* (John M. Stahl, 1935) and *Lloyds of London* (Henry King, 1936) respectively. Despite having the lead role and appearing in almost every scene, Power received fourth billing after child actor Freddie Bartholomew, leading lady Madeleine Carroll and Sir Guy Standing. Since his most substantial role thus far had been the somewhat limited part as Young's romantic interest in *Ladies in Love*, it appears that Twentieth Century-Fox was playing it safe by promoting bigger star names above its potential new leading man. Despite his billing, Power was evidently given the studio's full star treatment in terms of screen time, lighting, privileged shots and so forth, as discussed in Chapter 1. The film was a tremendous success, not only becoming the studio's most popular film of the year but its only one to make over $2 million (Solomon 1988: 33); it also received Oscar nominations for Best Art Direction and Best Film Editing. Most importantly for this study, it made a star out of the twenty-two-year-old Power, who remained a leading man and top star until his death.

A British acting legacy

Although both lost their fathers, thus the dominant male presence in their lives, early on (Power at seventeen and Taylor at twenty-two), one of the chief differences between the actors lies in their genealogy. While

Taylor's father was a grain merchant-turned doctor, changing careers to aid his ailing wife (who outlived both her husband and son), Power was born into an acting dynasty and was the third to bear the name 'Tyrone Power' after his great-grandfather and father, both stage performers. Consequently, he is sometimes referred to as Tyrone Power III. As noted, although this is not a biography and it makes no claims to uncover the 'real' man behind the constructed image of 'Tyrone Power', it is important to briefly discuss Power's background and genealogy since his star image and many of his roles were strongly tied to his British and Irish heritage, and less so to his Americanness.

Before the subject of this book was even born, Montrose Jonas Moses included a chapter on the Powers in his *Famous Actor-Families in America* (1906). The first actor to publicly perform under the stage name 'Tyrone Power' was Power's great-grandfather, born William Grattan Tyrone Power (1797–1841) in Kilmacthomas, County Waterford, Ireland. Now known as Tyrone Power I or Tyrone Power the Elder, he was famous not only as an actor, comedian and theatrical manager but was also an accomplished playwright and author, which the subject of this book also aspired to be. Indeed, both Guiles (1979) and Romina Power (2014) include several extracts from a semi-autobiographical novel Power began writing while on active war duty, but which was never finished nor published. As well as dramatic and comical plays, the elder Power penned *Impressions of America* (1836), a two-volume non-fiction account based on observations he made between 1833 and 1835 while visiting the country, thus providing the family's first link to America. Perhaps the strangest coincidence linking the two men is that they died at almost the same age. In 1841, the elder Power was sailing on the *SS President* on the North Atlantic when the ship was lost at sea and all 136 passengers and crew were pronounced dead. He was forty-three years old.

Although the name skipped a generation, Power's father was born Frederick Tyrone Edmond Power in London, England in 1869 and became a well-known stage actor for thirty years (Winter [1913] 2018). Due to his grandfather's legacy, he was sometimes billed as Tyrone Power II. He moved into cinema while it was still in its infancy, making his cinematic debut in Paramount's *Aristocracy* (Thomas N. Heffron) in 1914, the same year that his namesake son was born. As with many early films, it is now considered lost. Overall, he appeared in close to forty films, the bulk of which were made in the 1920s, and in 1924 alone he made eight films. His final screen role was also his only sound film, the Western *The Big Trail* (Raoul Walsh, 1930), which is best known for giving John Wayne his first starring role after more than twenty uncredited parts. Set to star in a remake of the Lon Chaney vehicle *The Miracle Man* (George Loane Tucker, 1919), which was to include a small part for his seventeen-year-old son who had some theatrical experience behind him, Power Sr died of a heart attack two days before Christmas 1931. *The Miracle Man* was recast with Chester Morris and there was no longer a part for Power's son.

The first Tyrone Power to be born in America, and the subject of this book, was born Tyrone Edmund Power III in Cincinnati, Ohio on 5 May 1914 to Tyrone Power II and his wife, Helen Emma Reaume (known as Patia), a Shakespearean actress and drama coach who taught her son dictation and who appeared in three of her husband's cinematic releases. She would outlive her son by almost a year, and when she died on 29 September 1959 it is said that she was unaware of her son's passing as, due to her own ill health after a series of strokes, it was thought best not to inform her (Guiles 1979; Arce 1979; Power 2014).

As a result of his lineage, Power's strong connections to Britain, particularly Ireland and England, became a major element of both his on- and off-screen personas throughout his career. On-screen, for example, he came closest to character acting in *The Long Gray Line*, in which he adopted a rather impressive Irish brogue for the duration of the film. Likewise, in *The Luck of the Irish* (Henry Koster, 1948), his American journalist of Irish descent visits the country of his roots and falls in love with both the land and an Irish colleen.

Similarly, the year before his death, Power narrated John Ford's anthology *The Rising of the Moon* (1957), a non-commercial film in three vignettes depicting traditional Irish life, values and culture. Although Power was extremely enthusiastic about getting involved in this project, Ford objected to Power's presence since he felt the American actor destroyed its Irish flavour given that the entire cast was Irish. However, as Ronald L. Davis notes, Power's participation was essential if the film were to receive backing from a Hollywood studio (1995: 282). Although Columbia had initially intended to release the film, they backed out amid fears of its lack of commercial value, perhaps due to their collaboration on *The Long Gray Line* not doing as well as hoped. It was eventually distributed by Warner Bros, which was also doubtful about its box office appeal (Davis 1995: 282). Fittingly, the film made its world debut in Dublin on 16 May 1957 to an enthusiastic crowd. However, it was dismissed 'with faint praise' by both British and American critics, and even banned in Dublin (Davis 1995: 282). Thus, Power's work with

Ford may have been creatively invigorating for the actor, allowing him to expand his range, but neither film did well at the box office, which is what really mattered to the studios.

The film begins with Power opening the front door of a house strongly resembling the London home belonging to his character in *The House in the Square*, also known as *I'll Never Forget You* (Roy Ward Baker, 1951). At the time, Power was also living in London and working on the stage, and although it is highly doubtful this was his actual home we are being asked to read it as such since he is playing 'himself'. Looking into the camera, as if surprised by our presence, he smiles and addresses us directly with a friendly 'well, hello'. He introduces himself, as if this is necessary, before conferring his strong connection with Ireland. He begins with his biography: 'My name is Tyrone Power. I'm an actor and, by grace of God, of Irish descent, my family having come from Kilmacthomas in the county of Waterford'. After relaying historical and statistical facts about the country, he adopts an Irish accent similar to that used to portray Maher, concluding his monologue with 'we're a quiet and peace-loving people' (thus including himself as an Irishman), and noting that 'nothing much ever seems to happen in Ireland', before returning to his own recognisable voice to introduce the first of three short stories. He is seen or heard only intermittently as a disembodied voice for the rest of the film. Off-screen, his biographers note that when he discovered that his third wife Debbie was pregnant in 1958, he began inquiring about property for sale in Ireland in hopes of settling down there with his new family (Guiles 1979; Arce 1979). The authors further speculate that Power was ready to turn his back on Hollywood permanently but, unfortunately, he was to die later that year before any potential plans could be finalised.

Continuing the extensive family legacy, Power's own son, born Tyrone William Power IV in Los Angeles, California on 22 January 1959, two months after his father's death, uses the name Tyrone Power Jr. His name honours not only his father and grandfather, but more so his great-great-grandfather since it inverts the name of the first performing Tyrone Power: William Tyrone Power. According to his biographers, Power was intent on having a son who could carry on his famous name, but first wife Annabella was unable to conceive after her first child with a previous husband, and second wife Christian had three miscarriages (including two boys) before giving birth to daughters Romina and Taryn (Power 2014). Power Jr has carried on the acting tradition, making his screen debut in *Cocoon* (Ron Howard, 1985) alongside Don Ameche, his father's regular 1930s co-star. The film was produced almost fifty years after they first appeared together on-screen. Power Jr has one child, a son with his ex-wife, actress DeLane Matthews, who was born in 1998 and for whom they have chosen the name Tyrone Keenan Power V.

Twentieth Century-Fox

When Robert Taylor signed with MGM in 1934, the studio billed itself as having 'more stars than there are in heaven', underlining that Taylor would be competing for roles with the studio's already established leading men such as Clark Gable and Robert Montgomery, as well as other recent newcomers like James Stewart. However, when Power was hired by Twentieth Century-Fox in 1936 the studio was only recently formed, the result of a May 1935 merger between existing studios Fox Film Corporation and Twentieth Century Pictures. While Fox was formed by William Fox in 1915, the latter was an independent company set up in 1933 by former United Artists president Joseph Schenck and Zanuck, who had worked at Warner Brothers before moving to Twentieth Century as Production Chief. Thus, Power signed with a studio that was still in its infancy and certainly not yet the major power it would soon become.

Its biggest star draws were child actress Shirley Temple and the middle-aged Will Rogers; however, both these artists had limited runs, since Temple soon became an adolescent and Rogers died in a plane crash in 1935. As Wheeler Winston Dixon declares, it was solely due to Temple's popularity that Fox survived the Depression, but she was abruptly dropped when *The Blue Bird* (Walter Lang, 1940) was a box office failure and lost money. Thereafter, the studio 'relied on the dashing charm of Tyrone Power and lush beauty of Linda Darnell and Gene Tierney' (2006: 18), both of whom co-starred with Power several times. Although MGM had the biggest 'stable of male stars', Twentieth Century-Fox relied on Power, Ameche and Henry Fonda as its top leading men, with Schatz calling Power 'the most vital company asset' (1988: 98), and Ameche and Fonda both supported him on screen. Further indicating Power's importance to the studio, Robyn Karney notes that Zanuck demonstrated the efficacy of the star system by developing 'a new group of distinct star personalities', including Power, Ameche, Alice Faye and Sonja Henie, who all aided in helping it become one of Hollywood's most powerful studios (1984: 41). Moreover, in the late 1930s and early 1940s these four players worked together extensively.

Finler feels that, although Power's films with Faye were the best of his early work, he was initially cast in 'forgettable pictures designed to boost new female stars': Faye, Henie and Loretta Young (1984: 84). However, although Young would become Power's most regular co-star throughout the 1930s, her career went much further back than his, in fact to the silent era when she made her film debut as a child in 1917. By the time she was paired with Power in *Ladies in Love,* Young had over sixty-five screen credits to her name, while it was only his fourth film and first substantial role. Likewise, although Faye had arrived in Hollywood around the same time as Power, she established herself as a star name far quicker and was even able to request him as her leading man in *Sing, Baby, Sing* (Sidney Lanfield, 1936). Although Power began shooting, and photographs of the two of them on-set exist (see Belafonte 1979: 14), Power was replaced by Michael Whelan after Twentieth Century-Fox decided they wanted an established 'name' in the role (Belafonte 1979: 12). Whelan, twelve years Power's senior, had only made five films prior to this and, ironically, his fame never came close to reaching the heights of Power's despite his working consistently into the 1960s.

Although Power was never nominated for an Academy Award, many of his films and co-stars were, indicating that he was not taken seriously because of his looks. Furthermore, Zanuck received Oscar nominations for 'Outstanding Production' on three films in which Power played the lead: *In Old Chicago* in 1938, *Alexander's Ragtime Band* (Henry King) the following year, and *The Razor's Edge* (Edmund Goulding, 1946) almost a decade later.[1] The latter marked Power's return to the screen after a three-year absence while he undertook active duty. Many of Power's films earned huge profits for Twentieth Century-Fox, beginning with his debut as a leading man in *Lloyds of London.* In the twenty-two years between this film and *The Sun Also Rises* (Henry King, 1957), there were only five years when a film starring Power did not make the studio's highest earners list; an enormous feat for any actor. These were 1943–6 (when he was doing his military service),[2] 1956 (the first year he was no longer under contract to the studio), and 1958 (the year he died). In 1953, Power turned down the lead in *The Robe* (Henry Koster), the very first CinemaScope production, to return to the stage. With Richard Burton in the lead, the film became the biggest money-maker to date, grossing $17.5 million.

In addition to the longevity of his profitability, on several occasions more than one Power film made the list in a single year. For example, in 1937, therefore extremely early in his career, four of the five top earners starred Power. The biggest money-maker was *In Old Chicago* at $2.5 million, and $1 million higher than the second-ranked film, *Life Begins in College* (William A. Seiter) starring the Ritz Brothers. Power's films *Thin Ice* (Sidney Lanfield), *Love is News* and *Café Metropole* (Edward H. Griffith) rounded off the list. The following year, the studio's top three money-makers were all Power films: *Jesse James, Alexander's Ragtime Band* and *Suez*, collectively earning the studio $8 million.[3] Another notable film, *The Black Swan* (Henry King, 1942), made $3.5 million and was not only the highest earner of 1942 but the first Twentieth Century-Fox film to surpass $3 million.[4] Power's return to the screen after the war in *The Razor's Edge* earned $5 million, second only to *Forever Amber* (Otto Preminger, 1947), based on Kathleen Winsor's controversial book of the same name and the studio's answer to MGM's *Gone with the Wind* (Victor Fleming, 1939). In total, thirty-one of the forty-three films in which Power was the leading man made the top earners' list, resulting in a profit of over $69 million for the studio (which, if we consider this figure at the end of his career, equates to around $642.5 million today). This can be broken down to an average of $2.2 million a year across the twenty-two years (even after he was no longer under contract) or, if only considering the fifteen years he had a film on the top earners' list, an average of $4.6 million a year. These impressive figures reveal how much of an asset Power was to the studio, and not just in a certain timeframe but for the length of his career, his films continuing to turn high profits for over two decades.

In early 2019, Twentieth Century-Fox became a subsidiary of Walt Disney Studios, prompting the publication of numerous news articles exploring the studio's vast history spanning more than eighty years. Despite Power being the studio's first and most successful leading man in the initial phase of its existence and for over twenty years thereafter, neither Power nor his films were mentioned in any articles I accessed, further supporting the fact that he continues to remain elusive and curiously forgotten even within the history of his home studio.

Bit parts and the early years: 1932–5

Before exploring Power's films within their defined genres, I conclude this introduction with a discussion of his initial screen work as a bit part player in his first five films where he was either uncredited or billed as Tyrone

Power, Jr. Thus the genre chapters commence with his star-making film *Lloyds of London*.

Power's 1932 screen debut was in the relatively minor role of Cadet Donald MacKenzie in *Tom Brown of Culver*. Much of the film focuses on the title character (played by actor Tom Brown), but Power appears frequently as one of a small assemblage of cadets and has a few lines of dialogue. In several scenes depicting the group's military training, Power is placed directly beside Brown, therefore is often in the frame even when Brown is meant to be the focus. As the tallest member of the group, having the darkest features and, arguably, the most pleasant face (in a boyish way), Power is not easily missed. However, at this point he was still very young and thin, with an adolescent frame and features, his looks having not yet reached their true potential. Additionally, on the three occasions when he is given lines to speak, his voice is high and somewhat strained and his movements quite deliberate, as if he is not yet comfortable with acting in front of a camera, perhaps as a result of his extensive stage work and theatrical training. Nevertheless, the dialogue he delivers includes phrases like 'swell', 'the dame's old enough to be his mother' and 'the nut' (about a fellow cadet), revealing a wisecracking and likeable, if not fully developed, character. Furthermore, as Donald and his classmates laugh at a cadet who is forced to read aloud his love letter to a famous actress, we receive the first screen reveal of the wide grin that would become a major part of Power's star image, and appeal, for the rest of his career.

What followed was an even smaller role as an unnamed and uncredited cadet in *Flirtation Walk* (1934). Marking the fifth pairing of Dick Powell and Ruby Keeler, much of the film takes place at West Point military academy, with Power indistinguishable from the dozens of other young actors. He receives no close-ups and no dialogue, and has no interactions with the leading players. Similarly, the following year he played an uncredited and unnamed Mountie in *Northern Frontier*, a star vehicle for Western hero Kermit Maynard.

The year after that, however, Power's roles became progressively more substantial. His next film, *Girls' Dormitory*, starred French actress Simone Simon in her American cinematic debut. Simon portrays schoolgirl Marie Claudel, who is in love with headmaster Dr Stephen Dominick (played by British actor Herbert Marshall), a feeling that is reciprocated. Although Power makes his entrance a mere seven minutes before the film's conclusion, he still makes an impression. Dressed in a dark suit and tie, and carrying white gloves, a hat and cane, he knocks on the door of

Figure I.1   Power makes his entrance in *Girls' Dormitory* (1936)

Stephen's office before bursting in, grinning widely (perhaps too widely) and announcing, 'Marie, they told me I'd find you here' (Figure I.1). Simon moves towards him and he kisses her hair, but upon noticing Marshall his smile fades and he utters, 'Oh, I beg your pardon', before bowing slightly. Marie, who has been trying to convince Stephen that she is not in love with him so that he can marry someone closer to his own age, introduces Jacques (Power) as her fiancé (it is not clear whether Jacques is also meant to be French). While Power's entrance is somewhat theatrical, we get an early glimpse of his ability to use more subtle acting techniques better suited to the screen. Particularly noteworthy are his use of facial expressions, predominantly his eyes and eyebrows, which would become an important tool for him throughout his career. Power's momentary look of confusion suggests that Marie is lying, but his silence aids with her deception. Although the scene includes several close-ups of Marshall and, predominantly, of Simon, the camera remains at a distance while filming Power, presenting him chiefly in a medium-long shot while Simon grips his arm. Leaving the office, he bows once more to Marshall, excuses himself and closes the door with a large grin just as he had opened it less than a minute before, demonstrating that his character has decided to play along. In helping Marie, it is not just his physical appearance that is appealing to audiences, but also his gallantry and quick thinking.

We soon learn that Jacques is Marie's cousin, therefore removing any romance between the two. Marie is also genuinely in love with Stephen, merely using her ruse with Jacques to convince him otherwise so he may marry a more suitable woman also in love with him. With Jacques no longer posing a threat to Stephen, due to his familial connection to Marie, in the final scene Power appears in both an outfit and setting that would become standard for him throughout the coming decades: wearing evening clothes in a nightclub. While the rest of their party are dancing, Jacques asks Marie what will cheer her up: 'a diamond bracelet, a million francs or a dance with me?' When she informs him she does not feel like dancing he tells her to 'have a drink of champagne', while touching her glass, before adding, 'or maybe I could entertain you with a few . . . card tricks', twisting his wrist before uttering the final two words. When Stephen appears and asks Marie for a dance she rushes off, leaving Jacques alone at the table, holding a glass of champagne, and it is here that Power exits the film. Having now entered his twenties, he appears less boyish and is developing into the recognisable Power who would soon become a star. However, his movements remain too pronounced and not refined enough for the intricacies of screen acting. Likewise, he delivers his lines in a high-pitched, almost strained voice that has an unnatural quality to it. He deliberately pronounces each word with a lilt more closely resembling Fred Astaire's voice than the familiar tone that Power would soon develop, and that remained an important component of his star persona. Significantly, this was the first of several times he played a nobleman in the 1930s. Billed as Count Jacques Vallais here, he also portrayed counts in *Ladies in Love* and *Marie Antoinette*. In *Thin Ice* he is a prince disguised as a commoner and in *Café Metropole* a commoner masquerading as a prince.

As noted, the plot of Power's next film *Ladies in Love* revolves around the female leads, Young, Gaynor and Bennett, and their convoluted love affairs with Power, Ameche and Lucas's characters respectively. Only Gaynor and Ameche end up as a couple at the film's conclusion, with Power's Count Karl Lanyi calling off his romance with Young's Susie to marry a woman of his own class (played by Virginia Field), and John (Lucas) leaving Yoli (Bennett) for his sixteen-year-old cousin (again played by Simon). Although Power and Ameche do not appear together on screen, they worked together several times in the forthcoming years, and Ameche acted as best man at Power's 1939 wedding to Annabella. Furthermore, although Power shares no screen time with Gaynor, nor were they ever paired together on-screen, they did become an off-screen couple for a time, seen together at several film premieres and receiving much press attention, as discussed in Chapter 7.

Susie has trouble with the safety latch on the women's apartment door while attempting to let John in. During the first part of this exchange, Lukas is framed in the doorway, however, when she pulls the door open a second time Power stands in the spot previously occupied by Lukas, telling her she must close the door before she can open it (Figure I.2). Again, Power is revealed to the audience and other characters by the opening of a door, only this time he is presented from Young's point of view. Shot from below as she looks up at him, he is partially framed in the doorway while also slightly obscured by Young's hair, hand and the latch. The shadow of her face projected on the wall shows her surprised expression before the camera cuts to a close-up of her staring at him and uttering a breathless 'What?' As with his entrance in *Girls'*

Figure I.2   Power's introduction in *Ladies in Love* (1936)

Dormitory, Power wears a tailored suit and tie (but in a lighter shade) and a wide grin, before exiting within a minute. However brief, his initial appearance leaves a lasting impression on Susie, who continues to stare at Karl throughout the film. Attending a party that night, Power is again seen in evening dress, and Yoli needs to shout Susie's name to stop her unconsciously gaping at him, thus acting as surrogate for the audience. Although she understands the vast difference in their social status, she becomes besotted by him so quickly that when they inevitably break up so he may marry a countess, she tells him that she loves him so much 'that losing you is like losing a part of me'. In his final appearance, Power wears full military dress as Young watches the wedding procession from across the street before attempting to commit suicide with poison, which Gaynor's character drinks by mistake.

Although his role was again somewhat limited, it helped set the foundations of Power's developing star image as an extremely beautiful and desirable man whom women cannot help staring at and falling in love with almost instantly, with Twentieth Century-Fox hoping that audiences felt the same way. As Richard Maltby notes, 'the real influence of stars lay not with their employers, but with the paying public', since stars, rather than film types, draw the most audiences (1995: 89). Maltby draws parallels between the way a star repeats performance elements across his/her films and an understanding of genre. The use of repeated traits results in 'the consolidation of that performance as a set of gestures and behavior patterns recognizable to the audience', thus making it easier to envisage what a star may do in future roles. Therefore, he suggests, star acting provides audiences with a simultaneously autonomous and integrated performance, since a star is both a 'production value' and a 'known bundle of personality traits', resulting in the star performing his or her persona in a movie autonomously while also disappearing into their role as an actor (1995: 250). Although Power was not yet a star at this point, his home studio seemed to be marketing him as such.

In Power's case, his personality traits included a wide grin and a charming, but roguish, disposition that often expanded into his being viewed as a cad or, as Betty Grable's character repeatedly calls him in *A Yank in the RAF* (Henry King, 1941), 'a worm'. These traits, evident in his early films and constructed via camera and editing choices helped create a recognisable star persona for Power almost instantly. His characters frequently have complicated relationships with women (plural, as there is usually more than one love interest in any given film), and since the narrative frequently allows him the opportunity to dance with women, audiences are regularly presented with images of Power immaculately dressed in evening clothes, both modern and historical, which highlight his elegant frame. Undeniably, clothing, or its lack, became a key factor in Power's appeal to female characters and audiences, with several scenes presenting him in a state of undress, generally without a shirt but at times in underpants, trunks or tight, form-fitting outfits that help accentuate his figure (most obviously *The Mark of Zorro, Son of Fury* and *Blood and Sand*). In several films his character is involved in physical fights, gets drunk and avoids trouble that he has created with a wide grin, easy charm and some cunning. Given his extreme good looks, these measures were perhaps Twentieth Century-Fox's way of making sure Power avoided some of the negative, lightweight labels placed on Robert Taylor by the press (including the likes of 'powderpuff') due to his beautiful face and early roles in melodramas. Thus, it appears the studio was learning from the manufacture of stars at rival studios and attempted to build a new and improved model with Power.

Power was, first and foremost, a product of the Hollywood film industry and became an important star during its heyday of the 1930s, a decade of glamorous stars and the studio system at its peak. Although all his films are covered, to a greater or lesser degree, analysis of specific scenes in selected films reveal how Power subtly used his face, body and voice to embody his characters. By focusing on specific moments that highlight his recognisable yet diverse performance skills across both individual films and genres, this study illustrates Power's excellent performance skills, which have long been overlooked because of his outstanding beauty, proving that the two are not exclusive and that a beautiful performer can indeed be a skilled one. Thus, the book explores ideas around the constructed nature of stardom, while suggesting that the very thing that made Power a star (his looks) undermined recognition of his talent both during his career and since.

Notes

1. Between 1925 and 1962, Zanuck received sixteen Oscar nominations, winning 'Outstanding Motion Picture' for *How Green Was My Valley* (John Ford, 1941), *Gentleman's Agreement* (Elia Kazan, 1947) and *All About Eve* (Joseph L. Mankiewicz, 1950), which all won multiple Oscars.

2. Even then, the highest earner for 1943 was *Sweet Rosie O'Grady* (Irving Cummings, 1943), a musical remake of Power's comedy *Love is News*, starring Robert Young in Power's role and Betty Grable in Loretta Young's, and earning $3.5 million.
3. *Jesse James* and *Alexander's Ragtime Band* both made $3 million, and *Suez* $2 million for the studio.
4. Tying with the Betty Grable musical *Springtime in the Rockies* (Irving Cummings, 1942), and also earning $3.5 million.

Chapter 1

The dramatic performer

Overview

Because he starred so successfully in the likes of *The Mark of Zorro*, Power tends to be remembered primarily today as a cinematic 'swashbuckler' (Solomon 1988; Mayer and McDonnell 2007). However, almost a third of his oeuvre, sixteen films, is comprised of dramas. Both his 1932 screen debut in *Tom Brown of Culver* and his final film *Witness for the Prosecution* (Billy Wilder, 1957) were dramas, thus making it the genre he appeared in most often and over the longest period of time. Furthermore, most of his stage and radio work was in drama, as was his only fictionalised television appearance: *Armchair Theatre*'s episode 'Miss Julie' (1956).

Six of the twenty films Power made in the 1930s were dramas. While the three he appeared in as a bit part player are discussed in the last chapter (*Tom Brown of Culver, Northern Frontier* and *Girls' Dormitory*), it was his fourth film, *Lloyds of London*, that made him a star. His final two dramas of the decade were *Marie Antoinette*, made while on loan to MGM, and *Suez*, the first drama for which he received top billing. Although World War II interrupted Power's screen career for three years while he undertook war duty, he made another four dramas in the 1940s: *Johnny Apollo* (Henry Hathaway, 1940) and *Blood and Sand* in the pre-war years and *The Razor's Edge* and *Nightmare Alley* directly after his post-war return to Hollywood. In the 1950s, the final decade of his career, he starred in an additional six dramas with a variety of themes and characterisations: *The House in the Square, Diplomatic Courier* (Henry Hathaway, 1952), *The Long Gray Line, The Eddy Duchin Story, The Sun Also Rises* and *Witness for the Prosecution*, his final completed film before his death.

Power's appearance in drama was also more consistent across his career than in any other genre. In the 1930s, his total filmic output was evenly spread across dramas, comedies and musicals, with six in each genre. Additionally, he starred in his first Western (*Jesse James*) and action-adventure film (*The Rains Came* [Clarence Brown, 1939]). Because of his three-year wartime absence from the screen, his 1940s output was slightly lower with fifteen films, which can be categorised into four dramas, two comedies, three war films and six action-adventure films, thus making it the only decade in which another genre exceeded his dramatic output. Power made no Westerns or musicals in the 1940s; in fact, he made no musicals beyond the 1930s (so long as we do not classify *The Eddy Duchin Story*, which leans more towards drama, as a musical). In the 1950s, Power made an additional fourteen films before his death in 1958: six dramas, three Westerns, four action-adventure films and one war film.

Since his first three dramas were dealt with in the introduction, I begin here with the first truly important film in Power's career trajectory: *Lloyds of London*, exploring techniques such as lighting, framing and editing, along with Power's appearance and performance skills within the film. I then chronologically discuss the rest of his work in drama, stressing the most important films and discussing ways in which these helped develop and progress Power's star image and screen presence, before concluding with a detailed discussion of his final completed film, *Witness for the Prosecution*. Made over twenty years apart, *Lloyds of London* and *Witness for the Prosecution* are both set in London and feature Power's character on trial in The Old Bailey, thus bringing his career full circle. A comparison of these films from either side of his career provides a clear illustration of how Power's screen image had developed over time, likewise showing the progression and refinement of his acting skills, voice projection and use of gestures, as well as the obvious and inevitable changes in his physical appearance as he aged, all of which are discussed.

A star is constructed: *Lloyds of London*

Power's first 'starring' role came in 1936 with *Lloyds of London*. This was also an important film in the actor's oeuvre since it marked the first of eleven films he made with director Henry King, crossing several genres and culminating in *The Sun Also Rises* the year before Power's death. It was also his first time working with regular co-star George Sanders, with whom Power was filming a duelling scene when he collapsed on the set of *Solomon and Sheba* and subsequently died.

Aubrey Solomon suggests that Zanuck took a risk by casting the unknown Power, placing 'an $800,000 "A" picture in his hands' (1988: 32). But the risk paid off, and not only did the film become the studio's biggest money-maker of the year, but the only one to cross the $2 million threshold (Solomon 1988: 33). However, I qualify the term 'starring' because, although the plot of this almost two-hour long historical drama revolves around Power's character Jonathan Blake, he received fourth billing since, despite his acting heritage, he lacked the star name to carry such an expensive and lavish production at this time. Nevertheless, while watching the film it becomes transparently obvious that Twentieth Century-Fox was grooming Power for stardom.

Top billed was established child actor Freddie Bartholomew, a twelve-year-old whose career had begun around the same time as Power's. Although Bartholomew appeared in some uncredited roles between 1930 and 1932, his portrayal of the title character in MGM's Oscar nominated *David Copperfield* (George Cukor, 1935) meant that his star was already ascending, thereby giving him much higher standing than Power. Second billing went to leading lady Madeleine Carroll, born in 1906 and therefore eight years' Power's senior. Having begun her career in 1928, Carroll had made close to thirty films, and is probably best remembered for her role as Pamela in Alfred Hitchcock's *The 39 Steps* (1935). Elder actor Sir Guy Standing received third billing, and would make just one more film before his death of a suspected heart attack. Billed below Power were veteran actor C. Aubrey Smith and actress Virginia Field, making Power the sole American actor in the principal cast.

The film commences in Norfolk, England in 1770, and for the initial thirty-three minutes Bartholomew portrays protagonist Jonathan Blake. The top-billed star then exits the film (returning only briefly for a minute-long flashback at the end), with Power taking over as the adult version of Jonathan for the duration. Before Power even makes his entrance, Jonathan's attraction to women is made obvious. Learning that he has been arrested as a 'Peeping Tom', waitress Polly (Field) baulks at the idea, brazenly calling it 'a likely tale. I've been trying to make him look at me for a whole year.' The film then moves to The Old Bailey, where we are first introduced to his accuser: a plain-looking woman whom the judge does not appear to believe. The camera then follows the judge's glance towards Power, whom we see for the first time, thus giving his introduction greater impact. Brightly lit and placed in the centre of the frame between two rather unattractive guards, Power stares with wide-eyed wonderment at the accuser and then at the judge as he pleads his innocence. Through the utterance of his first few lines, it becomes apparent that Power is attempting to speak with an English accent, which works at some points but not at others. Indeed, he seems to shift between accents from different regions on words like 'trespassing' (clipping the 'g'), 'spyglass' (elongating the letters after 'g') and 'telegraph'. Additionally, while his 'believe me' has somewhat of an Irish lilt, his 'aye, sir' sounds Scottish. When explaining that he is an inventor and was merely 'experimenting', Power's own American accent begins to creep in. Perhaps due to the rather stilted dialogue he has been given, or his attempts at producing a convincing English accent, the words sound forced, and he speaks them much more slowly than required. What he does manage to do here, however, that he did not achieve in *Girls' Dormitory*, is to bring the timbre of his voice down so as not to sound too high-pitched, strained or nervous when saying his lines. Indeed, it is obvious that Power has become much more comfortable in front of the camera and successfully delivers his copious amounts of dialogue to a high standard throughout, even if it is in a range of accents. Jonathan informs the court that he has no romantic interest in the accuser and was merely working on his telegraph when he fell in her bedroom window. Convincing an influential gentleman to look at his invention, Power flashes the wide grin we saw in his previous films and would see a lot more in the future.

His initial meeting with Carroll's Lady Elizabeth takes place in France where all English people are being arrested. Having taken on the guise of a French priest, he addresses her in English but with a French accent. Subsequently travelling together in a carriage in very close proximity, Power is somewhat desexualised through his all-enveloping costume and masquerade as a priest (later repeated in *The Mark of Zorro* with Linda Darnell), alongside the fact that the accent he has now acquired sounds more like Peter Lorre (who was not even French) than Charles Boyer. However, it is possible that Power decided to employ a purposely bad accent (as with *Café Metropole*), since we already know this is a façade and he is most definitely not a priest. Certainly, since Jonathan, and by extension Power, adopts the persona to avoid detection, the accent does not need to be believable (at least to the audience), whereas his English accent should sound authentic throughout since it is part of Blake's true identity. After the two escape on a small fishing boat, he replaces the priest's robes with a sailor outfit, becoming more dirty, unshaven and, by extension, manly as the trip progresses. Nevertheless, despite these hypermasculine associations, Power's young, beautiful and unlined face remains brightly lit in multiple close-ups, and he receives considerably more screen time than Carroll. Moreover, throughout this scene, Power is filmed in full face, staring off into the distance as he speaks, whereas Carroll is consistently filmed looking at Power, resulting in less of her face being visible and allowing the focus of her attention to be on the object of Elizabeth's desire and, it is hoped by the studio, the audience's too as we trace her gaze to Power's beautiful face.

Although Carroll was the bigger star, her role is minor in comparison to Power's who receives far more screen time. Additionally, he is privileged in shots in which they both feature and gets many more individual close-ups in their shared scenes. The sequence following their return to England is a particularly noteworthy illustration of this. After finishing their meal, the pair ascend the stairs to retire to their respective rooms. Standing in the hallway, Power faces the camera while we only see Carroll's back. This full body shot of Power also allows audiences to view his complete figure in a tight-fitting period costume, the light-coloured trousers and short, dark jacket drawing particular attention to his crotch. While Carroll disappears into her room, the camera remains stationary at the end of the hallway, continuing to film Power's entire body until he moves across the hall and exits the frame. There is then a cut to a medium close-up of Power as he turns around and looks intensely and longingly at Carroll, and therefore also at the camera/us. Again, he is positioned in the centre of the frame and filmed in full face, his features lit so brightly that they appear not dissimilar to Valentino's in the silent era. While nothing impedes our view of Power's face, Carroll peers through a half open door, which results in her face being in semi-darkness and partially obstructed by the door frame. The camera lingers on Power as he continues to stare at Carroll before marching across the hallway and kissing her. Carroll then closes her door, thereby exiting the scene, so we do not get to experience her reaction to this passionate exchange. Instead, the camera stays with Power and follows him into his own room where he is again shot in full body, only this time from a low angle which makes him appear taller and more virile than previously, and thus (perhaps) more desirable. He rushes to the window, throws it open and jumps onto the bed, breaking it, before again grinning widely as the scene fades out. Throughout the film his elaborate historical costumes draw attention to his body, while a long wig pulled back into a bow impeccably frames his beautiful face. Persistent bright white lighting gives him an almost unearthly quality, making his skin appear like porcelain, and complements his wavy hair, glossy lips and slender frame. Additionally, his dark, expressive eyes and long eyelashes aid in creating this ethereal quality. He is very obviously a beautiful man, and Twentieth Century-Fox evidently wanted to do everything possible to demonstrate this to cinematic audiences to make them notice him and his star potential.

The final scene opens with the brightly lit Power lying in bed. Despite his character being gravely ill, his face and hair remain impeccable. The two women who love him stand on either side like bookends, Carroll's and Field's blondeness strongly contrasting with and complementing Power's dark features. When he weakly rises and walks towards the window to watch a procession below, the camera slowly pulls in for an extreme close-up of his face (Figure 1.1). The shot isolates and accentuates Power's features, fragmenting him from chin to forehead and highlighting the significance and importance of his face while the camera lingers there for a full two minutes. For half this time, however, a flashback of Bartholomew is superimposed over Power's face, thus allowing a minor break in our intensive gaze so that we may feel less voyeuristic (particularly relevant to historical audiences viewing the film on a large cinema screen), but he is still fully recognisable behind the image. Power then gives the slightest hint of a melancholic smile

Figure 1.1 *Lloyds of London's* final scene (1936)

before his eyes fill up with tears and he casts his eyes downward, his tremendously long eyelashes particularly apparent in this moment. Camille Paglia proposes that 'light makes beautiful boys incandescent' (1990: 118), and this could certainly be applied to Power here.

He is momentarily joined by Carroll in the film's final few seconds, but she again remains in the background and in semi-darkness while Power is fully exposed by the light from the window and his positioning in the centre of the frame; thus she continues to be incidental while he is singled out as the object of the camera's, and thereby the audience's, gaze. It is Power's face that we are asked to look at and study at length, with his smooth skin, defined cheekbones, long eyelashes and a strategically placed single section of hair falling onto his forehead. As Steven L. Davis suggests, men's hair that is neatly styled save for a few stray hairs can be read as 'a combination of ruggedness and style, freedom and discipline' (2008: 66), which unquestionably describes both character and actor here, as well as what will be the habitual presentation of Power going forward. These individual elements combine to present a visual construction of extreme male beauty, while indicating an underlying manliness that would appeal to female audiences in the object of their erotic desire, and that came to the fore even more dominantly in Power's future cinematic endeavours. Moreover, this extreme close-up is the image audiences are being asked to take away with them at the fade out: a study of Power's immensely magnified face. Immanuel Kant declared that beauty, both natural and artificial, may be described as 'the expression of aesthetical ideas; only . . . in beautiful art this idea must be occasioned by a concept of the object' (1964: 323). He adds that the beautiful pleases immediately and apart from any interest, 'the freedom of the imagination (and therefore of the sensibility of our faculty) is represented in judging the beautiful as harmonious with the conformity to law of the understanding', and therefore, 'the subjective principle in judging the beautiful is represented as universal' (1964: 342). Kant's ideas may explain why Power became an international star so quickly, since his undeniable, but technically assisted, beauty is repeatedly put on display to be judged as harmonious and universal. Consequently, but perhaps unsurprisingly, this film marks the point where Power was no longer an incidental player and it is obvious throughout that he was receiving Twentieth Century-Fox's full star treatment. This evidently worked since the film made him a star, which he remained until his death over twenty years later.

Davis suggests that the 1930s saw a growing importance placed on men's appearances in popular culture, particularly within a 'visual discourse on male beauty' (2008: 63), highlighting Clark Gable as cinema's leading male sex symbol and Johnny Weissmuller's loincloth in the *Tarzan* films as examples of male beauty. However, I would argue that Gable's looks were less beautiful and more akin to a darkly sexual and somewhat dangerous rugged handsomeness, while Weissmuller's near-naked body was objectified much more than his face. Power's 1930s image fits much more readily with Davis's notion of male beauty and how it was displayed for audiences, since he presents both a beautiful face and a well-proportioned body. Davis further suggests that visual representations of the male body 'register the specific historical conditions in which they are designed', therefore we must understand the historical conditions that shape the visual (and narrative) representations of masculinity (2008: 75–6). But, I would add, this undoubtedly depends on the appearance of the man in question, and by taking into account a number of elements, not least age since Power can be read as being much more 'beautiful' in his twenties than in his 40s, when his body became broader and his face more hardened. Thus, later on he may no longer have been 'pretty', although he was still extremely attractive and recognisable as such. As will become apparent in the forthcoming chapters, as well as making Power a star and allowing audiences to safely gaze at his beautiful face without the fear of his looking back, *Lloyds of London* introduced several tropes and themes that resurfaced throughout Power's career.

Early stardom

In the almost twenty years that Power was under contract to Twentieth Century-Fox, the studio loaned him out just once, for MGM's lavish historical drama *Marie Antoinette* (1938). A star vehicle for the recently widowed Norma Shearer, whose producer-husband Irving Thalberg had died suddenly at the age of thirty-seven, Power's role as Count Axel de Fersen lacks any real substance and does nothing to advance his emerging star persona. However, it did provide audiences with some breathtakingly beautiful shots of his face and, by now, quite muscular frame. The role seems more suited to a player already under contract to MGM, such as the equally beautiful Robert Taylor, who was also in the first few years of his career and establishing himself as a leading man in need of the exposure that a film on this scale would have provided. In the words of a *Film Weekly* review, Power's role gave him 'few chances' (Anon 1939c: 33), and is not dissimilar to Taylor's Armand in *Camille*, neither man being allowed to display much acting ability since the roles require little more than looking desirable in period costumes while providing romantic interludes for their leading ladies.

As with MGM's *Gone with the Wind*, released the following year, this two-and-a-half-hour epic includes both an overture and interlude; the official trailer noted that it was in preparation for four years, meaning that neither Power nor Taylor would have been in the running at the start. Set over a twenty-year period, it boasts of having ninety-eight massive sets, 152 speaking roles and 5,500 extras.[1] Thus, it is noteworthy that Power was given second billing (to Shearer, of course) above the title in such a prestigious production this early in his career. Axel is Power's third on-screen count, and his entrance is again delayed until thirty-eight minutes into the film, when he is seen walking down a dark street dressed in historical costuming of tight trousers, a fitted coat and frilled shirt. Accompanied by an older gentleman, who quickly leaves the scene, Axel enters a grand building at the request of Marie (Shearer). Unable to see his features, since she has called to him from an upper-storey balcony, upon entering the brightly lit house he ascends the staircase towards her and the camera (Figure 1.2), as her wide smile fades and she appears astonished. Initially rendered speechless by his attractiveness, she looks him over before declaring, 'But how perfect'. When Marie asks him to pretend to be Russian so that she might win a bet, he informs her that he is Swedish, although Power uses his own distinct American accent throughout. Leading him into the room so that her friends may view her 'prize', one woman asks, 'Is he really a Russian?', before looking into his face and adding, 'Oh and a handsome one too. Don't you think, Philip?' The man addressed as Philip examines him through a monocle before replying, 'Not bad'. Power is stationary and in the centre of the frame while the guests fuss over him, particularly the women and not least Shearer, who spins him around in order to show him off from all sides, while the men admit their jealousy. When one woman audaciously asks, 'What's Russian for kiss me?' Marie scolds her, saying, 'He's mine, I forbid you to touch him', before examining his appearance and clothing. Showing discomfort at being put on display, he attempts to leave, but when he leans forward to kiss Shearer's hand, she grabs him and kisses him on the lips before he exits angrily.

Figure 1.2 The brightly lit Power in *Marie Antoinette* (1938)

Although Power re-enters the film twenty minutes later in screen time it is much later in the narrative when the pair share their first love scene together. This time, however, it is he who takes the initiative, making him the dominant party and allowing him to appear manlier than in their last encounter. Subsequently, he often visits her in the palace gardens, but puts an end to their affair when she becomes Queen of France, much to her dismay and distress but to his too, as is made obvious by Power's performance here. As they embrace, his eyes desperately trace her face as if trying to memorise it; he then leans down and kisses her slowly and softly before pulling away. Without breaking his intense gaze, he stands upright, squares his shoulders and clenches his jaw, flashing his eyes just once. Slightly opening his mouth and licking his lips as if to show Axel's determination and his growing courage, he abruptly breaks his gaze and walks away without looking back. Music swells as Power strides towards the camera, which follows him in full length for a full twenty seconds before he disappears out of frame. Watching him go, Shearer becomes a tiny figure in the background, and as he passes the camera, she reaches out a hand towards him before turning away and hiding her face. A fade out then leaves the audience with this striking image as the intermission commences.

Power is seen only sporadically thereafter, reappearing as an older gentleman almost two hours into the film, his age depicted by a slight greying at the temples but no apparent ageing to his beautiful face. Half an hour later he returns for the film's conclusion when, instead of seeing Marie's execution, we are shown Axel's emotional reaction to witnessing it. The blade of the guillotine rises ominously before there is a cut to Power standing at the top of a tall building across the street, his body limp as he looks down dejected and alone. As Marie is decapitated off-screen, we receive a close-up of Power's face, wincing at first before opening his mouth in silent horror, but unable to look away. As with *Lloyds of London*'s conclusion, Power casts his eyes slowly downwards as the camera follows his gaze to his clenched fist, and the ring Marie had given Axel years ago, at the final fadeout.

Neal Benezra and Olga M. Viso suggest that 'the Classical belief in beauty's objective qualities has led to an endless search for ideal standards', with the ancient Greeks seeking to rationalise beauty and define the perfect proportions of physical beauty (1999: 89). They further note that Ancient Greece's view that beauty is a mathematical development has deeply affected Western culture, perhaps no more so than with the Renaissance masters, 'for whom Classical models were often interpreted as the best guides to "improving nature"' (1999: 89). In their scenes together, particularly the close-ups, it becomes extremely apparent that Power is much more beautiful than Shearer, either in full face or profile. Here, perhaps more than any other film, and due in part to the extreme bright lighting that MGM famously bestowed on its stars, Power strongly resembles the beautiful sculptures of Greek Gods with their features in perfect proportion to one another. Although the same lighting is used for both performers, profile shots help emphasise Power's jet-black hair, heavy-set eyebrows, rounded nose, strong jawline and extensive eyelashes, the sum parts combining to accentuate his extraordinary beauty. This contrasts sharply with Shearer's pale skin and light-coloured wigs, which almost wash her out while also exposing her rather pointed features. This did not make a kind comparison for MGM's foremost female star but an inescapable one when the two shared the screen. Although Shearer was dubbed 'the Queen of MGM' and the studio's leading female performer while Thalberg was alive, she was not one of the studio's great beauties, a fact made more obvious by pairings like this. Furthermore, the age difference that was slightly obvious between the twenty-five-year-old Taylor and the thirty-one-year-old Garbo in *Camille* is more noticeable here, with the twenty-four-year-old Power looking considerably younger than Shearer at thirty-six. Despite her elaborate costumes and hairstyles, Power is very much the erotic spectacle for both Marie and the audience, which is where the film is dissimilar to *Camille*, since Garbo and Taylor can be argued to be as beautiful as each other.

There is a softness in Power's face and body in this film, though less so than in *Lloyds of London*, which can partially be attributed to his youth, but also to the lighting, his elaborately frilled costumes and the composition of shots that consistently reveal his stunning beauty. Certainly, his every move appears deliberate and forced in order to best show him off to audiences, just as Marie displays him to her friends. As the object of Marie's, and by extension, the audience's, desire, Power's body is displayed in several elaborate but form-fitting costumes and his long, glossy hair is tied back in an oversized ribbon. Paglia calls Greek art's beautiful boy one of the West's great sexual personae, 'an androgyne, luminously masculine and feminine', who has both 'male muscle structure but a dewy girlishness' (1990: 110). In Greece, she notes, 'the beautiful boy was always beardless, frozen in time ... his beauty could not last and so was caught full-flower by Apollonian sculpture' (1990: 114), the beautiful boy representing 'a hopeless attempt to separate imagination from death and decay' (1990: 118). Like the traditional arts of sculpture or painting, cinema works to capture and record an actor's beauty before he ages and/or dies, and his beauty is lost to the world. Thus we can still marvel over and be affected by recorded images, made over eighty years ago, of Power as a beautiful youth that defies his death in 1958 and keeps his beauty ever-present for modern audiences.

Back at Twentieth Century-Fox, Power made his final film of the decade, *Suez*, a historical drama about the building of the Suez Canal. The film opens in 1850 in Paris where Power's Ferdinand de Lesseps is introduced playing tennis, losing a set because he is preoccupied with smiling at Loretta Young's Countess Eugenie. Attending a formal ball that night, Power dons historical evening dress and, as in *Marie Antoinette*, the brightly lit actor engages in romantic embraces with

Young. However, in this film, the last of their five on-screen pairings, their characters do not end up together. In fact, their romance ends thirteen minutes into the film when Eugenie refuses to marry him and follow him to Egypt. Although, unusually for Power, he subsequently engages in no more romantic scenes, the familiar trope of two women being in love with him remains ever present. While Eugenie never ceases loving Ferdinand, she marries Louis Napoleon and becomes Empress of France. Similarly, Annabella's Toni falls for him at first sight and loves him unrequitedly until she dies in a desert storm while saving his life. Power was permitted to be much more physically active in this film, portraying the strong, virile leader of the men undertaking the gruelling work of building the canal, and is thus placed in a purely homosocial situation after Toni's death. Although a nobleman by birth, as demonstrated by his elaborate costumes in the early scenes, his clothing gets less fussy and more utilitarian as the film progresses. He moves from evening dress and ruffled collars to a white three-piece suit, and finally to an open-necked shirt and casual trousers, which not only look quite modern, but also illustrate Ferdinand's journey from aristocracy to working man with an obsessive goal. Another European character, Ferdinand is a Frenchman but Power's American voice jars with Annabella's strong French accent.

Suez was not only his final film with Young, but his only on-screen appearance with future wife Annabella, although the two did work together on stage and in radio.[2] Upon meeting him, Toni tells Ferdinand, 'We heard you were good looking', pausing to look him up and down before adding, 'And you are'. Obviously, this line would only work for an attractive performer since it is spoken to the character (Ferdinand) who looks like the actor (Power). Responding merely with a disapproving face, Power demonstrates that men may 'regard compliments as potential face-threatening acts and find compliments on their appearance particularly discomforting' (Holmes 2011: 85). From this point on, Toni consistently pursues him, trying to kiss and seduce him regularly despite her feelings clearly not being reciprocated. However, when she dies saving his life, Ferdinand regrets how he has treated her and, as with *Lloyds of London*, the film ends on a close-up of Power's beautiful face with tear-filled eyes as he views the completed canal, still hearing her voice in his head (Figure 1.3).

Figure 1.3 The closing image of *Suez* (1938)

Pre-war dramas

Although in the 1940s Power starred in only four dramas, these films were diverse and, taken together, create the most significant phase of both his career and image development. While two were released in the pre-war years (for the US), the other two were made when he returned to Hollywood after his active duty. The earliest of these, *Johnny Apollo*, was not only Power's first drama of the 1940s but his first film of the decade. Although it begins in familiar territory, with a widely grinning Power sporting mussed-up hair and very little clothing, it soon veers off in a different direction for the actor. According to Fran Mason, this film, along with *Johnny Eager* (Mervyn LeRoy, 1941) starring Robert Taylor, helped demonstrate the romantic hero's tough side, which was used not only to revisit existing gangster conventions but also as 'a framework within which the star's masculinity could be measured' (2002: 53).

Before Power physically enters the film, he is introduced via a framed photograph on the cluttered desk of his millionaire father, Wall Street broker Robert Cain (Edward Arnold), who receives a telephone call

Figure 1.4   Power's 'entrance' in *Johnny Apollo* (1940)

informing him that he is being indicted for embezzlement. A close-up of the photograph then introduces the character of Bob/Robert Cain Jr, the telephone's cord running across the front of the image foreshadowing how Bob will soon become entwined in the situation (Figure 1.4). Dressed in a lightly coloured suit and tie, Power passively looks away from the camera, a wide smile not only displaying his happy-go-lucky, youthful appearance and perfectly white teeth but making the dimple on his left cheek prominent. As Paglia proposes, 'the beautiful boy, the object of all eyes, looks downward or away' (1990: 122), which echoes Dyer's discussion of the white male pin-up who 'might be there for his face and body to be gazed at', though the pose of looking 'up and off camera' suggests that 'his mind is on higher things' (1982: 63). The fact that this image is a professional headshot of Power used by Twentieth Century-Fox to promote the actor blurs the lines between performer and character. Furthermore, his being named 'Jr' and in the shadow of his famous father, at least at the start, was also a significant component of Power's early image. A second photograph linking Power's on- and off-screen lives is that of Bob's mother, placed prominently on his bedroom wall as he confronts his father. Although identified within the narrative as representing Bob's dead mother, it is, in fact, a photograph of Power's mother Patia (who would outlive her husband and son). Furthermore, although Power portrayed a range of nationalities on-screen, this was the only time he began a film by embodying the all-American college student often played by Taylor, such as in *A Yank at Oxford* (Jack Conway, 1938). Additionally, the name 'Bob' is not only a quintessentially all-American diminutive of Robert, but it was consistently used by the press when discussing Taylor.

Having been introduced to the viewer via the photograph, Power makes his actual entrance shortly afterwards, immediately greeting a photographer and his father's attorney with a wide grin reflecting the one in the portrait. However, the corporeal Power has messy hair and wears only a pair of tight trunks, attributed to the fact that Bob has just taken part in a college boat race. Unlike the passive photograph, the act of rowing suggests an active pursuit requiring a strong, disciplined body and, since the camera mostly films Power from below the knee throughout this scene, his body is put on display for audiences to gaze at and admire. Returning to ancient Greek philosophy, in *Rhetoric, Book I* Aristotle suggests that a young man's beauty 'is the possession of a body fit to endure the exertion of running and of contests of strength; which means he is pleasant to look at', therefore 'all-round athletes are the most beautiful, being naturally adapted both for contests of strength and for speed' ([4 BCE] 1964: 96). Bob then learns of his father's predicament from a newspaper handed to him by the attorney. Now isolated from his teammates with a pane of glass separating them physically, Power allows his smile to slowly fade, gives a brief but expressive glance at his carefree classmates, then at the attorney and back to the newspaper. Without using any words, Power effectively portrays that Bob's own happy-go-lucky youth has abruptly ended, while signifying the distance he now feels from his fellow students. It is a subtle but effective piece of acting, and although exhibited with his toned torso on display in a manner that might be read as gratuitous or 'beefcake' at the hands of another actor (for example, Victor Mature), it is Power's expressive face and eyes depicting Bob's conflicting emotions that we focus on. Paradoxically, this brief initial presentation of Power's statuesque body illustrates its parallels with ancient Greek sculpture, thus awarding us not only a brief erotic display but foreshadowing Bob's reinvention as Johnny Apollo, which he will soon undertake in order to enter the criminal underworld in his quest to free his father from jail.

Bob gets mixed up with the perpetually drunk lawyer Brennan (Charley Grapewin), gangster's moll 'Lucky' (Dorothy Lamour) and several undesirable characters from the criminal underworld, not least Mickey Dwyer (Lloyd Nolan), who was sentenced at the same time as his father but paroled. Wishing to conceal his real name, Bob introduces himself to Lucky as Johnny, another quintessential all-American name. When pressed by Brennan for a surname, Power slightly shifts his eyeline to a neon sign flashing across the street, before answering 'Apollo'. This advertisement for The Health Institution carries the message 'be a he-man, Apollo', a clever indication of the changes that Bob must undergo to fit into a world that is alien to him, while also directly inviting him to 'be a he-man', which he currently is not.

Moreover, Apollo is an apt name for Power. As a star to be looked at, he perfectly fits George Wilson Knight's remark that 'the Apollonian is the created ideal, forms of visionary beauty that can be seen' (1967: 268). In Ancient Greece, the beautiful boy inhabited 'the world of hard masculine action. His body was on view, striving nude in the palestra' (Paglia 1990: 110). Power's near nudity at the start of the film is rendered safe and non-homoerotic by the cover of a sporting event, a physical endeavour involving masculine action. As Paglia adds, the beautiful boy's 'broad-shouldered, narrow-waisted body was a masterwork of Apollonian articulation, every muscle group edged and contoured', while he was 'the focus of Apollonian space. All eyes were on him' (1990: 110). This is also true of a beautiful cinematic performer like Power, repeatedly put on display to be looked at by audiences and other characters. Paglia calls Apollo 'the integrity and unity of western personality, a firm-outlined shape of sculptural definitiveness. He is a fabricated form' (1990: 73). The initial display of Power in trunks allows the audience a tantalising glimpse of his beautiful body, which is then concealed beneath a more socially acceptable suit and tie. According to Paglia, 'Greek art transformed Apollo from the virile bearded god', the likes of which Power portrayed in the incomplete Solomon and Sheba, 'to a beautiful young man or ephebe' as he was here (1990: 73). She further remarks that in the revival of pagan culture, Apollo 'was hailed as the supreme creation of classical mythology' (1990: 81), just as Power's star image was the 'supreme creation' of the Hollywood star and studio systems, and Twentieth Century-Fox more specifically.

Elizabeth Prettejohn notes that in eighteenth-century Germany, Johann Joachim Winckelmann referred to beauty as 'not the precondition but rather the result of aesthetic contemplation, of a kind of collaboration between the viewer and the work' (2005: 22). We can apply this to the visual medium of cinema, particularly when discussing stars with great aesthetic appeal. Furthermore, given that Winckelmann's chief interest lay in the statue of *Apollo Belvedere*, this link to Power is particularly noteworthy. While in Greek mythology, Apollo, the son of Zeus, is the god considered to be the most beautiful, the *Apollo Belvedere* is celebrated for perfectly capturing the beauty of the human male form, and is described by Winckelmann as the 'highest ideal of art' with its mix of 'pleasing youth' and 'alluring virility' (Williams 2013: 34). Similarly, while discussing the male body, Rudolph Arnheim declares that 'perfection of the body and mind comes from being a god' (1994: 151). Thus the name Apollo also connects Power with the long-held view of movie stars being like modern gods (see de Cordova 2001). As Michael Williams notes, 'stars are *not* gods, and yet an institutionalised discourse apparently would have us believe that they are'; thus it is 'no accident that it is the Apollos, Venuses and Herculeses that first come to mind in describing star beauty and persona types' (2013: 17, original emphasis). Williams adds that, in the early decades of cinema, male stars 'tended to follow ideals already established in Western art', with the two male types categorised as Apollo and Hercules. He declares that Valentino, Ramon Novarro and Ivor Novello were 'termed Apollo at one point or another', because they were the 'most handsome and moderately athletic leading men' (2013: 49); they were also Power's most apparent predecessors, both in looks and the star type that he would embody in the classical era. While James Harvey describes Power's contemporary Joel McCrea as 'Apollo crossed with a small-town storekeeper' (1987: 294), Power can be viewed as a Greek god incarnate. His near-naked introduction shows a lean, athletic, muscular body depicting health and male beauty, which is exactly what sculptures and paintings of Apollo depict; thus, the name that Bob adopts, merely by chance, appears a deliberate one by the filmmakers. Ironically, aside from beauty, Apollo was also the god of truth, which shows the complex nature of his character since, by adopting the name, Bob has begun to spin his own web of lies.

Upon meeting Bob, Dwyer asks him to bail out an associate, with whom he must get tough when the man attempts to escape, giving Bob a black eye in the process. Displaying his first bout of violence, Bob cracks the man's head off the pavement before returning him to Dwyer. While Dwyer gives him a piece of raw steak for his eye and Lucky sings the appropriately titled 'This is the Beginning of the End', Bob is initiated into the group. A cut from a brightly lit close-up of Lamour to a low-angle shot of a much harder-looking Power reflects the life that Bob is about to enter. He looks older than before: shadows and lines are now etched on his face and the wide grin replaced with a clenched jaw and anxious expression. Breaking out of a trance-like stare, Power looks down at the steak he is gripping and holds his breath as he notices blood on his hand, another occurrence of foreshadowing. Slowly moving his thumb away from the steak and looking at the blood, he flashes his eyes once before closing his fist, indicating Bob's repulsion at his situation. Again, without dialogue, Power uses his eyes to show Bob's contradictory emotions, from shock and fear through disgust and finally determination. There are no close-ups of the steak or Power's hand, which would overtly guide the viewer where to look and the moment could easily be lost. Instead, it is chillingly conveyed by Power through this understated performance. Thus, *Johnny Apollo* was important in expanding Power's performance skills and, unusually at this stage in his career, allowed him to appear as a 'tough guy' in a film primarily aimed at male audiences. There do, however, remain several recognisable tropes, not least the exposure of his body, but also his costume of evening dress, this time a perfectly tailored modern tuxedo. Furthermore, like Shearer in *Marie Antoinette*, after Lamour's Lucky invites him to kiss her, he gives her a gentle peck on the cheek just before she grabs his face with both hands and forcefully kisses him on the mouth.

Power's final pre-war drama, *Blood and Sand* (1941), was based on Vicente Blasco Ibáñez's 1909 novel of the same name. As Paglia contends, many Western conceptions about the body are based on sexual personae originated by the Greeks. She examines, for example, what lies behind the lasting power of mythic male individuals such as Don Juan, Lord Byron, Elvis Presley and Valentino (1990). As a dark, brooding movie heartthrob, Valentino was the obvious choice as the lead in the 1922 silent version of *Blood and Sand* (Fred Niblo). One reviewer not only called the Power version one of Hollywood's strongest releases in 'many a season', but suggested that 'they can stop talking about ... Valentino ... This is stated with no disrespect or irrelevance for Valentino or his picture', but Zanuck's film is 'almost perfection in motion picture entertainment' (Anon 1941b: 9). As well as similarities in their looks and audience appeal, Valentino and Power both suffered untimely deaths during active careers. Why then, we may ask, is Valentino so much better remembered today, even by those who have never seen his films? Perhaps it is because he was not only one of the first movie stars, but one of the screen's first heartthrobs. Perhaps it was the press coverage of the hysteria surrounding his death and the reports of women committing suicide at his funeral, or maybe the myth of the mysterious 'Lady in Black' who placed roses on Valentino's grave for decades and whose true identity has often been disputed.[3]

Even though it was his twenty-fourth film, *Blood and Sand* was only the second of Power's films to be shot in colour (the first being *Jesse James*); it won the Best Colour Cinematography Oscar and was nominated for Best Art Direction. While *Johnny Apollo* earned the studio an impressive $1 million, *Blood and Sand* made $1.75 million (Solomon 1988). Furthermore, even though the film boasted two leading ladies, the first title card reads 'Twentieth Century Fox presents Tyrone Power', confirming the actor's importance to the production and the studio's pride in its top leading man. The film's title is on the second card and a third adds 'with Linda Darnell and Rita Hayworth', the use of 'with' reducing the women to the status of supporting players. The film was indeed very much a star vehicle for Power, just as *Marie Antoinette* had been for Shearer. Power's Juan Gallardo may be Spanish, but there are several parallels with the actor's own life. Juan seeks success and fame as a matador, a profession for which his deceased father was famous and greatly respected, and which he died undertaking. Juan's own fame soon eclipses his father's until, admired by men and adored by women, he also dies young while undertaking his job, predeceasing his mother in the process. Although bullfighting is an extremely active, hypermasculine pursuit within an explicitly homosocial community, this provided cover for *Blood and Sand* to be the first film to present Power explicitly as a spectacle to be looked at for prolonged periods by both diegetic and non-diegetic audiences.

Like several of his other films (*Lloyds of London, In Old Chicago, Son of Fury*), the story begins in flashback to Juan's childhood, so that Power's entrance is delayed for twenty-two minutes. His face is revealed from behind a newspaper, his hair combed forward in a rather unflattering style, as he grips a cigar between his teeth and grins widely. Noticing a photograph of himself in the newspaper but unable to read, he asks a man to read it for him. We are shown the article, which describes Juan in unflattering terms such as 'fifth-rate' and untalented, leading the man to invent a positive story while the smiling Juan proudly rips out the page and puts it in his pocket. Returning home to marry childhood sweetheart Carmen (Darnell), he boastfully asks her to read the clipping, which she reluctantly does while quickly realising he cannot read. She intersperses her reading by repeatedly asking when they will be married, demonstrating that she does not care if he is a failure; she is also the one to instigate their first kiss as adults.

Alongside *The Mark of Zorro*, David Thomson suggests that *Blood and Sand* shows Power at 'his iconographic best' (1994: 600), and both films do their upmost to display his body as an erotic spectacle. Power is often presented in a state of undress in *Blood and Sand*, including being shirtless in bed for a whole scene while eating breakfast and romancing Darnell. The most obvious example, however, is when he sits bare-chested on an elaborate chair resembling a throne, with an audience of over fifteen fully clothed men there to observe the spectacle of his being dressed for the ring. Given this contrast and his positioning, Power's near-nakedness particularly stands out on this occasion. Once he is fully clothed in a royal blue matador outfit edged with an extravagant gold trim and a jewel-encrusted cape, he poses for Carmen and asks her how he looks, thus reversing traditional gender roles. With her hair tied back, wearing very little make-up and clothed in a plain grey dress, the usually beautiful Darnell resembles a dowdy peahen in contrast to Power's dazzling and showy peacock or, in the words of Colin McDowell, Power, presents us with an image of 'male as visual peacock' (1997: 45). He is unquestionably the true beauty of this scene, and the focus of our attention, while Darnell almost merges with the background. In his discussion of masculine curves, McDowell notes that a man's bottom is the 'only part of his anatomy to rival the female shape for curvaceousness', and that, although it has always been considered an erogenous zone, it tends to be 'decently covered but occasionally allowed to burst into glorious sexuality' (1997: 10). For Power, this is never truer than in *Blood and Sand*, where costumes, lingering shots and his positioning in the bullring draw particular attention to his buttocks, which are enrobed in a range of tight, form-fitting matador outfits while he is exhibited for both the on-screen and theatre audiences.

As is common with Power's characters, women look him over throughout the film, principally Hayworth's Doña Sol. In one noteworthy scene, she attempts to seduce him by singing and fingering her guitar. Realising that Juan has fallen asleep, she stands up abruptly, but her expression quickly changes from anger and disappointment to an excited smile as she casts her gaze over his entire body, and she can view him safely, since he cannot return her gaze. The audience is given the same thrill through a point-of-view shot as the camera slowly pans the length of Power's body from his feet to his face, so that we too may relish what Doña sees and very much approves of. Murray Pomerance has discussed actors Gary Cooper and Fredric March 'performing sleep' in *Design for Living* (Ernst Lubitsch, 1933), while their characters are unknowingly watched by Miriam Hopkins's Gilda. Pomerance suggests that, because 'she is working her vision in a territory outside … their performance space, their consciousness, this female is a voyeuse' (2019: 38). These characters, travelling in a train carriage, are unaware of Gilda's presence since she enters while they sleep, but Juan falls asleep at Doña's house and is fully aware of her presence beforehand. Nevertheless, his being rendered unconscious does not justify her lustful gaze, since he is both unaware of it and unable to return it, meaning she too can be deemed a voyeuse. But, as Pomerance states, an actor 'can still perform while sleeping, or when "sleeping", as long as an audience is in place to watch' (2019: 38). Thus, Power (the actor) is not actually asleep whereas Juan (the character) is; perhaps, then, we are less voyeuristic than Doña since Power performs sleep for us, but Juan does not perform sleep for her. Although Dyer suggests that the point-of-view shot, which is 'one of the building blocks of filmic storytelling', is mostly that of a 'white male character scrutinising, appraising or savouring black and/or female characters than vice versa' (1997: 45), this is not true of Power's films, since it is often the woman who scrutinises, appraises and savours his face and body as Doña does here. However, many of his characters also actively look, so that he is never rendered fully passive or emasculated and, consequently, is still active and masculine as well.

The film's most erotically charged scene occurs a short time later as Power plays bull to Hayworth's torero in what appears a convoluted form of foreplay, with her taunting him with a cape and shouting, 'Toro, Toro'. She is in full control as he moves from a kneeling position near her breast, slowly sliding his hands up her body until he too is standing upright and facing her. Hayworth holds him at arm's length by tightly gripping and tugging his hair, pushing his head back as he leans in to kiss her (Figure 1.5). Power's body trembles as he moves forward against her resistance before she finally breaks away, leaving him looking bewildered and confused at this anti-climax. However, it is Juan's unfulfilled passion that fuels his desire for Doña and renders this an extremely sexual scene even though the promised kiss does not occur. Their affair comes to an end while Doña is dancing with up-and-coming matador Manolo de Palma (Anthony Quinn). Shots

Figure 1.5 Power and Hayworth in *Blood and Sand* (1941)

of Hayworth and Quinn moving provocatively are interjected with those of Power watching, half in shadow, from a corner table. His furrowed brow and downturned mouth reveal Juan's fury, and for the most part he remains stationary while staring at their sensual exhibition. When he does move, his actions are quick and jerky as he looks at his glass, drinks the champagne down in one and quickly returns to glaring at them. The sexual tension builds as their dance concludes with Quinn holding Hayworth in his arms and breathing heavily before a final cut shows Power, without averting his gaze, squeezing his glass so hard that it shatters into numerous fragments, symbolising his delayed ejaculation and release before he walks out, finally free from her clutches. Quinn sits down in his place and uses his sleeve to wipe the particles off the table before asking for a new glass, a significant move since he will soon replace Juan in the bullring as well as in Doña's affections.

At the film's conclusion, Juan reluctantly agrees to retire after one last bullfight for the sake of Carmen and his mother, but as he plays up to the adoring crowd he is gored from behind and dies shortly afterwards. Since bullfighting has become his whole existence, and that of his father before him, he cannot truly envision a life outside of the ring, and death means he no longer has to. Manolo immediately takes his place in the ring and in the affections of the fickle crowd, as well as Doña's, as the camera pans to reveal the mark Juan has left in the ring: both the literal and symbolic blood on the sand, as the film fades out. Although he would make several more films before enlisting in the Marine Corps, this was to be Power's last drama for five years before he returned to the genre after the war. During his absence from the screen, like Juan, he too was replaced by new leading men, both at Twentieth Century-Fox and on movie screens more generally, although unlike his character he would return to the screen as a leading man, if not to his full glory as displayed in *Blood and Sand*.

Sex and power: the post-war dramas

When Schatz notes how the penchant for realism and social critique in the post-war era significantly impacted many of Hollywood's productions, with 'maladjusted males ... alienation and anxiety clearly invok[ing] the general postwar climate' (1997: 4–5), he could be referring to Power's Larry Darrell in *The Razor's Edge* (1946). Concurrently, he could also be talking about Power and his return to the uncertainty of post-war Hollywood after his military service, and off-screen work, for more than three years. Based on Somerset Maugham's best-selling novel of the same name, Twentieth Century-Fox had paid $50,000 for the rights (Casper 2007: 45). Drew Casper refers to *The Razor's Edge* as not only a male melodrama but the 'period- and genre-defining' film, with Power as both 'Fox's primo male attraction' and its 'genre icon' (2007: 252). This suggests that Power's post-war return to Hollywood, and the genre, was extremely successful. Indeed, as the figures quoted in the introduction show, *The Razor's Edge* earned the studio $5 million and was its second biggest money-maker after *Forever Amber*.

In the film, Maugham becomes a character (portrayed by Herbert Marshall) and the narrator of Larry's story. Power enters the film once the other principal characters have been introduced, and it is a grand entrance indeed. Arriving at the vast building where an elaborate party is going on, he is first at a distance before the camera finds and focuses in on him across the crowded room. The camera then dollies in on his face, seen on-screen for the first time in three years but as handsome as ever, the studio obviously delighted to have him back and show him off. As the diegetic music fades, Marshall's voiceover begins, 'this is the young man of whom I write', which hints at the importance Power's character will have to the plot. He concludes his speech with the words, 'long after his death perhaps it may be realised that there lived in this age a very remarkable creature', which could just as easily be applied to Power himself. Indeed, there are several parallels between actor and character.

Made just after World War II but set immediately after World War I, Larry is an ex-flier who has just returned from the horrors of war and wants to do more with his life than sell bonds. Casper calls the film 'a cultural touchstone for the post-war ex-serviceman' and 'an emblem of the individual vs. the group mentality', with Larry 'a conscious pursuer of spirituality' (2007: 251–2). Seeing it as an unconventional film, and a 'career about-face' for Power (2007: 553), Casper views the actor's first post-war film as 'a decided career switch from his classical persona of a dashing lover and/or peerless wielder of derring-do' and finally giving him something to play (2007: 252). He suggests that the film's theme displaces 'the culture's traditional criteria for male maturity' by suggesting that marriage, fatherhood and a well-paid job were 'not what it was all about', with Larry's continual search for the meaning of life encompassing the idea of fulfilment through the 'virtues of altruism, self-sacrifice, and celibacy' (2007: 253). Despite other performers receiving Oscar nominations or awards for the film, Power's Larry is the central character holding it all together, as does the actor with his understated performance, but yet again even a nomination eluded him.

It is a familiar Power who enters the film, as if he has never been away (Figure 1.6). Dashingly handsome in a tuxedo and black tie, he grins widely, kisses girlfriend Isabel (Gene Tierney) and dances with her in the garden. Within seven minutes of his entrance, however, his usually breezy manner switches to a darker one indicative of the post-war sensibility, which is played out through a combination of Power's words, vocal intonation and gestures. Although both the lines of dialogue and Power's performance are highly dramatic and his voice almost melodic, the scene is fully believable, particularly when we consider that, like Larry, Power had also just returned from active war duty during which he must have witnessed some horrific sights. Shot in profile, he silently stares at Tierney from over his shoulder for an uncomfortably long time, both for her character and the audience, until she finally asks, 'Yes?' Continuing to stare, as if seeing her for the first time, he turns his whole body around slowly until he is facing both her and the camera, never breaking his

Figure 1.6 Power's post-war return to the screen in *The Razor's Edge* (1946)

gaze. Adopting a deadpan voice as he ominously states, 'the dead look so terribly dead when they're dead' makes it a chilling moment. When she questions what he means, he replies in the same deep, flat tone, 'just that', while continuing to stare as if in a trance. Finally breaking his gaze and turning away, Power begins to talk more naturally while his back is turned, before spinning around violently and emotionally recounting how he witnessed a man's death. Like the expressive reading of a poem or the performance of a song, Power's voice adopts a variety of styles and registers across the scene, which flow seamlessly together to express Larry's pain and confusion at recalling this harrowing event. Additionally, although the actor allows the character's contrasting emotions to show on his face, we are likewise required to pay close attention in reading his subtle gestures since they are devoid of any theatrics. Faintly smiling now, and with his speech a little lighter, he notes that a minute before the man died, he was 'full of life and fun and then . . . '. His voice trails off and he pauses, lowering his eyebrows and closing his mouth tightly, before flashing his eyes just once. Although physically looking at Tierney, he also appears to be looking through her, as if not really seeing her, as his mind goes back and he fully becomes his character. With a break in his voice, he adds, 'He was dead'; these final three words are said in a low and barely audible voice as if he cannot bring himself to utter them. Looking off to the side, he exhales sharply as if in physical pain, and slowly turns from Tierney, as he recalls seeing many men die but this was different. Power spins around quickly to face Tierney again, his voice louder and steadier now: 'It was the last day of the war, almost the last moment'. Another pause before his speech becomes more rapid and his voice filled with emotion as he rushes out the words: 'He could have saved himself, but he didn't, he saved me and . . .' Another pause follows before he adds 'died' in an even lower register. Power takes a deep breath and allows his voice to return to a more natural tone and pace as he adds, 'so he's gone and I'm here alive'. A single beat follows before he steps towards Tierney and shouts, 'Why?', the word almost merging with the 'alive' of his last sentence and so unexpected that it feels like a sudden punch in the face for the viewer. It is a highly impactful scene, not only because of the nature of the dialogue and Power's actions, but particularly because of the varied and skilful way Power manipulates his voice throughout, not only with variation in tone and intonation, but in the perfectly executed pauses, which almost say more than the words themselves. The scene proves that Power has not forgotten how to act after several years away. If anything, his absence from Hollywood had given his characterisations more depth and rawness; perhaps because he could draw on his personal experience of the war, which was still very recent.

Although a darker style of filmmaking began to emerge during the war, Schatz feels that it was only through 'the paranoia, pessimism and social angst' of the post-war years that it 'reached full maturity' (1997: 235). Likewise, Dixon refers to this period in American history as a climate of 'hyper-surveillant paranoia', resulting in a glut of Hollywood films reflecting the public mood and demonstrating how America had changed as a society. These films, in Dixon's words, portrayed 'a spiritual terrain of bleak and unrelenting despair' (2006: 9). Dixon's account of *film noir*, depicting an entirely amoral, cynical world in which there were really only two classes: winners and losers (2006: 9), can be applied to the bleak post-war drama, *Nightmare Alley* and Power's portrayal of how his character Stanton (Stan) Carlisle viewed himself and those around him. Although it has been widely reported that Zanuck and Twentieth Century-Fox were greatly opposed to Power playing such a merciless role, Stan actually provided a better fit with Power's post-war mentality, and that of the country as a whole, and with much more clarity, than any of the swashbucklers the studio had him star in afterwards, such as the inter-changeable and quite forgettable *Prince of Foxes* (Henry King, 1949) and *The Black Rose* (Henry Hathaway, 1950). As Stan, Power makes a lasting impression and it is one of the few roles he is still known for today, while the aforementioned action-adventure films are largely forgotten.

Many films of the late 1940s, such as *The Lost Weekend* (Billy Wilder, 1945) and *Gentleman's Agreement* (Elia Kazan, 1947), aimed to analyse critically the problems facing contemporary American society (Shindler 1979: 100). There was also a dominant trend in dark dramas at this time, with many of these films subsequently being labelled *film noir* (including *The Lost Weekend*). According to Colin Shindler, this type of film suggests 'an attitude to life that was black, harsh and fatalistic' (1979: 101), a description that perfectly encapsulates *Nightmare Alley*. Given its extremely grim subject matter and treatment, the film is often discussed under the heading *film noir* and appears in several books on the topic (Silver and Ward 1980; Stephens 1995; Mayer and McDonnell 2007). For the purposes of this book, however, *Nightmare Alley* is classified as a drama, albeit an extremely dark one, since this is how it was initially produced and marketed to audiences. Furthermore, I would argue that, even retrospectively, it is not quite a *noir* given the absence of any truly unscrupulous women, or *femme fatales*, to manipulate the hero, although I do draw on some *noir* elements important for the historical positioning of both the film and Power's performance within it. It is Stan, the male protagonist, who manipulates the women around him, primarily using his physical attractiveness to do so, thereby rendering him neither victim nor 'hero' in the traditional sense. The film includes numerous dark settings, highly contrasted chiaroscuro lighting, and a sense of evil on the screen emanating from Stan that relies predominantly on Power's performance skills.

World War II brought about a change in America's self-image, which is also true of the Hollywood film industry and many of its cinematic stars. Not only did archetypes, such as the hero, undergo basic changes, but so too did genres as they hybridised and took on 'previously taboo subject matter ... [which] explored the seamier side of life' (Byars 1991: 112). Venturing into these previously undiscussed areas made cinema distinct from television, which was rising in popularity and deemed suitable for all the family. Thus, these films were aimed at 'an adult audience and provided controversial stories, often based on popular novels and plays that had already proven lucrative' (Byars 1991: 88). Just as *The Lost*

Weekend, based on Charles Jackson's novel, allowed a sharp change in direction for its star Ray Milland, who won an Oscar for his unrelenting depiction of an alcoholic, *Nightmare Alley* was adapted from William Lindsay Gresham's shocking 1946 novel depicting the seedy side of carnival life as the lowest form of showbusiness and, in Stan's case, the lowest form of human life. In his analysis of *Gun Crazy* (Joseph H. Lewis, 1950), Jim Kitses declares that venues like carnivals cater to people's need for release by providing an escape from both the everyday and oneself. In seeking this kind of release, however, characters often find themselves 'embarking on a dark journey', the carnival 'potent in feeding the appetite for pleasure and fantasy', while also operating as a 'distorted, deviant double of the normal world' (1996: 25). In *Nightmare Alley*, the world of the carnival is presented as grimy and sleazy, and it offers audiences the physically beautiful Power at his most grotesque in terms of personality and later looks. While Kitses feels that the carnival in *Gun Crazy* acts as 'a grotesque comment on capitalism and the work ethic' (1996: 25), Stan ubiquitously manipulates those around him in his egocentric drive to get to the top. Carnival life has become normal and everyday for him, and he wishes to escape and lose himself in the 'ordinary' world outside. He does this through devious means, most obviously by seducing and sleeping with the three women so that they will do his bidding; indeed, *Nightmare Alley* is mostly about sex and power.

Michael L. Stephens suggests that the film provided Power with the rare opportunity to prove that he could act, referring to his performance as both 'excellent' (1995: 272) and 'great' (1995: 293). While calling it 'one of the most unrelenting depressing *film noirs*' and unusual material for both Power and director Edmund Goulding, best known for 'his glossy MGM entertainments', Stephens also proposes that the film is flawed but gives no details as to why (1995: 271–2). He does, however, highlight Gresham's obsession with the dark side of show business and the 'unrelenting views of shysters, half-wits, and the madness of carnival life' of which he had first-hand experience (1995: 272), thus giving the story a sense of legitimacy.

Although both cocky and self-assured, Stan possesses none of the optimism of *A Yank in the RAF*'s Tim Baker. Similarly, he lacks the compassionate drive behind Jesse James's and Bob Cain's descent into a life of crime. Even Barton Dewitt Clinton, heading to jail at the close of *Rose of Washington Square* (Gregory Ratoff, 1939), shows some shame and remorse in his actions, weeping openly at the realisation of how deeply he has hurt Rose and handing himself in to the police. In brief, Stanton Carlisle is a deplorable human who eventually falls lower than he, or anyone else, could have imagined as he is rendered almost non-human as a sideshow freak. Indeed, the film comes full circle, since Stan is first seen staring at the geek, beginning to walk off and looking back as it devours live chickens. He pensively tells a fellow employee, 'The guy fascinates me', before the camera moves in for a closer shot of Power as he asks, 'How do you get a guy to be a geek? Is that the only one? I mean, is a guy born that way?' without receiving a response to any of his inquiries. He continues this dialogue with Zeena (Joan Blondell), stating that he cannot understand how anybody can get so low as he buttons up his jacket. When she dismissively replies, 'It can happen', he pauses in his task and quickly turns to look at her, foreshadowing Stan's own descent into the manifestation of the geek at the film's close.

After an establishing shot of the carnival we are introduced to Zeena, standing silently and stationary as Stan makes his way through the crowd. We watch Blondell watching Stan before being presented with the object of her gaze: Power looking magnificent in a tight white t-shirt. His jet-black hair and stature instantly make him stand out from the crowd, while the t-shirt clings to his form and displays his impressive arms and torso. Three women smile at him, look him up and down and discuss him as he walks past, but he ignores them. Chewing nonchalantly, he stops at a wooden post, raises an arm and flexes his muscles as he grabs hold of a rope and leans against the post. Discussing Marlon Brando's tight white t-shirt and jeans in *A Streetcar Named Desire* (Elia Kazan, 1951), Steven Cohan calls this costuming 'especially important in emphasizing that performativity and sexuality interact' (1997: 248). Far from being random attire, Cohan notes that the outfit is actually a 'look' used to 'produce a calculated effect, both dramatically and cinematically, in the way it veils and exposes the male body with the kind of attention conventionally given to costuming a female star' (1997: 248). Here, four years earlier than Brando, Power wears an almost identical outfit which adds a dangerous, earthy sexuality to his star image, and to the character. Power displays his muscularity in tight white t-shirts and vests while seducing Zeena (Figure 1.7) and Molly (Coleen Gray), whom he is forced to marry after he sleeps with her.

When seducing Dr Lilith Ritter (Helen Walker), however, Power dresses in a more formal and expensive-looking dark pinstripe suit, shirt and tie, complete with a pocket handkerchief and white carnation on the lapel, reminiscent of the one his felon wore in *Rose of Washington Square*.

Figure 1.7   Stanton (Power) seduces Zeena (Joan Blondell) in *Nightmare Alley* (1947)

McDowell calls the striped suit the dress of authority that has an aura of respectability (1997: 186) and, while carnival performers Zeena and Molly succumb to his primitive and animalistic seduction in tight t-shirts that exhibit his brawniness, the sophisticated doctor may not have been so susceptible to this lower-class coded item of clothing. In fact, the masculine cut of her business suit almost mirrors his, thus putting them on the same level, visually at least if not also morally. Furthermore, although his costumes are tailored to fit his frame and accentuate his broad shoulders and chest, Power's form is now fully covered.

Stan uses his physical beauty and immense appeal to women throughout to climb the ladder of success, but his downfall is also accompanied by a sharp loss of looks, which shocks the viewer. Discussing Oscar Wilde's *The Picture of Dorian Gray*, Paglia notes that the novel 'makes complicated use of the western ideal of hierarchies. Beautiful persons are *aristoi*, "the best." They are Dostoyevsky's "extraordinary men," who have the Sadean "right to commit any crime." The ugly belong to a lower order of being' (1990: 515). Something similar happens to Stan. Throughout *Nightmare Alley*, the beautiful Power, with his well-groomed black hair, seductive eyes and toned physique attired in a range of tight tops, tailored suits and tuxedos, seduces women to do his bidding, Stan's confidence in the power of his looks aids him in his thirst for fame and fortune. However, when his beauty fades due to hard living, alcohol abuse and his downright contemptibleness, he is alone, alcoholic and desperate for a job.

He finds a carnival and begs for any kind of work. At the pinnacle moment when the carnival owner offers him a job as a geek, Power is looking down. Upon hearing the word 'geek', he slowly looks up and bewilderingly repeats it almost in a whisper, rephrasing it as a question. When the man asks if he knows what a geek is, Power laughs lightly at the irony and replies, 'Sure, I know what a geek is', while continuing to stare pathetically at the man. Power then allows a small smile to play around the sides of his mouth, lets his intense stare relax and raises his glass before confidently and steadily replying to the enquiry as to whether he can handle the part: 'Mister, I was made for it'. Throughout the scene, Power is filmed from above and in stark, low-key lighting. Upon raising his head, we witness his 'otherness' for the first time, and he is almost unrecognisable as the character who had been making love to women just an hour previously. Gone are his good looks, replaced with craggy skin around the eyes, a drooping jawline and a gaunt face; his hair is a tangled mess and his complexion dull, creating a disturbing contrast to the brash, virile man we have followed throughout.

At the film's close, Stan has fully embodied the geek that so fascinated him at the start. Dressed in a baggy shirt and trousers appearing three sizes too large for him, thus masking his once exposed and desirable body and making him look small and pitiful, he is reduced to a primitive creature unable to form a sentence. With shrill, inaudible cries he runs feral while attempting to escape both the men chasing him and his own fate. The line 'how does a guy get so low?', which was uttered by the arrogant Stan at the start, is reprised here. Only this time it is chillingly asked of Stan rather than by him, his final descent to the depths of humanity complete. Given Stan's consistently wide grin, charm and fast talk, it is a particularly disturbing ending that also renders Power 'the Hollywood star' practically unrecognisable and is almost certainly why Zanuck had issues with him taking on the role. Much safer was his next film, *Captain from Castile* (Henry King, 1947), a historical action-adventure film that was a throwback to *The Mark of Zorro*, therefore a step back for Power's screen image, and nowhere near as impactful or demanding as *Nightmare Alley*.

As Higham and Greenberg note, after the war, 'the cessation of hostilities seemed to create more problems than it solved'. and although major male stars like Power, James Stewart, Clark Gable and Henry Fonda 'returned to sound-stage duty . . . Hollywood had still to put itself in a stable peace-time basis' (1968: 14). This is perhaps why Twentieth Century-Fox allowed Power to make *Nightmare Alley* at this time, whereas they may not have in the pre-war years. As the authors note, in 1947, the year of the film's release, '28% of films given a Motion Picture Association Code seal had a "problem" content' (1968: 16). They highlight that this was also a time when many relatively inexpensive 'quality' pictures were made: 'the psychological melodrama in black-and-white with mainly indoor sets and small casts' (1968: 16). Indeed, aside from the necessary nightclub sequences with lush sets showing Power dressed in a tuxedo (a major part of his pre-war image) and Gray in a floor-length evening dress, the remainder of the film takes place in a series of small, almost claustrophobic spaces, mostly stark and basic (motel rooms, carnival wagons, Ritter's office) with the cast primarily limited to six carnival performers and Ritter.

Now considered one of Power's most important films, *Nightmare Alley* is also the one that most obviously shows his depth as a performer. Although advancing Power's reputation as an actor beyond his long-established image as a beautiful star and romantic lead, it was a high-risk role given his recognised status as a leading Hollywood heartthrob. As Sarah Thomas highlights in her study of Peter Lorre, 'the concepts of "artistry" and "typecasting" are as much deliberate industrial marketing strategies which aim to give a sense of coherence to an otherwise disparate career, as they are evaluative critiques of a performer's work' (2012: 54). Despite Power's seemingly being typecast as a swashbuckler, therefore strongly associated with action-adventure films, he actually moved fluidly across genres throughout his career. Even his work in dramatic films, the genre he appeared in most often, greatly varies in themes, historical and geographical settings and characterisations. Moreover, Davis calls offbeat casting 'a frequent device for adding interest to a picture, and performers generally welcomed such departures' (1993: 107). *Nightmare Alley* is particularly unusual in Power's trajectory, and by all accounts it was he who pushed for the role after reading Gresham's novel. Twentieth Century-Fox grudgingly agreed but purposely did not promote it widely, giving it a limited theatrical run so that not many audiences would see it (Power 2014). However offbeat the casting, Power was one of the few stars who could have played Stan so effectively, since his consistent manipulation of the women around him needs to be principally tied to his physical appearance and sexual prowess, which he uses for his selfish gain. Thus, Power applies a performative style that was familiar to his image, while maintaining a distance between actor and role, particularly when he becomes 'othered' as the geek, sporting a macabre appearance and rendered almost speechless. Although elements of the film remain disturbing and shocking, the performance was in keeping with Gresham's obsession with the seedy underworld of carnivals.

The final decade: 1950s dramas

The last two dramas Power made while under contract to Twentieth Century-Fox were rather formalistic and unexceptional, particularly after his performance in *Nightmare Alley*. *The House in the Square*, also known as *I'll Never Forget You*, is a fantasy piece in which Power's twentieth-century atomic physician, Peter Standish, is struck by lightning and transported back to 1700s London, complete with historical costuming, where he romances both Ann Blyth's Helen Pettigrew and her sister. At the start, the film is shot in black and white and Power wears a modern business suit, but when he enters eighteenth-century London the film changes to colour and he is dressed in appropriate clothing for the time.

Paglia's discussion of *The Picture of Dorian Gray* suggests that Wilde 'shows the strange symbiosis between a beautiful boy and a painting, that is, between a charismatic androgyne and his portrait' (1990: 512). We could make the same comparisons with Power here and in his earlier screen performances, which were captured like paintings and can be revisited despite the passing of time. Equally, we can apply it to the portrait of Peter's eponymous ancestor that hangs in his Victorian London home and has been painted in the likeness of Power but dressed in eighteenth-century frills and ruffles. Thus, unlike the photograph in *Johnny Apollo*, this painting looks like Power and we recognise it as Power but it is not meant to represent Power, instead it signifies Peter's long-dead predecessor who still 'lives' in the portrait and looks identical to the actor in face and form. Yet even these boundaries are blurred, since Peter will adopt this costuming for much of the film when he goes back in time and masquerades as his forebear. The film fails to add much to Power's repertoire, but again allows the actor to be presented in a range of tight-fitting historical clothing, get involved romantically with two women and dance in evening clothes where he is again depicted as spectacle. Power's costumes echo those he wore thirteen years earlier in *Marie Antoinette*, only this time he portrays a twentieth-century man masquerading as his eighteenth-century ancestor. Furthermore, the actor is now thirty-seven and sporting manlier features; the soft prettiness of his youth replaced by a more solid and rugged handsomeness.

Similarly, *Diplomatic Courier* is a Cold War drama that, although rather routine for Hollywood at the time, was a different kind of film for Power and the only one of its kind that he made, although it shares the familiar narrative pattern of having two women (played by Hildegarde Neff, also known as Kneff, and the extremely forceful Patricia Neal) vying for his affections. As R. Barton Palmer notes, these Cold War films dealt with various developments in Europe and the intrigues of foreign politics (2014: 91). They offer little opportunity for star spectacle. However, ten minutes before the film's conclusion Power's Mike Kells is injured, and the audience is granted a prolonged four-minute scene during which a shirtless Power is shot from several angles as he discusses the case with two fully clothed military officers (Stephen McNally and Karl Malden). Asking for his clothes, Power removes the blanket covering his lower body and begins putting on his shirt while sitting in his underpants before the scene fades out. The latter part of this scene, in particular, seems merely there for spectacle since the cut-away could have been made much earlier and, even though he wears a range of business suits during the rest of the film, the official posters mostly carry images of the shirtless Power. Moreover, despite Neal not actually being in this scene, the posters feature her wearing a red dress and holding a gun at the semi-naked Power, an incident that does not happen in the film. Palmer calls the film 'a dark, suspenseful tale of postwar espionage in the divided city of Trieste', and notes that it ends with 'the improbable, if ideologically satisfying, conversion of the beautiful Russian agent (Hildegarde Neff) to democratic principles as well as a romantic commitment to her handsome American counterpart' played by Power (2014: 91).

Independent drama

Power's next two dramas were Technicolor biopics, both over two hours long. Made for Columbia, they marked the first dramas Power made away from Twentieth Century-Fox since his loan-out to MGM for *Marie Antoinette* almost two decades earlier. This also meant that Power was once again on trend since, as Casper points out, '1955 witnessed a quintuple summation of the classical bio which every studio continued to turn out' with big studio luminaries (2007: 170). Both films are highly emotive and allow Power to display a vast array of performance skills through his portrayal of complex, real-life characterisations, although, significantly, neither role relied on his looks. First, he starred in *The Long Gray Line* (1955), depicting Martin Maher's life and distinguished West Point career, which spanned over fifty years as he rose from waiter to master sergeant and was adored by generations of cadets in the process. It is the film in which Power comes his closest to character acting, his work at Columbia allowing him to tap into new acting skills that showed the diversity of his performance and relied less on his physical appearance. He was also permitted to age considerably in the film and adopts an Irish brogue for the duration, his first attempt at an accent since *Lloyds of London*, and far more convincing. In both biopics, Power arrives in a strange place as a brash young man with a suitcase, dressed in a flat cap and light-coloured suit. *The Long Gray Line* was based on Maher's 1951 memoir *Bringing Up the Brass*, and its subject was still alive when the film was made. In fact, Maher outlived Power, dying in 1961 at the age of eighty-four.

Martin gets his start at West Point as a waiter, dressed in whites and with a mass of curly hair to make Power look younger. Several scenes then follow in which Power convincingly, and unusually, displays a range of physical, almost slapstick, comedy including falling over and breaking piles of dishes, trying to load a canon the wrong way and repeatedly getting knocked down in a boxing ring. Similarly, during his initial meeting with future wife Mary O'Donnell (Maureen O'Hara), he wears a baseball cap and carries an armful of boxing gloves. Here, Power's performance more closely resembles a Charlie Chaplin or Jerry Lewis sketch rather than the courtship of a romantic leading man, as he silently stares at her while dropping the gloves one by one. Martin is almost completely desexualised throughout the film, which is a tribute to Power's excellent acting skills since, for the most part, he still looks like Power. Once he has proposed to Mary, the film moves forward some years and Power now sports a bushy moustache as Martin is hired as a swimming instructor even though he cannot swim, and his pupils have to save him from drowning after he accidentally, and comically, falls into the pool.

Although Power plays the first hour and ten minutes of the film with overt physical comedy, when the couple's only child dies at birth and Mary is told she cannot have any more children the film shifts to high drama. Power's understated performance when initially hearing the news, and later when visiting Mary in the hospital, makes the event even more poignant, particularly since he has been so animated up to this point. When World War I breaks out, many of the cadets whom the couple have come to view as their own children are killed. Martin's grief and despair are shown through Power's slower movements in everyday tasks, his disappearing inside himself and his lack of humour; now he is rarely shown smiling. The film again moves forward in time as the third generation of cadets Martin will be working with are enrolling. Martin has now been promoted to sergeant, with Power sporting spectacles and distinguished grey hair and moustache, several lines on his face and jowls beginning to appear. When Mary dies, Martin becomes a lonely old man unable to take care of himself. His house is a mess, the kitchen full of unwashed dishes and piles of rubbish everywhere. When the cadets come to visit him on Christmas day, one gives him a new pipe and they sing while putting up a Christmas tree for him. Although Martin becomes emotional at their generosity, he tries not to show it. It is a poignant performance from Power and, more than any other role before or after, shows his range of performance skills. Although make-up is used to show Martin has visually aged, Power also alters his posture, his manner and his voice, and we are given a glimpse of what Power may have looked like as a mature man had he lived (Figure 1.8). Despite the wonderfully real and touching performances from Power and the rest of the cast, the film was not a success at the box office and critics branded it 'mawkish, even though

Figure 1.8   Power is almost unrecognisable in *The Long Gray Line* (1955)

they found its characters loveable and warm' (Davis 1995: 266). However, it is arguably Power's greatest screen performance, and although the film is not readily remembered today, Power gives a touching, believable and very real depiction of Maher's extraordinary life and proves that he was much more than a pretty face.

The Eddy Duchin Story also allowed Power some character acting as the famed pianist of the film's title, though less so than as Maher. Duchin, who was also a friend of Power's, died of leukaemia in 1951 at the age of forty-one, only five years before the film was released. This time, it was one of the year's biggest successes and took over $5 million at the box office; Casper calls it the 'mega-hit' with which ex-MGM director George Sidney began his tenure at Columbia (2007: 69). At the start of the film, Eddy secures his first job playing the piano in a nightclub while the band takes a break and customers eat. Perhaps as an in-joke, given the number of times Power had been seen wearing one on-screen and in publicity shots, Eddy is asked if he owns a tuxedo, which he does not. Borrowing an ill-fitting one with sleeves and trouser legs that are too short, he looks uncomfortable as he buttons and unbuttons the over-large jacket in an attempt to make it look better. A montage then follows in which he is seen playing bigger and better pianos in larger and ritzier nightclubs; the fit and quality of his clothing slowly improving with each performance until we are presented with a familiar Power in fitted evening dress, his dark hair slicked back and a huge smile on his face.

Another montage follows that depicts Eddy and Marjorie (Kim Novak) falling in love, and which ends with an artistic shot of their reflections in a puddle as they kiss. After Marjorie prompts a proposal from him, they are married, and she instigates the first kiss on their wedding night. As they dance in their nightclothes to a record of Duchin's own music, the most sensual scene of Power's career unfolds. As they slowly move around the floor, Power slides his hand inside Novak's robe and she shudders with delight. She moans as they circle around, sharing a long kiss before he bites her lip and she giggles. When she puts her head back, he kisses her neck before she whispers to him and they walk out to the balcony. He grabs her face with both hands and she places her hands over his, telling him she loves his hands before kissing the palms of both and adding 'not just for the sweet music they make, but physically, they excite me just to look at them', and he looks at her seductively. Her emphasis on the word 'physically' means that his hands are not just tied to his skills as a pianist, but also coded with sexual power.

Power faced an intensely emotional scene when the Mahers' baby died, and here it is Marjorie who dies after childbirth. Talking to her as she lies in the hospital bed, he attempts to hold a normal conversation while knowing she will not recover. Power's voice is full of emotion as he depicts Eddy trying to get the words out as naturally as possible, taking pauses, stuttering, swallowing hard and allowing his voice to break at times. With a tear in his voice, his eyes well up and as he is talking, he looks down and realises she is dead. He stops speaking and stares at her before rising slowly. In the scene that follows, Power walks slowly into a dark and empty nightclub as if in a daze. Sitting down near the piano, Eddy's most comfortable place to be, he picks up a streamer left over from the Christmas party from earlier that evening and looks up at the lit Christmas tree (although in real life Marjorie died in August, the change of season makes the scene more emotional). A close-up of Power then shows his character's emotional state. Smiling slightly, he says, 'Merry Christmas' in a normal tone. Looking around the room, he repeats, 'Merry Christmas' more softly, almost in a whisper, as he nods and starts to well up again. He then sniffs, allowing his lip to start trembling; a tear now on his cheek, he repeats the words in a questioning and bewildered way, as if asking the empty room how it could possibly be a merry Christmas since his wife has just died. Finally, in complete despair he gasps, squeezes his eyes together and shouts, 'Merry Christmas' as he breaks down completely, throwing himself on the ground and weeping uncontrollably while the camera slowly pans out until he is a small figure, alone in the large room, before the scene fades out. As Power repeats these two words over and over, each time with new meanings attached to them, we see flashes of anger, disappointment, regret, nostalgia, love, denial, fear, despair, loss and utter heartache projected through Power's facial expressions and vocal intonation in just a few seconds of film time.

When he returns from the war, Eddy tries to build a relationship with his son, Peter (played by Mickey Maga at age five and Rex Thompson at age nine), whom he had previously refused to see since he blamed him for Marjorie's death. Just as he gets close to Peter and starts to fall for his nanny Chiquita (Victoria Shaw), Eddy discovers he is dying. Power must then depict another range of emotions to convey Eddy's fear, shock, anger, hurt and finally acceptance. A particularly poignant scene occurs when Eddy takes Peter to a play park to try and lessen the blow of his 'going away' as he puts it. Power gives a very restrained and controlled performance while delivering the devastating news and, when

Peter gets angry because he thinks his father is choosing to leave again, he tells him that it is not his choice and the boy finally understands. As Murray Pomerance notes, when the subject of a biopic is no longer living at the time of the film's release, their 'cinematic "death" ... must be made sacrosanct and elaborate' so as to 'vie in emotional tone with the death of fictional subjects in conventional dramas, who, adopted into the audience's zone of care, provoke suffering when they leave the scene' (2019: 151). Although it is almost inevitable that the audience would be aware of Duchin's recent death when viewing the film, foreshadowing to the event is played out by Power tensing his hand as if it is going into spasms, which greatly alarms Eddy when it first occurs as he is playing the piano. However, it soon becomes part of his everyday life as he must come to terms with the fact that he is dying.

In the film's poignant final scene, Duchin and Peter are playing a duet on pianos facing each other as Chiquita observes. Power glances at Shaw before moving behind her and holding her close, his face registering a complex combination of pain and acceptance. He then sits beside Thompson, remarking on how good Peter is getting before returning to his own stool. The boy, now crying, has stopped playing and Power steals a painful glance at Shaw, wincing slightly and dropping his shoulders just a fraction as he looks back at the boy, dejected and powerless to help. With a mix of emotions registering in his eyes, he begins to forcefully pound on the keys to get the boy's attention; the ploy works, and he stops crying and joins in as they smile widely at each other. In his final moment on screen, Power is framed by the open piano lids, which ominously resemble an open casket, before we move to a close-up of his hands playing the piano from his point of view. His left hand cramps up and he hits the wrong key; a rapid cut to Shaw shows her looking shocked, closing her eyes and turning away. When the camera returns to Power's hands, he slowly withdraws them from the frame leaving Thompson playing alone and, as the camera pulls out, we are presented with Eddy's empty piano seat, thus Duchin's death is symbolised without the need to show it. It is a powerful final image created through the absence of the star.

The Sun Also Rises is a CinemaScope spectacle, again over two hours long, and was the final drama Power made for Twentieth Century-Fox, although he was no longer under contract to the studio at this point. Based on Ernest Hemingway's novel of the same name, Gene D. Philips calls it the most underrated of the Hemingway movies (1980: 133). He also suggests that, along with *The Snows of Kilimanjaro* (made into a 1952 film starring Gregory

Peck, Susan Hayward and Ava Gardner), it is a perfect example of 'the kind of dark tale set in the sunlight which one critic has dubbed Hemingway's nightmares at noonday' (1980: 116). The film marks Power's only pairing with Ava Gardner and former heartthrob and contemporary Errol Flynn. Once more expanding his range and acting against type, given the potent sexuality consistently attached to Power's image, he portrays ex-soldier Jake Barnes whose injuries in World War I have rendered him impotent. As Philips notes, Barnes is semi-autobiographical since Hemingway was wounded in the war, though not so severely. Finding pieces of his uniform had infected his scrotum, Hemingway had to recuperate in the genitourinary ward of a hospital, where he encountered a patient who had 'lost his penis but retained his testicles, meaning that, as Hemingway put it, "he was capable of all normal feelings as a man, but incapable of consummating them". This is precisely the frustration Jake feels, particularly 'in his hopeless love for the nymphomaniacal Brett' (Philips 1980: 120). Like Maher, Jake is desexualised, not through how he looks or what he does, but through what he does not do. Jake looks exactly like Power and is thus presented as a physically attractive and desirable man, whom ex-lover Brett Ashley (Gardner) confesses her love for before adding 'I know it's no good', meaning that she knows he cannot satisfy her sexually. Repeating these words several times throughout the film, she even asks him to kiss her in the back of a taxi, indicating that women just cannot resist Power in any form. Although Jake's physical presence still excites Brett, just as a star's image on screen might, it is all a façade and she must, therefore, seek her sexual pleasure elsewhere; she does so with a variety of men, including Mike Campbell (Flynn) and young bullfighter Pedro Romero (Robert Evans). Putting Power into the position of portraying an impotent character may also be understood as an in-joke, given his consistently sexualised persona, his stunning looks, his numerous romantic encounters on-screen and his many reported affairs off-screen.

With its bullfighting theme, the film links Power back to his earlier role in *Blood and Sand* but also allows his screen image to come full circle, since he now acts as a spectator while young toreros parade around the ring in almost identical outfits to those he wore sixteen years previously. In fact, the blue and gold outfit Romero sports, and the scenes in which he plays to the crowd could almost be footage of Power left over from the earlier film. By this point, Power's looks had begun to harden into a somewhat mature handsomeness but he does look older than his years, especially in full face; his frame has filled out and his voice is deeper and more sombre, even more so than in the previous biopics, and carries the weight of too many cigarettes.

Being impotent takes away Jake's masculinity, rendering him non-threatening to the men and women around him; in fact, he almost takes on the role of gay best friend for Brett as she discusses her sexual conquests with him and he remains non-threatening to the men who pursue her. However, Power's queer positioning as everyone's conscience and chaperone, the friend who tries to solve their many (mostly sexual) problems while remaining a bystander, is very much like Larry in *The Razor's Edge*. The clear difference is that Larry chooses a life of celibacy, whereas it is thrust on Jake. But even here two women are sexually interested in Jake: Brett and Georgette (Juliette Greco) who, after a date with him asks, 'Don't you like me?', because he has not tried to get her into bed. When he replies that he was 'hurt in the war', her desire turns to pity.

Power gives a mature, extremely composed performance, which makes the only time Jake loses his temper stand out. When Brett starts to flirt outrageously with Romero, Jake leaves them and walks silently down the street past a row of posters presenting the virile Romero in a series of masculine poses while fighting a bull, highly reminiscent of those used in publicity for Power in *Blood and Sand*. With every poster he passes, Jake gets more frustrated at his own lack of masculinity, identifying with the impotent steer rather than the hypermasculine matador. His frustrations come to a climax when he throws a glass of red wine over one of the posters, which both resembles blood (perhaps another in-joke, given how *Blood and Sand* ended) and an 'unnatural' ejaculation (just as Juan shattered his glass). Jake also gets embroiled in a physical fight, though it is not of his own doing, and while Brett sleeps around, Mike gets drunk and Robert (Mel Ferrer) pines over Brett, Jake is the only level-headed one. But Power's restrained performance, the way he uses his eyes and voice, and his interactions with Gardner show that Jake is being eaten up inside, that he feels like an outsider and different from the other men, although he never lets the others see this.

Philips highlights Jake's impotence as 'a metaphor for the spiritual condition of these emotionally exhausted, physically sterile individuals [his group of friends] who, like himself, are awash in postwar disillusionment and unable to sustain any fruitful and lasting relationships' (1980: 122). As with the novel, Philips adds, Jake's impotence symbolises the 'incapacity of the disillusioned postwar generation to feel and to love deeply', while his 'abiding respect for Romero ... also comes through in the film, as does his consequent recognition of the bullfighter as the norm of conduct against which he judges himself and his companions' (1980: 125). Casper, citing Jake as an example, notes that, as with any form of melodrama set against a crucial time in a nation's history, emphasis is placed on an individual's psychic state; 'how the event affects the character's personality, relationships, and situations is central, not the event itself' (2007: 258). Mel Gussow claims that Zanuck thought Power best for the role because he was 'in a sense something of a symbolic Jake Barnes, to Zanuck, the truest, the handsomest, the best of the lot. He was a good choice for the part, except for his age – forty-three' (1971: 193). However, Philips notes that while film historian Roy Pickard sees all the actors as too old for their parts, the film's director, Henry King, says that because the film takes place several years after the war, the characters are meant to 'look dissipated and worn out . . . a dimension of their personalities would have been lost' with younger actors (1980: 130).

Philips calls the final scene with Jake and Brett, again alone in the back of a taxi, inconsistent with the rest of the film, since repeatedly 'the pair articulate their despair of ever forging a satisfying relationship' (1980: 126). To Brett, Jake's impotence is the only problem, but Jake gradually realises the problem is more extensive and that they both 'came out of the war unable to love genuinely ever again'. Jake knows there is no 'cure' because 'they have both lost the moral and emotional stamina required to sustain a deep, lasting relationship', which would be true with or without his impotence. Thus, by the end, Jake is no longer deceiving himself and must shed his 'romantic illusions about life, including those involving himself and Brett' (Philips 1980: 127). Philips also feels it would have been beneficial to have Jake as the film's narrator, rather than an unattached and disembodied voice, which 'would have provided continuity with the flashbacks which occur later in the film and would also have supplied a better hook on which to hang the movie's single fantasy sequence' (1980: 129). I would add that it would also have given the audience the familiar and distinct voice of Power to guide them along, making it more of his story than that of the group and, since it is really Jake's story, it seems an unwise choice for the filmmakers to have made.

The final film: *Witness for the Prosecution*

Witness for the Prosecution, the final film discussed in this chapter, is important for several reasons. First, it was the only time Power worked with either director Billy Wilder or co-star Marlene Dietrich. Although it was his third film with Elsa Lanchester (who appeared briefly in *Son of Fury* and *The Razor's Edge*), it was also the first time he appeared on-screen with her husband Charles Laughton, who had directed Power in a 1953 stage production of Stephen Vincent Benét's epic poem *John Brown's Body* alongside Judith Anderson and Raymond Massey. Most importantly, it was Power's final completed film and thus a careful study of it demonstrates where his star image and performance skills stood at the end of his still active career, as well as how they had developed since his first dramatic performances in the 1930s.

The film is based on Agatha Christie's short story of the same name, which had been adapted into a stage play performed in London's Winter Garden Theatre in 1953 and on Broadway in 1954. Actress Una O'Connor reprised her stage performance as housekeeper Janet MacKenzie in the film adaptation, which cost $3 million to make. However, it became one of the most popular films of the year, taking $9 million at the box office and being nominated for several prestigious awards, including six Academy Awards including Best Picture, Best Director for Wilder, Best Actor for Laughton and Best Supporting Actress for Lanchester, although it failed to win any. Additionally, it gained several Golden Globe nominations, including Dietrich as Best Actress, though only Lanchester won. Laughton was also nominated for a BAFTA award and won the Italian David di Donatello award for Best Foreign Actor. As with previous films, Power's name is distinctively absent from all award nominations, but his performance as Leonard Vole shows a maturing depth to his character acting that could have carried him into middle-aged and more elderly roles had he lived. His voice control, vocal intonation and understated performance skills are widely used throughout, demonstrating how he had truly developed as an actor of great competence over the two-and-a-half decades since his career had begun.

Several of Power's early roles had seen him depict loveable rogues and cads, most notably his comedies with Loretta Young, *Day-Time Wife* (Gregory Ratoff, 1939) and *A Yank in the RAF*, in which Grable's character frequently calls him a 'worm' and yet remains romantically attached to him. In each case, his character flashes a grin and charms the woman with a few well-chosen words so that she remains faithful to him, even if he strays. Similarly, these earlier characters do not suffer any real repercussions for their indiscretions and, even in films in which he portrays criminals, his actions are justified to audiences, usually through family connections. In

Jesse James, his good-natured farm boy turns outlaw after the railroad men try to take his mother's land and she dies in the process, triggering his life of crime. Likewise, *Johnny Apollo*'s Bob is an upstanding college student who only becomes involved with criminals in his quest to get his father released from jail. As noted, it was not until *Nightmare Alley* that Power was permitted to demonstrate a much darker screen persona, when the unscrupulous Stan uses several women to climb to the top. But even here, we see that he really has come to love Molly (despite being forced to marry her), revealed through Power's gestures and facial expressions as he puts her on a train to keep her safe. Ten years later, in *Witness for the Prosecution*, Power uses this familiar and, quite literally, murderous charm to manipulate men and women from all walks of life into doing exactly what he wants for his own personal gain, and employs several of his previously exercised performance techniques to achieve this.

Although the top-billed star, Power receives the least amount of dialogue of the principal players, yet he is the core around which they all move. Vole's looks and charm, fundamental to Power's star image throughout his career, are again proposed as the reason that women will do anything for him. In his final screen appearance, he impressively has three generations of women romantically interested in him: the elderly Emily French (Norma Varden), his devoted wife Christine (Dietrich) and his much younger girlfriend Diana (Ruta Lee). After Mrs French takes a fancy to him, Vole abuses her trust, murders her and inherits her money, while Christine perjures herself in court through a concoction of lies and deceit so that he might live, and he repays her by planning to run off with Diana.

Stephen Farber names *Witness for the Prosecution* as among Wilder's best films, confronting 'the darker side of American life with a bracingly sardonic wit', and calls the director the 'most colorful and renowned cynic [who] never surrendered to sentimentality or sanctimoniousness' (2001: 161). Likewise, Richard Lemon suggests that the hallmarks of Wilder's filmic style are 'realism, cynicism, and a convoluted approach to the matter of sex', marked by a low view of life and love (2001: 45). Dale M. Pollock further points out that disguise, deception and death are key themes of the director's work (2011: 39), all of which are explored here, particularly through Power's and Dietrich's characterisations as Leonard and Christine Vole. Most notable is how Christine deceives both Sir Wilfred Roberts (Laughton) and the court in order to save Leonard's life, and how Leonard deceives everyone around him, including Christine.

The only one who does not fall for his act is Janet, who is excessively dedicated to her dead mistress, much like Mrs Danvers in *Rebecca* (Alfred Hitchcock, 1940), and overly jealous of her obvious romantic interest in Vole. Janet is rude and inhospitable to him in flashbacks and tries to get him convicted of murder in court but, as with his accuser in *Lloyds of London*, the court does not believe her.

Many of Wilder's films during this period have flashback scenes, including *Double Indemnity* (1944) and *Sunset Boulevard* (1950), and it is through this filmic technique that we learn how Leonard met both Mrs French and Christine. In a way, Power's performance fits with Naremore's discussion of *Double Indemnity*, in which he notes that *film noir* frequently demands that actors dramatise situations in which the expressive coherence of a character either breaks down or is revealed as an act, with characters succeeding or failing at maintaining expressive coherence. Thus his description of Barbara Stanwyck's Phyllis Dietrichson as 'a cool and skilful performer who seldom steps out of character' could be applied to Power's Vole (1988: 70). Naremore further notes that the audience is sometimes taken in by a performance as much as the characters are, which is true here because we believe Leonard to be innocent until the revelation of the shocking ending. As Naremore points out, 'sometimes we know that a character is behaving falsely because the plot has given us that information', which happens with Power in many films including *Lloyds of London*, *Love is News*, *Café Metropole*, *That Wonderful Urge*, *Thin Ice*, *The Mark of Zorro* and *Prince of Foxes*, and sometimes 'we can see indications of deception in a player's expression even when these signs are invisible to others' (1988: 70).

Naremore suggests that a performer can reveal their acting skills in films that contain a moment when a character is clearly shown to be wearing a mask. In moments like these, the performer sends out conflicting signs, with 'the vivid contrast between facial expressions giv[ing] the "acted image" an emotional richness, a strong sense of dramatic irony' (Naremore 1988: 76). Certain character traits are particularly apt for creating incoherence, and villainy is a favourite among actors, since it normally 'takes the form of an insincere or duplicitous performance' (1988: 76). It is not until the film's final four minutes that Vole reveals his true identity, of a conceited, swaggering and downright obnoxious personality that is exposed to the other characters and the audience. When it is revealed that he did, in fact, kill Mrs French, Power uses his performance skills to flaunt the fact that Leonard knows he cannot be tried again for the same crime. The moment he returns to the dock in his raincoat, signifying his freedom, we realise that Vole has been acting all along in order to gain the sympathy of the court and the confidence of Sir Wilfred. His false, wide-eyed surprise and cries of innocence are gone, replaced by a brash arrogance as he smirks at Wilfred and rolls his eyes at Christine. Calmly discussing how he will use the dead woman's money, he cheerfully announces that he will buy a new hearing aid for Janet, who admitted her lack of hearing on the stand, one of the reasons her evidence against him was dismissed. Picking up the flask Sir Wilfred used in court each day, he merrily announces that he will get him a fourteen-carat gold version, as well as the best defence possible for Christine's perjury case. Throughout the scene, Power smiles his familiar wide grin, but it now resembles a sneer, which suggests that Vole is internally laughing at the foolishness of those around him. Christine admits that she constructed her elaborate act simply because she loves Vole ('there's never been anyone but Leonard'), but his villainy takes a further turn when she attempts to embrace him and he shrugs her off as Diana runs over and kisses him passionately. Squaring his jaw, he rolls his eyes at Christine's protests, arrogantly sticking his tongue into a back tooth to show boredom at her obsession for him. Scoffing arrogantly, he grabs her roughly by the shoulders, shakes her and pushes her forcefully down onto a wooden chair before turning to leave with the young woman, but in a jealous rage Christine kills him: if she cannot have him, no woman will.

In this, Power's final screen performance, Vole carries the weight of all his earlier performances and seems to embody the darkest version of his recognisable screen image. The wartime flashback, in which he first meets Christine, echoes the widely grinning ladies' man in military uniform, alluding to *A Yank in the RAF* and *Crash Dive* (Archie Mayo, 1943), as well as Power's own real-life war duty. When he enters the film, he informs Sir Wilfred about his version of events, and in the flashback scenes with Mrs French, we are presented with the familiar chatty charmer of many of Power's earlier films, particularly his comedies. His breezy, easy manner and high-pitched tone of voice as he declares his innocence ('but I haven't done anything') is reminiscent of the younger Power, and this masquerade is maintained until the end when he has completely fooled both the audience and other characters. There are moments at the start, however, when Vole's behaviour seems rather strange: for example, his wide-eyed innocence, which contradicts his physical appearance as he plays with a cigarette and tells the secretaries, with a smile, that he may be arrested at any minute. There is a sense of eeriness about his performance at this point: when asked what he might be arrested for, he pauses before adding, 'Well, for murder', as he flicks the ashes of his cigarette into a wastepaper basket, his voice rising as if making a throwaway comment about the weather. This suggests that either Vole has psychotic tendencies and feels no remorse or that he is completely innocent; it is the latter judgement that the other characters and audience must gravitate towards for the film to work. Consequently, much rests on Power's performance as a guilty man masquerading as an innocent one, and one who does not give too much, if anything, away until he spills his guts as his 'real' self when the trial is over. Indeed, ambiguity is the key to the role, and once more Power plays a character who is performing; when talking to Sir Wilfred, and in the courtroom, it is hard to know where Vole's performance ends and his reality begins. Particularly ambiguous is his sudden explosion in the courtroom as he screams, 'It's not true, Christine' and 'Why are you saying these things?' when his wife 'confesses' that they are not actually married and that she has a lover called Max, which he knows are false statements. Furthermore, he performs affection for Mrs French in the flashbacks and love for Christine when apparently he feels nothing; we are not even sure if he has feelings for Diana, or indeed if he can feel at all. Thus Power's complex performance as a murderer who performs as an innocent man before becoming 'himself' as he remains ambiguous throughout must be taken into account.

Despite Power's physical appearance, the film tries to emphasise that he can still play a youthful man. When Christine confronts Leonard as to who 'this girl' is, Diana responds with 'I'm not this girl, I'm his girl'. Even in his final role (leaving aside the few scenes that have survived from the incomplete *Solomon and Sheba*), Power's character juggles two women who would do anything for him. In the end, Christine 'executes him', in the words of Sir Wilfred, and Power's final moment on screen is, unfortunately, as Vole's dead body lying on the courtroom floor (Figure 1.9). Even here, he is surrounded by women, with the two women in love with Vole placed at either side of the scene with his body between them.

As Naremore points out, there are three elements of characterisation that go into creating a star performance (1988: 158). First, the actor: the corporal presence who brings their voice, accent, vocal quirks and acting techniques to the part. The performer also brings physical attributes that cannot be as readily altered, such as height, build, ethnicity and so forth (although it is not impossible to alter these, especially with special effects). Second, the character. In the case of Leonard Vole, he had been created by Christie for her short story before being rewritten and acted on stage

Figure 1.9 Power's final moment on-screen, as a corpse in *Witness for the Prosecution* (1957)

by the original performers a few years before the film began shooting. The character would also be predetermined, perhaps even before the actor was chosen for the role. Finally, the star image is brought into play, and with over twenty years' worth of screen work, Power's biography, his appearances in newspapers and fan magazines, publicity photographs and candid images, film posters and so forth, could be in the minds of audiences while watching Power's depiction. Indeed, the film's intertextuality reaches its culmination when Vole attends a cinema screening of a film about Jesse James that alludes to Power's own screen performance as the outlaw in 1939, while also suggesting Vole's tendencies for thinking he is above the law and foreshadowing his sudden death at the hands of someone he trusted. In fact, *Jesse James* was the first film in which one of Power's characters dies on-screen and *Witness for the Prosecution* was the last, before Power's own untimely death the following year. In relation to his celebrated looks, at the end of his career Power continued to look young and still very much recognisable when shot in profile, but the stark nature of his altering looks face on, particularly around the eyes as they started to droop, cannot be glossed over. It is still a recognisable Power we are presented with in *Witness for the Prosecution*, but he looks older and more tired, sporting a hardened handsomeness and a more solid masculinity at the end.

Notes

1. The 1938 theatrical trailer for *Marie Antoinette* can be viewed on YouTube at https://www.youtube.com/watch?v=R_gc6V76PCQ (accessed 14 August 2019).
2. Power reprised his on-screen role as Juan in *Blood and Sand* for Lux Radio Theatre, with Annabella adopting Linda Darnell's role as Carmen (aired 23 December 1941). The two appeared together on stage at the Country Playhouse, Westport, Connecticut in *Liliom* for two weeks starting on 11 August 1941.
3. In the forthcoming drama, *Silent Life* (Vladislav Kozlov, 2020), Power's *King of the Khyber Rifles* co-star Terry Moore portrays the Lady in Black.

Chapter 2

The comedic actor

Overview

It was through his work in comedies that Power mostly played the typical cocky young American who did not take the world, or himself, too seriously and wanted nothing more than to chase thrills and woman. His comedic pairings with Loretta Young, in particular, helped to cement his 'loveable rogue' persona early on, and this persona is most overtly exhibited in their 1937 pairings *Love is News*, *Café Metropole* and *Second Honeymoon* (Walter Lang). These films allowed Power to express a diverse range of facial expressions, distinct vocal intonation and wide grins, which soon became established features of his star image. Combined with his extreme good looks, these factors held a strong appeal to (predominantly female) audiences and helped to make, and keep, Power Twentieth Century-Fox's top male star for almost two decades. Perhaps most importantly for his developing star image, analysis of these films reveals how Power was being established as a star with erotic appeal whom audiences are invited to gaze at and desire. The extreme bright lighting usually reserved for female stars was repeatedly used on Power throughout the 1930s, and the camera frequently lingers on his face and body longer than is necessary for the narrative. This resulted in Power becoming slightly emasculated, given his beautiful face, and meant that his physical appearance began to overpower his actorly skills. His physical appearance being so striking is perhaps why his comedy characters are often smart-talking journalists who drink hard and play hard, thus allowing them to be somewhat animated and active on-screen. Furthermore, Power's casting in the title role of *Jesse James* at the close of the decade allowed his image to take on a more brutal masculinity, despite his beautiful face. These decisions surely helped him avoid much, though not all, of the negative press endured by Robert Taylor because of his beautiful face and Taylor's frequent roles in romantic comedies and dramas in the 1930s.

In contrast to the longevity of his dramas, most of Power's comedies appeared in the mid to late 1930s and could be categorised under the subgenre of screwball comedy. While permitting him to exhibit a flair for both oral and physical comedy, therefore expanding his repertoire, since all his comedies were set in modern times his body was displayed in a range of contemporary tailored suits and evening clothes; this acted as an alternative to his many historical costume pictures. Although he made a further two comedies in 1948, these were sandwiched between two historical action-adventure films and can be read as nostalgic throwbacks to his 1930s comedies. In fact, and rather unusually, Power's final comedy, *That Wonderful Urge*, was a direct remake of *Love is News*, the first comedy he had starred in a decade earlier. A more extreme case of this involves Clark Gable who starred in both the 1932 pre-Code drama *Red Dust* (Victor Fleming) and its 1953 remake *Mogambo* (John Ford). Gable was thirty-one years old in the original, while co-stars Jean Harlow and Mary Astor were twenty-one and twenty-six, respectively; however, in the remake, the fifty-two-year-old Gable was romantically paired with thirty-one-year-old Ava Gardner and Grace Kelly, who was just twenty-four. Another example of an actor appearing in two versions of the same film is Herbert Marshall, who appeared in both screen adaptations of the 1927 Somerset Maugham play *The Letter* (Jean de Limur, 1929; William Wyler, 1940).[1] However, while in the earlier film the thirty-nine-year-old Marshall plays the protagonist's lover, her passion for him driving her to commit murder, by 1940 the fifty-year-old actor had been relegated to the role of her gullible and doting husband, played by Reginald Owen in the earlier version. Indeed, although Power continued to play romantic leads for the rest of his career, because of his early death, it is unknown whether he would have moved into character parts as he aged.

As Janice Anderson notes, the coming of sound at the end of the 1920s profoundly changed the nature of film comedy and resulted in cinema being viewed as more sophisticated and appealing to a wider audience (1985: 58). Highlighting the obvious teething problems with this new technology, as famously parodied in *Singin' in the Rain* (Gene Kelly and Stanley Donen, 1952), the 1930s became the 'great age' of the talking comedy. Putting the films of this decade into their historical context, Anderson says the Great Depression actually helped their popularity; since tickets were inexpensive and cinema was viewed as an unrivalled form of escapism, 'attendance figures sky-rocketed everywhere' (1985: 60). Hollywood produced two distinct forms of comedy in the 1930s, which were soon emulated by the remainder of the Western world. One form was the wholesome, family-friendly 'folksy' comedies of

Will Rogers and Shirley Temple, and the Andy Hardy movies starring Mickey Rooney. The other, under which Power's comedies fall, were sophisticated and mildly satirical, in which the 'battle of the sexes and a certain anti-romantic cynicism added a witty spice' (1985: 61). Deleyto quotes Northrop Frye, who argued in 1957 that the focus of romantic comedy was to create a more adult and complex identity, its most crucial factor being the protagonist's discovery of a more profound sexuality (2009: 28). Expanding on this, Deleyto suggests that laughter and humour allow the genre to convey stories about 'interpersonal affective and erotic relationships', using a comic perspective on the cultural discourses of love and desire to convey an artistic transformation of the 'everyday reality of human relationships' (2009: 30). Likewise, Schatz calls the basic screwball plot a 'socially-conscious battles of the sexes', which dominated Depression-era comedy by 'restricting the fast-paced upper-crust romance' and providing the most 'significant and engaging social commentary' of the period, first established by Frank Capra's *It Happened One Night* in 1934 (1981: 150). Schatz adds that, 'regardless of their social antics, the final embrace of two representatives from disparate socioeconomic backgrounds certainly carried prosocial implications in the early days of the genre' (1981: 160). This is just how *Love is News*, *Café Metropole* and *That Wonderful Urge* conclude. While, in *Day-Time Wife*, Power's character is by no means affluent, he is comfortably well-off and lives in a well-furnished apartment. In *The Luck of the Irish* his character rejects the glamorous life of a modern New York apartment and well-paid job in favour of a basic, but homely, Irish inn.

James Harvey suggests that, although Twentieth Century-Fox 'didn't seem to have much knack for screwball comedy', it kept trying nevertheless, turning out a great deal of these films while they were in vogue (1987: 291). He adds that, except on occasion, the studio's screwball comedies were 'imitative and pale, never first-rate or even quite convincing', identifying William Powell's performance in *The Baroness and the Butler* (Walter Lang, 1938) – in which he played opposite Power's first wife Annabella – as an exception (1987: 291). Harvey suggests that this was a result of contract stars like Power, Young, Ameche, Alice Faye and Sonja Henie being used, believing them to be 'consistently so much less interesting than the stars at the other studios' such as Powell, Gable, Myrna Loy or Claudette Colbert, and views it as 'one of the oddities of . . . Zanuck's tenure as studio production head' (1987: 291). However, not only was Power a rising star at the time, and one that was being promoted heavily, but the studio itself was in its infancy since it had only been established a few years previously, thus contract players were the best, and cheapest, option at this time, especially for 'quickie' comedies. Likewise, if *Love is News* had not done well for the studio, it is doubtful that it would have been remade over a decade later, and even less so with the original star reprising his role. In fact, it was between 1937 and 1939, the years in which Power was starring in this sort of comedy, that he was the second highest ranking box office star, positioned between Mickey Rooney and Spencer Tracy (Balio 1993: 152). *Love is News* is important not only for being Power's first film after *Lloyds of London*, but for being the first time he received top billing, with his name appearing above Young's.

Remaking an original

Love is News and *That Wonderful Urge* follow the thread of earlier films like *It Happened One Night* and *Platinum Blonde* (Frank Capra, 1931), also starring Young, by having Power's journalist get entangled with a spoiled heiress. However, while in *It Happened One Night*, Gable's tough and virile Peter Warren must protect the unworldly Ellen Andrews (Claudette Colbert), Power's films fit more into the battle-of-the-sexes mould, where the woman gives as good, if not more, than she gets. His wisecracking reporters are both manipulative and manipulated, but the women show him what it is like to live in a 'goldfish bowl' because of their inherited wealth and status while he teaches them about real life and real problems. By the close of each film, the couple realises that, despite their differences, they are in love and strike a final compromise. When Deleyto declares that Western *Rio Bravo* uses a 'process of apparent male humiliation at the hands of the woman, a process which in reality is making him a better person' (2009: 15), he could just as easily have been referring to these films (or *Day-Time Wife*).

Discussing Power's first and final comedies as different versions of the same film but made over a decade apart reveals much about the dynamic of Power's performance over time, along with how his star image and characterisations had developed or remained stable. The opening credits for both films are extremely similar and feature a background image of overlapping newspapers, their front page headlines slightly obscured by the names of the players and other film personnel, and we can only read snippets of them. This helps not only to establish that the film is about journalism, but hints at what will unfold within the narrative. In *Love is News* the words 'reporter lands', 'heiress', 'million dollar' and '$1,000,000' stand out on the front pages of publications such as the *New York Chronicle*, while the names of cast and crew appear in love hearts and the title song 'Love is News' plays. With *That Wonderful Urge*, we can read much more of the headlines, such as the *New York Observer* stating, 'Woman's Club protests insult to American womanhood', the *New York Express* carrying the headline 'Cinderella man sues heiress' and the *New York Observer* mentioning the names 'Tom-Tom' and 'Sara'. The credits on the later film look more sophisticated; reflecting the newspaper print, the names appear in white with a black outline, which makes them stand out over the mass of wording on the overlapping newspapers below, and this time the tune has no lyrics.

As *Love is News* opens, Power's journalist Steve Layton enters the newspaper office of the *Daily Express*, his arms full of flowers as he quips that this is a wake for their 'beloved newspaper', which has met an untimely death. His fast-paced speech sounds like a breaking news story he would telephone in to a tabloid newspaper office as he describes the new city editor, Martin J. Canavan (Ameche), in the alliterative terms 'sinister spawn of Satan', 'perfumed pig' and 'rose watered rat' just as he walks in. The casual posture of Power, his hands in the pockets of his open overcoat and a fedora pushed back on his head, contrasts with Ameche's appearance, which looks more stereotypically British than American: his dark buttoned-up coat, bowler hat, high cravat, gloves and walking cane reflect Canavan's stuffy nature, and a small, neat moustache completes the look. Although an obviously close bond exists between the men, it is a love–hate relationship, and Canavan repeatedly fires and rehires Steve. In one instance, a line that seems to have been written specifically for Power is uttered by Ameche as Steve is thrown out of the office: 'if I ever see that pretty puss of yours'.

Steve tricks heiress Tony Gateson (Young) into giving him an exclusive story for the *Daily Express*, but his scheme soon backfires when she gives her own 'exclusive' story to every newspaper in town except his. Tony concocts a phoney engagement between herself and Steve, resulting in his becoming front page news and experiencing first-hand the unwanted attention that Tony receives on a daily basis because of reporters like him. Before long Steve is besieged wherever he goes, mobbed on the street by autograph hunters and people trying to sell him things, requests for personal appearances and so on. Given Power's own fast rise to fame just prior to this film, it may also be a comment on how the actor was suddenly being pursued by fans wanting autographs and reporters wishing stories for their publications.

Although Tony has the upper hand for most of the film, with Steve looking and sounding persistently angry at her, once he kisses her, she decides to call the phoney engagement off after realising that she has taken things too far. His virility is proven in that moment and the film ends with her chasing him down a street and begging him to kiss her again, which he does, to the cheers of an onlooking crowd. As discussed, women asking Power to kiss them is a theme that runs through his films but it is especially pertinent in his pairings with Young. Another common occurrence is his being seen in various stages of undress. In one scene, a group of men trying to sell him various items burst through his bathroom door as he is about to remove his pyjama trousers to take a shower, at which he jumps in the shower and closes the curtain behind him. Some publicity stills for this scene, however, show a more risqué scenario with Power surrounded by fully clothed men as he exits the shower, his bare chest and leg displayed to the thigh and the shower curtain meeting in the middle to protect his modesty. In another scene he removes his trousers to sew them, and while he is standing in his shirt and underpants, Tony arrives at his door. Entering, she looks him up and down for a prolonged period. The camera focuses in on her while she takes in his physique, a smile spreading across her face before she remarks, 'That's a nice tie you're wearing', gesturing to his crotch area with her eyes. He looks down, widens his eyes in panic and rushes behind the curtain that divides his kitchen from the bedroom/living area of his tiny flat. Since we have spent time with Power before she comes to the door, and have actually witnessed him removing his trousers, we are able to gaze at him, uninterrupted and for longer, therefore we know how Tony feels when she encounters him in this state.

Power's tough reporter plays drinking games, knows tricks to beat slot machines and both gives and receives punches to the face. He lives in the overtly homosocial world of the newspaper office, using coarse language and conniving tricks to get exclusive scoops, much like the characters Gable often played. He also has several witty lines of dialogue, which he delivers with comic flair and which keep the film moving at a fast pace. One outstanding comedy moment occurs as he is walking down the highway after Steve and Tony have been arrested and then released from a county jail. He completely ignores her presence as she drives beside him, stopping her expensive looking car at his side as he continues to walk at a fast pace, eyes forward and unflinching. When she drives up beside him a second time she cheerily asks, 'What's the matter, haven't you got a thumb?' Without even a sideward glance, he bitterly replies, 'Yeah, I'd like to stick it in your eye', while keeping up the same pace, hands in pockets and a scowl on his face. It is a brilliantly cutting moment that shows Power's finesse for perfect oral comedic timing.

When *That Wonderful Urge* was released in 1948, Zanuck wrote a memo to writer-producer Nunnally Johnson stating that, although it was a remake with Power 'playing exactly the same role' from over a decade earlier, and got wonderful notices, 'the strange part is that not one reviewer mentioned it as a remake in spite of the fact that we did not change any basic situation and that Tyrone was playing the same role he played before' (Zanuck 1993: 163). However, if we consider the volume of films that would have been consistently released in the interim, some with extremely similar plots, and the vast number of reviews these journalists would have written during that time, if indeed they had been employed as such back in 1937, it is easy to see why they may have missed the fact that it was a remake of Power's earlier film. It is also important to note here that historical audiences, had they seen *Love is News* upon its initial release when Power was still a rising star, would have waited over a decade before seeing *That Wonderful Urge* so may also have forgotten the plot, or never even seen the original, depending on their age. Therefore, although it is easy for a modern viewer to watch these films one after the other at home, this would not have been possible at the time unless the original had been rereleased. It may also have been counterproductive for both the studio, since they were rehashing their own material, and Power, whose career had come a long way since the first film. Furthermore, since he made three romantic comedies with Young in 1937, it is possible that some of the plotlines and gags may have overlapped in viewers' minds, and therefore *That Wonderful Urge* eleven years later may have seemed fresh to them. Although Zanuck notes that Power played 'exactly the same role', neither the plot nor characterisations are identical (including their names), but there are unquestionable similarities and some repetition between the two. While both films have autograph hunters, in *Love is News* these were mostly middle-aged women, whereas in the remake they are screaming teenagers who mob him *en masse* outside his home and destroy his clothes, which is probably closer to the way Power was treated by fans off-screen. Some gags that are reused are the radio station dedicating 'Thanks a Million' to his character, and several skits from the jail scene, including her biting his hand when he tries to give her a puff of his cigarette through prison bars.

That Wonderful Urge begins differently, with Power's Thomas Jefferson Tyler introducing himself as Tom Thomas and fooling not only heiress Sara Farley (Tierney) with his masquerade, but the audience too (as Power would do more ominously in *Witness for the Prosecution*). Posing as small-town reporter Tom, Tyler pretends not to know much about journalism but notes his contempt for Tyler and the articles he has written about Sara. Being taken in by him completely and believing him to be as unworldly as he appears, Sara provides 'Tom' with a detailed account of her life story while the two spend the afternoon alone in a ski chalet. Upon later discovering she has given her exclusive to the underhanded Thomas Jefferson Tyler, she is livid.

Deeply hurt and humiliated by his deceit, Sara goes a step further than Tony by announcing to the waiting reporters that she and Tom are married. Unlike Steve, Tom has a love interest, Jessica (Arleen Whelan), whom he very unromantically asks to marry him to prove he is not married to Sara. Jessica agrees, despite doubts of his sincerity, but Sara is alerted and stops the nuptials by announcing that he will be arrested for bigamy. Sara even has a background check done on Tom, which results in her calling him a wolf; when he protests this, she reads the names of all of the women he has been involved with, ending with Jessica, whom, she declares stony-faced, makes it 'an even dozen' while he smirks at his impressive list of conquests.

One standout scene occurs when Tom and Jessica plan to cook dinner at her apartment but only have four dollars between them. As she carefully peruses the shelves to see what they can afford, he walks along the aisles with his hands in his pockets. Glancing at a shelf, he stops dead, takes his hands out of his pockets and grabs a tin of soup. A close-up of the tin reveals that it says 'Farley's vegetable soup', and he looks around at the décor, realising that it says 'Farley' everywhere. Grinning widely, he announces that they are in a Farley store before quickly heading for the caviar and piles dozens of tins into their cart. When she reminds him they only have four dollars, he smugly announces 'Never mind money, I'm married to a rich woman', since Sara is the heiress to the Farley company. Taking two full carts to the till, he asks the clerk where the champagne is. Told there is none, he tuts and arrogantly remarks, 'No champagne? A low type of store. Probably have boll weevils in the flour', while Jessica scowls at him. As the clerk tries to add up the total for the products, Tom keeps interrupting and tells him he can stop counting. The clerk nervously replies that he must keep counting before Tom calmly announces that he is not paying because 'I own this stuff', gesturing to the products. The clerk calls the manager as Tom stands calmly, his arms folded defiantly but stealing glances at Jessica and the clerk, who both look nervous. After the manager arrives, Power produces a newspaper from his pocket that announces Tom's marriage to Sara, saying, 'Perhaps you don't know who I am. Here, take a look at that', as he hands it over. The manager begins grovelling, calling him 'Mr Farley' before Power glares at him and snatches the newspaper back indignantly, a wonderfully subtle piece of acting almost lost in all the action, and the man corrects himself to 'Mr Tyler'. Tom introduces Jessica as his fiancée before adding 'my wife is very broadminded' as they leave with the free food.

Sara claims that they were married but that Tom does not remember since he was knocked unconscious by a tree and thrown from a dog sledge. At the conclusion, neither Tom nor we know if they are actually married, only Sara does. When the judge throws the case out of court, Tom asks him how they can avoid annulling the marriage, to which the older man advises him to 'remove the grounds'. Questioning what he means, the judge merely repeats the words while Power stands with furrowed brows, blinks a few times and looks confused. Finally realising that the judge means he must sleep with Sara, he smiles and walks out with his hands in his pockets. When Sara enters her bedroom in the next scene, she does not know Tom is there but, as she starts to undress, we see the image of Power lying on her bed reflected in the mirror. A close-up reveals he is reading the controversial Kinsey Report on *Sexual Behavior in the Human Male* (1948), which includes chapters on both pre-marital and marital intercourse. When he moves towards her and puts a hand on her waist, she screams and tells him to get out. The sequence of events that follows resembles rough foreplay as he first sits on a chair and grips her by the wrists before she pulls away and he falls off the chair. Crawling towards her, he grabs her legs and pulls her to the floor, before holding her down with the force of his body. When she begins to shout for help, he covers her mouth, but she bites him and breaks free of his grip. Propping herself against the bed, he moves towards her and tells her he loves her and she melts instantly. He leans in to kiss her before pulling back, much to her dismay, before asking again if they are really married. When she smiles and replies, 'That's something you'll never know', he tells her he needs to know especially if, he stutters embarrassedly, they have children. She tells him they will get married again to satisfy him, although as they passionately kiss on her bedroom floor at the fadeout it is doubtful that they will be remarried before consummating their 'marriage'.

Power shows much more composure as an actor in the latter film, a decade of work in various genres helping him to hone his skills. Gone is the high-pitched tone of youth, replaced by the deeper, more controlled voice of a mature man. Likewise, his slight frame of *Love is News*, which was often hidden behind a large overcoat, although still desirable, had developed into a broader, more manly physique adorned by a range of tailored suits and white shirts. Power's size and strength are perhaps most apparent in the final scene when he overpowers Tierney before she surrenders to his animal magnetism and virility, much as Alice Faye did when he wrestled her to the floor in *In Old Chicago* back in 1938.

Young stars

Café Metropole was Power's third on-screen pairing with Young, and it allowed a continuation of this cocky young American persona, but with a twist. In order to pay off a gambling debt, his penniless character, Alexander Brown, must use his performance skills, or lack thereof, to masquerade as a Russian prince and woo Laura Ridgeway, another of Young's heiresses. As Deleyto highlights, in Shakespeare's comedies a character embarks on a 'circulate journey' that begins in their own society and concludes back there, during which 'through disguise, masquerade and mistakes of identity' they learn something about themselves that they did not know (2009: 31), which is a major element not only of Power's comedic image but his overall screen persona. While Alex tries to establish convincingly the (false) persona of Prince Alexis for a diegetic audience (Laura), which the non-diegetic audience is in on, Power must also convincingly portray the 'real' Alexander Brown for both café owner Victor (Adolphe Menjou) and us, thus allowing several layers of his performance to form. In other words, what Power the performer must do is act convincingly when portraying the 'real' Alex and poorly when Alex masquerades as the prince: Power must act well to ensure that Alex acts badly, particularly so that Laura becomes wise to his masquerade early on. This includes accidentally letting his accent slip (as the actor unintentionally does in *Lloyds of London*), or behaving in ways not appropriate for nobility, before correcting himself as if rehearsing an unfamiliar role. While Power is an actor, Alex is not, and his slippages provide a nod to the audience that we are aware of Power's performance skills on each level.

The film's establishing shot shows the outside of a prestigious-looking building, soon revealed as the Café Metropole of the title, a highbrow nightclub where much of the action takes place. A cut to the interior shows staff clearing up after closing time and, as the camera pans across the room, Power can be heard before we see him. Refusing to leave until he has been served 'roasted eagle', the intoxicated Alex protests that he will only eat 'a strong bird with a level head' while wagging a finger at the waiter. Power's hair is dishevelled, his movements jerky and his speech slurred as he delivers nonsensical dialogue that instantly places the film within the comedy genre. Dressed in a tuxedo and white tie, his elegant outfit and idiotic demands suggest a wealthy and spoiled young man, like Robert Taylor's role as Bob Merrick from *Magnificent Obsession* two years previously. As Victor holds his hat out to him, Power furrows his brow and looks at it in a confused state before garbling 'Why two hats?', thus effectively suggesting the inebriated Alex's double vision. Being escorted to the door (read thrown out), he trips on the stairs, hands Victor some money and waves back weakly while exiting on unsteady legs. Although we do not see the denomination of the banknote, Victor looks delighted and quickly puts it in his pocket, so we can only imagine it is a substantial amount and that Alex therefore has money to throw around.

In Power's second scene, his voice is again initially heard off-screen, only this time he shouts a coherent 'banko' before the camera reveals a more put together young man, with neat hair and still dressed in evening clothes, as he haughtily pulls at his cuffs. However, Power indicates that Alex is still inebriated by stumbling towards the gambling table while attempting to walk straight, using the back of the chair to steady himself and conceal his condition. Sitting down and squinting at his cards, which again suggests blurred vision, a smile spreads across his face as he tosses the cards down, throws up his hand and announces 'eight', before arrogantly leaning back in his chair. When Victor reveals that his cards trump Alex's, Power stares at them as his eyes slowly widen before shifting a panicked gaze at Menjou and then the others as if in complete disbelief. Throughout this exchange, Power keeps the rest of his body rigid and motionless, a cigarette sitting limply in his hand personifying his dejection. Swaying from side to side as he follows Victor into his office to write a cheque for his losses, he hesitantly signs the cheque before slamming the pen down, standing up abruptly and crumpling the paper up before announcing that he has no money and no bank account. Power slurs his words throughout the scene and implies Alex's unsteadiness on his feet by continuing to sway; he also keeps his eyes half shut as if it is a great effort to open them. Explaining why he cannot pay Victor, he takes a piece of paper, which he says represents the million dollars he has just inherited, and repeatedly tears away at it while listing the numerous taxes he has had to pay on it until he is left with a tiny scrap of paper on his fingertip. Staring at it at close range, he squints before closing one eye and announces that it represents his net inheritance of $6,000.85, the last of which he gave to Victor.

Arriving back at Victor's office the next day, sober and wearing a day suit and overcoat, Victor asks Alex to say 'banko' again, which he mutters at first. Asked to repeat it like he had the night before, his voice rings clear and confident and Victor praises his acting skills by informing him he fooled him completely. In order to pay off his debt and avoid jail, Victor asks him to pose as a Russian prince, and the destitute Alexander Brown is transformed into Prince Alexis Paneiev. Asked to read a telegram with a Russian accent, Power does a double take and laughs, 'I don't think so', before adding, 'Will any Russians hear me?', despite their being alone. He begins reading before correcting himself and starting again, much like an actor trying to get authenticity into his performance. Returning to the club that night to begin his 'job', he is again dressed in a tuxedo, making this the third of four scenes in which Power has worn one. Taking his new role seriously, he looks stony-faced while placing a monocle on his eye and looks like a forerunner to Laurence Olivier's prince in his self-directed *The Prince and the Showgirl* (1957) two decades later. Victor is not impressed by his overacting and dismissively tells him to go to the flower shop and get a boutonniere. Power's response is merely to raise an eyebrow, which makes the monocle fall into his hand, a perfectly timed comedic moment. While in the flower shop, the clerk is called away and Alex continues to browse just as Laura enters and mistakes him for the clerk. Power's back is turned to Young at first, but when he turns around she stares at him, as with their first meeting in *Ladies in Love*, unable to finish any sentence she begins. Alex pretends to be the clerk, another slight deviation in his masquerade, before re-entering the club as the Russian national anthem plays, symbolising the true start of his charade. As Power descends the staircase, his body is erect and he comically removes and replaces the monocle, much to Victor's annoyance. Young turns around and stares at him again, a huge smile spreading across her face, but Laura is also embarrassed for mistaking him for a clerk. When he approaches her table to ask for a dance, at Victor's insistence, Laura's elderly aunt also stares before watching him through eyeglasses as the young couple dance. Once more Power's character has charmed two women, but he has also reinforced his universal appeal since they belong to different generations.

When Alex takes Laura to a small restaurant they again dance, only in less grand surroundings and dressed in day clothes. Sitting down to eat, Alex repeatedly slips in and out of his fake accent before correcting himself and telling her, 'My accent, she comes and goes, comes and goes', while we get a privileged shot of his face looking exasperated at his situation. When a cut signifies that it is later, although in the same location, Alex now lies with his head on Laura's lap and his eyes shut. While a man draws Laura's portrait they discuss Alex, assuming he is asleep. We receive another privileged shot as Power opens his eyes, signalling that Alex is listening. Laura confesses her love for him as she plays with his hair and strokes his head. When the man encourages her to kiss the 'sleeping' Alex, she laughs, leans down and kisses his forehead. He then tells her to kiss him on the lips, to which Young looks down, smiles and bends down to kiss him on the mouth just as Power moves his head up and kisses her back, reaching a hand up to rest on her back. Laura is the dominant party here, both with her higher social position and her instigating their first kiss, although she needs to be prompted. Moreover, Power's passive, brightly lit 'sleeping' face is observed by both Laura and us, the contrast aiding in emphasising his dark features and remarkably beautiful face. Thus, we all look at Power but, with his eyes closed, he cannot (or will not) look back.

Laura's domination is most fully realised when she proposes to Alex because he will not ask her. She repeatedly begs him to marry her while on the cusp of hysterics, informing her family that her desire for him is so strong that she does not mind making a fool of herself. When Alex tells Victor he can no longer keep up the façade since he has real feelings for Laura, Victor tries to reveal him as a phoney, but Laura just laughs and tells him she knew it all along and can tell a Princeton man from a prince, hence an all-American boy from Russian royalty. Chasing after him to propose again, the film ends as they dance in the nightclub. When he asks her what she is thinking, she replies, in a deliberately poor Russian accent, 'I was thinking you give me big kiss now', turning her face upwards just like the end of *Love is News*. When he tells her that sort of accent gets people into trouble, she mocks his often-repeated phrase 'My accent, she comes and goes, comes and goes', before he interrupts her with a kiss and Alex is finally able to be 'himself' with Laura. Café Metropole is the comedy that most overtly puts Power's physique on display through form-fitting outfits and numerous full body shots. It also advanced his more animated 'loveable rogue' persona, which was an important development for his image, especially in his next comedy, *Second Honeymoon*, his final comedy pairing with Young.

Second Honeymoon opens with Young's Vicky Benton standing on the balcony of a glitzy apartment overlooking the sea. Turning towards the camera, she steps back in shock before a look of delight crosses her face and she declares, 'Raoul!' A cut shows the object of her reaction: Power's Raoul McLiesh grinning widely from the doorway and looking impeccable in a white dinner jacket and black bowtie. He greets her before rushing over and kissing her passionately, but she pulls away and they both start to act awkwardly. We soon learn why: they are a divorced couple and she has remarried. They casually discuss her new husband Bob (Lyle Talbot) as he attempts to kiss her again, which results in her panicking and leading him indoors to meet Bob, as if she cannot trust herself with him. Upon meeting Raoul, Bob comments to Vicky, 'You never told me he looked like Ronald Colman', to which Power replies, 'Only more sinister', with a huge grin. Vicky calls Raoul 'a waster' and 'a clown', noting that she divorced him because he made plans but did nothing but crack jokes, and we get much evidence of this throughout the film. Power's hair is styled slightly longer, wavier and less formally and, despite *Love is News* being released the same year, his frame appears broader here as if he has bulked up in the interim. Although Power's wide grin had become a familiar part of his image by this point, he smiles more in this film than in any other before or after, with most of his lines being delivered through an enormous grin that emphasises the dimple on his left cheek. Moreover, his comedy timing, physical movement and voice control have improved immensely, even from as recently as *Love is News*, and he appears remarkably more natural and relaxed in front of the camera in a short space of time. There are, however, a few scenes in which he is being asked to pose for the camera, and therefore for us, so that we may gaze at his beautiful face and form. For example, in one scene he sits on the beach with Young while looking off into the distance. Shot in profile, he holds a pipe in his mouth as he dreamily reminisces about their life together, a bright light shining across his dark eyes presenting us with a stunning image. But, for the most part, he plays the cocky clown whom everyone loves, except Bob, and it was as the loveable rogue that he appealed to audiences at this time.

Unlike many of Power's other characters, we are not informed about Raoul's nationality but assume that he is American. However, as he dances with Vicky she tells him, 'You will dance better than anyone else, you dog', but he merely grins and replies, 'It's the Spanish in me', while spinning her around. Although Raoul is the French equivalent of the Anglo-Germanic name Ralph or Rudolph, the Spanish version is Raul. Likewise, McLiesh (or McLeish) has early medieval Scottish origins so, perhaps like Power, Raoul has British, or at least European, roots.

When Bob is called back to New York, Vicky and Raoul become inseparable, and their feelings for each other soon resurface. Sitting alone on the beach once more, she instigates a passionate kiss, and although Raoul reciprocates, he becomes the serious party for once and tells her it cannot happen again, although the pair are clearly still in love. The scene advances the plot while also presenting the opportunity of having these two beautiful stars fall into each other's arms in breathtaking surroundings. Their carefully positioned pose shows off both their faces to great advantage, and more closely resembles a sensational publicity shot than an actual embrace (Figure 2.1).

Figure 2.1 Beautiful stars Power and Loretta Young in *Second Honeymoon* (1937)

Bob, with his plain appearance, uptight nature and lack of humour, let alone passion, provides a strong contrast to the carefree, wisecracking and exceedingly beautiful Raoul. Indeed, the viewer is asked to question why Vicky would leave Raoul in the first place, let alone for Bob. She admits that she wanted security and routine after her uncertain but passionate life with Raoul, and that is exactly what she received with the dependable Bob. However, seeing Raoul again stirs her old desires and makes her extremely unsatisfied with her life with Bob (particularly sexually); she quickly realises she craves Raoul's passion above Bob's security. Knowing she cannot possibly go back to her uneventful life with Bob after being with Raoul again, she and Raoul confess their love for each other, charter a private plane and another film ends with Young's character asking Power's to kiss her.

Enter Darnell

Day-Time Wife was Power's final film of the 1930s and his last comedy for almost a decade. It was also his first of several on-screen pairings with Linda Darnell who, although portraying his wife Jane, was only fifteen years old. Power's Kenneth (Ken) Norton is a roofing expert engaged in an extramarital affair with his secretary, Kitty (Wendy Barrie), as well as Power's biggest comedic heel. Furthermore, although the film deals with the serious subject of adultery, it fits the comedy mould described by Deleyto that, through humour, 'we indirectly acknowledge the humanity that is apparently being ridiculed as close to our own', and that acknowledging such in romantic comedy 'is crucial to understanding our attitude towards the lovers' predicament but this predicament is precisely the subject of the narrative' (2009: 21–2). Ken's predicament leads to several scenes of physical comedy directly related to his infidelity, with Power's actions and reactions making for highly entertaining and comedic situations.

The film opens with an establishing shot of a city skyline before the camera pans into the Nortons' bedroom, where they are asleep. Jane answers the telephone, while Ken, lying on his stomach and wearing an eye mask, does not stir. The call is a singing telegram informing the audience that this is the couple's second wedding anniversary, and in the rest of this scene Jane repeatedly tries to place a calendar in front of Ken. She even sends their dog, Goliath, into the bathroom with the calendar in his mouth as Ken shaves, but it soon becomes obvious that he has forgotten. That evening, Jane hosts an anniversary party, but since Ken is working late Jane's friend Blanche (Binnie Barnes) suggests they go to his office and surprise him. Arriving, they find only cleaners and Blanche discovers a bottle of expensive perfume in Kitty's desk. Through the fragrance's scandalous name, Foolish Night, we can imagine what sort of scent it is, and it soon becomes a trope.

Expecting Jane to be asleep, Ken sneaks into their bedroom and switches on the en suite light, Power does a double take at Darnell sitting in bed holding a book. He begins grinning guiltily and jokes about her playing a trick, but his face and words suggest the edginess of a naughty child who has been caught. Starting to undress, he energetically informs her of the stacks of work he got through, having left the office just minutes earlier. Noticing he has a package, she grabs for it and a look of panic spreads across his face, his eyes widen and he informs her that it is a surprise for her but that she must wait until morning. She rips it open and he looks horrified: it is a box of cigars evidently for himself (and potentially from Kitty). Flashing her another grin, he tells her he was so busy he forgot their anniversary. As he hugs her, she sniffs his shirt and whispers, 'Foolish night' before he brazenly heads to the bathroom, waving back and replying 'Good night'. Thus, Ken is immediately set up as a forgetful and unfaithful husband, as well as a compulsive liar who attempts to charm his way out of situations with a smile.

Jane confides in Blanche that she suspects Ken's infidelity but intends to hold onto him, but Blanche sends her a bottle of Foolish Night with the note 'maybe this will help'. Seeing Goliath begging, she douses him with perfume and what follows is Power's most comedic scene in the film, and arguably of his career, created through a sequence of small gestures.

While they eat dinner, Goliath sits at his feet and he gets a whiff of Foolish Night. Looking around, confused, Power sniffs his grapefruit before sheepishly grinning at Darnell and complimenting her perfume. When she informs him that she is not wearing any he looks really confused, chokes on the grapefruit and gestures and stutters that he meant the flowers. Clearly recognising the scent, he looks panicked as he tries to determine where it is coming from. First, he takes his handkerchief from his pocket and pretends to dab his face, taking a quick sniff and raising his eyebrows in a bemused fashion, since it has obviously come up negative. Pulling at his collar, he declares that it is stuffy before rushing to open a window. Breathing in some air, he smiles before returning to the table and the soup which has been served. He smiles awkwardly as he begins to eat, before getting another whiff of the perfume. Pausing with the spoon halfway to his mouth, he frowns and looks back at Darnell worriedly. Putting the spoon down, he glances around as if still trying to work out where the scent is coming from before absentmindedly picking up a cigarette which he soon exchanges for a cigar, telling her that it is a habit he picked up recently, another lie. Lighting it, he moves his head from side to side in a sneaky attempt to waft the smoke around him and mask the perfume. Taking a puff of the cigar and then a spoonful of soup, he smiles again, repeating these actions until he becomes short of breath and looks nauseous, his smiles getting less broad and sicklier with each puff until he takes his handkerchief out and dabs his forehead. When the maid comments on Goliath's smell, Power jerks his head around and looks across the room and then down before stubbing out the cigar with an arrogant grin, suggesting that the snug Ken thinks his affair has remained a secret.

Power's performance here is full of nuances, the progression of incidental gestures resembling pantomime or silent cinema performers like Buster Keaton, and one must pay close attention in order to appreciate its subtleties, which is often the case with Power's acting and perhaps a reason why his skills have long been overlooked. Furthermore, his ability to convincingly act out smelling without becoming theatrical should be noted, since it is difficult to get this across naturally on-screen, with the audience unable to see or hear it. A similar scene occurs when Kitty, unaware that Jane is Ken's wife, divulges their romantic secrets, including that he calls her 'Kitten', while Power cringes and squirms. Later Ken fights off her advances when she pounces on him for a kiss while Jane looks on, leading Kitty to comment that he did not act like that the previous night. Although Ken gets a taste of his own medicine when Jane takes a secretarial job and constructs a false romance with her boss, she forgives Ken and the film ends with the couple embracing, but the audience is left in little doubt that Ken will remain unfaithful. Thus even when Power plays the part of a married man, two women vie for the affections of his character.

More family connections

The Luck of the Irish is the film that most overtly links the actor's on- and off-screen lives through its strong ties to both his American identity and his Irish heritage, along with his character's personality traits. Like Power, the aptly named Stephen Fitzgerald is of Irish descent, and while on a visit to Ireland falls for both the scenery and Irish colleen Nora (Anne Baxter), who runs the local inn where he is staying. Although Stephen is another journalist, he is a different kind of reporter from Steve Layton and Thomas Jefferson Tyler. Firstly, he is a freelance writer who has recently accepted a well-paid position working exclusively for David Augur (Lee J. Cobb), whose daughter Frances (Jayne Meadows) he is also romancing. While Augur pays for Stephen's chic New York apartment it is decorated by Frances, much to Stephen's distaste, thus hinting early on at their incompatibility. Indeed, Stephen appears much more relaxed and himself in the small inn in a foreign country than he ever does in his own lush apartment. Stephen is the most amiable of Power's comedic characters, and until almost the conclusion both father and daughter tell him what to do and he does it, both in work and in his personal life, which makes Stephen the closest to the actor's own personality, given some of the answers Romina Power received from interviewees for her 2014 book. For example, she quotes Henry Fonda as calling Power 'beautiful and nice beyond description, lovable in every way' (74), and saying, 'I can't think of a single negative thing to say about him and I don't think anybody could' (73). While Bert Lazzarus called him 'a good and generous man' (31), ex-wife Annabella described him as 'totally unselfish. He wanted everyone to be happy' (2014: 60), while both actor Cesar Romero and Ray Sebastian, Power's make-up man for twenty-five years, used the same phrase when calling him 'as beautiful inside as he was outside' (82, 40). Romero added that Power's 'one weak spot' was that 'he loved beautiful girls, and how! Wherever he went, there were girls galore and they followed him as if he were the Pied Piper!' (82), which is like many of Power's on-screen characterisations too, therefore adding to their believability. Perhaps Rock Hudson's comment is the most complementary when he says, 'I honestly believe that he was the kindest man I ever met', before adding rather chillingly, 'but I think that he died because he was TOO good. He kept everything bottled up inside him; he never let off steam' (208). Echoing this sentiment, George Sanders states in his autobiography, 'I shall always remember Tyrone Power as a man who gave more of himself than it was wise to give. Until in the end he gave his life' (1960: 166).

When Stephen and friend Bill Clark (James Todd) get lost in the Irish countryside, Stephen heads off to try and find a path. He stumbles across an old man (Cecil Kellaway) mending shoes near a waterfall, who acts rather strangely but gives him directions to the local town. When Stephen turns around to thank him, the man is gone. Arriving at the local inn, he casually mentions the incident to proprietor Tatie (J. M. Kerrigan), who backs out of the room while talking to himself and denying any knowledge of the waterfall. Power pauses, looks up with one eyebrow down, before turning to watch him exit. Gesturing to Todd, he throws his hands in the air and asks, 'Is everyone in this country barmy?' and states that he will be glad to get back to New York, 'where things make sense'. Thus, although his American identity comes to the fore here, his unusual use of the British word 'barmy' hints at his roots. Additionally, he begins to talk in an Irish accent, which is much more convincing than his English accent in *Lloyds of London*, before laughing dismissively, throwing down the shoe he has just taken off and reverting to his own accent. When Bill informs Stephen that he likes the Irish, he replies, 'Well, you can have them. All of them, myself included', thus now identifying himself as an Irishman, at least partially.

Although Stephen complains about the simplicity of the place and the people, he appears much more relaxed and at ease in the Irish scenes than he ever does in New York. On his first night in the inn, he sits by the fire, puts his feet up on a chair and takes a pipe from his breast pocket. Taking his feet off the chair, he leans forward and tells Tatie that when he was a cub reporter in Tennessee he interviewed a man on his one hundred and tenth birthday who said the secret to his long life was drinking a pint of corn liquor every morning before breakfast. The gullible Tatie falls for the story, but Stephen's wink at Bill shows us that he has just made it up. While Tatie tells them the truth about the old man Stephen met, Power faces the camera so that we can see his changing reactions throughout. Filling his pipe and placing the pouch of tobacco in his pocket as Tatie begins his story, he gives Bill a disbelieving nod as Tatie tells him that there is no waterfall and that it was not a mortal man he had met. Taking the unlit pipe from his mouth, Power leans in and asks, in a humouring tone as if talking to a child, 'Who was it then?', before turning away again and placing the pipe back in his mouth. Kerrigan begins to whisper, and Power takes the pipe out of his mouth again, turning his ear to hear better as Tatie informs them that it was a leprechaun. Power looks at Kerrigan and groans a low 'Oh', before slamming his hand down on the table and looking back at Todd. He strikes a match, glances at Kerrigan and begins to light the pipe, sneaking a sideways glance at him as he puffs on it before stealing a look at Todd, and then looking between the two men as amusement spreads across his face. He then gestures with the pipe in his hand, asking what he should have done, and is informed that he should have grabbed him and made him hand over the pot of gold. Power looks back at Todd, tuts and mockingly quips, 'I wish I'd thought of that'. The Americans are not believing a word of Tatie's story; he is now telling of a man who caught the leprechaun but forgot to spit on the gold. Power removes the pipe abruptly, mouthing to Todd, 'Forgot to spit on the gold' in mock disappointment before shaking his head and turning back to Kerrigan. Blinking several times, he asks if you have to spit on the gold, but by this point seems genuinely interested as Tatie tells a story from the past. Stopping mid-flow, he prods Kerrigan's arm and asks to hear the rest, no longer interrupting, looking at his friend or making any sort of sarcastic facial gestures. Tatie is eventually interrupted by Nora, who scowls at him from the doorway, and he leaves the table. Although this is a simple scene, Power's subtle facial gestures and the slight variation in his vocal intonation make it an extremely entertaining one that flows very naturally. Even though Kerrigan is doing most of the talking, Power's positioning and reactions mean that we pay more attention to him throughout the scene.

Looking out of his window that evening, Stephen sees the leprechaun. Running after him through the woods, he knocks the small man to the ground as an Irish tune plays over the soundtrack. Closer to the camera and much larger than Kellaway, Power's physical frame is particularly impressive in this scene as he overpowers the man on the ground, his hair wet and messed up from running, his heavy breathing from exertion noticeable between assertive sentences as he asks the man for his pot of gold. Not believing Tatie's story, he looks amused and comments that they have gone in for this joke in a big way, with 'props and everything' when they dig up a pot of gold. Upon opening it, however, his smile fades as he picks out a handful of gold pieces and declares, 'They're real'. Standing up slowly, his hair still a mess, he examines them again before asking if the old man has stolen the gold. Handing the pot back, he informs the man he is not going to steal his savings 'or whatever they are', and tells him to bury them again; the old man is delighted and gives him a gold piece to remember him by. The coin becomes a trope throughout, reminding him of Ireland (and Nora) and acting as his conscience every time he takes it from his pocket and flips it in the air.

The sweet and gentle Nora, in her long skirts and knitted shawl, pumping water from an outside well and enjoying life's simple pleasures, strongly contrasts with fashionable New Yorker Frances, with her figure-hugging black dresses, pearl necklaces and fur coats. Frances has a predatory nature that is most overtly revealed in her lust for Stephen, which resulted in his getting the job with her father rather than one that uses his writing skills. She has even decorated his apartment in a style he does not like, and when he rearranges some items, she forces him to put them back the way they were even though he is the one living there. It is obvious who wears the pants in their relationship, and his easy-going nature means he does not put up an argument, becoming emasculated around her and this is another reason that we wish Stephen to choose Nora, so that he may become a 'real' man. When he sits down, Frances immediately places herself on his knee, the shot composed so that Meadows is above, and therefore dominating Power just as he has dominated Kellaway. When he attempts to get up for a drink, she will not let him. Leaning in, she asks if he wants to know why she hates him before looking down into his face and forcefully telling him, 'All the time you were away you kept coming between me and whatever I was doing. Because I saw your face in crowds on the street, in my mirror when I was alone in my room. Because I ate, dreamt, slept, lived you. You and your black magic.' He merely stares at her from his lower position. Her attempt at seduction clearly has not worked, and he tries once more to get up but she pushes him back down, rendering him immobile from her weight on top of him. She continues, 'I hate every inch of you. Your superiority. Your black Irish eyes and your arrogant nose.' As she presses his nose there is a diegetic buzzer noise, at which they both look shocked. Power jumps back before touching his nose in confusion, but when the buzzer sounds a second time, he realises it is the doorbell and gets up to answer it. It is Kellaway, telling him that his name is Horace and that he is from the Acme Employment Agency, here to work as his manservant. Sending Horace to the kitchen before realising who he reminds him of, Power stares forward before rushing to the kitchen and questioning him. He leaves the room, before peeking through the door again to stare at Horace. When Frances and Stephen crouch behind the bar to find a bottle of scotch, their faces are extremely close and he gives her a quick kiss, she then gives him a quick kiss back before moving in for a passionate one. They stand up before kissing again, Power leaning Meadows passionately backwards over the bar to embrace her before Horace appears and asks if he can help and they break apart, looking embarrassed.

When Stephen runs into Nora in the New York subway he thinks it is a chance meeting, but it has been arranged by Horace. Stephen has his wallet stolen, but Nora thinks he is penniless and takes him to dinner, making him eat several large plates of Irish stew while he protests. The café owner invites them to a wedding, at which Stephen is knocked out after an altercation with a firefighter, Nora having to revive him in the backroom. As she places a cold compress on his head he starts to stir, and although she is also in a dominant position over him since he is lying down, she does not have Frances's forceful nature and resembles a worried mother tending to her sick child. Not realising he is awake, she calls him 'darling' but he sits up and kisses her tenderly before opening his eyes and looking up, obviously remembering Frances. Visibly conflicted about his feelings, he squeezes her arm and says her name, as if trying to explain something before saying that he must go. He puts her shawl around her shoulders and softly tells her he will see her home. They silently walk to her apartment before he informs her that he is going to the country for the weekend with his fiancée, whom he is marrying in a month. His sombre tone suggests that he is less than thrilled at the prospect, and Nora puts on a brave face as she wishes him happiness before rushing off. After watching her go inside, Power turns slowly, his brow furrowed as he again flips the gold coin. However, when he looks down, it has become a pebble. Picking it up and examining it with a confused look, he looks up and then back down at it. Scowling, he licks his lips and rushes across the street. Arriving at his apartment, Stephen confronts Horace, who is mending shoes just as he was the first time they met. He pushes the pebble into the old man's face and asks him to explain it. A comedic chase around the apartment ensues before Power once more pins him to the ground. Accusing Horace of bringing Nora to New York, the old man informs Stephen that he brought her over himself in his mind, and that her physical presence made no difference. The crux of the story, and of Stephen's realisation of what he wants and does not want in life, comes when he asks Horace if he is trying to ruin his life. Horace looks at him and calmly replies, 'I offered you gold, 'tis not my fault that you prefer a pebble', as he stares back, wide eyed. Horace walks into the kitchen and Stephen follows, but the old man has disappeared.

There is a cut to Augur making a dinner speech, with everyone laughing at his feeble jokes except Stephen, who sits stony-faced with Frances at his side. Looking up through one raised eyebrow while fidgeting, he awkwardly looks the other way, clearly feeling uneasy, and sees Bill looking at him as Augur calls Stephen one of the best newspapermen of our time, a first-rate reporter and his replacement when he retires. Frances beams, but he looks at her uncomfortably out of the side of his eye, making it obvious that Stephen does not want to take the job, be engaged to Frances or even to be in the room. When Stephen is asked to make a speech, she claps his arm and back, gesturing for him to stand up. As he walks across the room, several men pat him on the back, but he ignores them all as if in a trance. Cameras flash in his face and he blinks several times before looking into the crowd, most of whom have now taken on Horace's form. Power's eyes move rapidly around the room, and there are quick cuts between Kellaway in different parts of the room and Power's face in extreme close-up, again from forehead to chin. He covers his eyes before looking out to the crowd again, who have reverted to their usual selves. He refuses the job, stating that Augur needs someone working for him who agrees with his policies. When the press ask about his plans, he puts his hands in his pockets and smiles, looking relaxed for the first time in New York as he states that he has no plans except to 'sit under a waterfall with an old friend of mine'. When Frances is asked if she is going to share the waterfall, she replies that she does not think she is invited, but even if she were, she is 'not cut out for the job' before bidding Stephen goodbye. Staring at her, he looks relieved, lifting a hand to shake hers before telling her goodbye, whispering an almost silent second goodbye and walking out. On his way out, Stephen slaps Bill on the shoulder, who runs out after him, and this is also their exit from New York.

The film's final four minutes takes place back in the Irish inn, Power once again smoking a pipe as he sits reading, his head resting on his hand and an arm casually propped on the back of his chair. Wearing an open-necked shirt and tank top, a much different style from the restrictive suits and unflattering bowler hat in New York, he looks relaxed. Nora walks down the stairs and asks if Stephen and Bill are going to sit arguing all night, before Bill replies, 'It's this pig-headed husband of yours', indicating that he and Nora have married, and the reason why he looks so contented and at home. As the couple walk upstairs, Power smacks Baxter's backside, and she tells him to go first so that he does not do it again. As she talks to Bill in the hallway, he pulls her into the bedroom and closes the door. Bill sees Stephen sneak back downstairs and place a bottle of whisky on the doorstep for 'an old friend', watching from his window as Horace comes and retrieves the bottle before saluting to him, he smiles and salutes back as Nora brushes her hair in the background, showing he is finally where he wants to be.

The film is unusual in that it is a fantasy-comedy, and the only one of its kind that Power made. But perhaps what is most unusual is that the scenes set in Ireland have a green tint to them, while those in New York are in black and white, thus creating a stark contrast between the two locations. The green adds a sense of warmth, connoting nature, freshness, new life and safety. Conversely, the harsh black and white of the New York offices and Stephen's luxury apartment suggest sophistication, wealth and a lack of emotion or, as Horace calls it, a 'cold and inhospitable city'. While the Irish inn is mostly made of wood, with a large fireplace and a homely feel, Stephen's apartment is modern, minimalist and decorated in someone else's taste; the two greatly contrast throughout, as do the two women in Stephen's life. Stephen lacks any sort of arrogance, thus making him very different from Steve in *Love is News*, *Day-Time Wife*'s Ken and Tom from *That Wonderful Urge*. Of all of Power's comedy characters, Stephen is most like Alexander Brown in that he is being asked to do things against his will, but he is an honest man in debt to no one, which Horace makes him realise. Thus he leaves an unhappy job and a cold existence behind for the warmth of a good woman and a simple Irish inn, whereas Alex marries into money by romancing an heiress, continuing to dine in expensive nightclubs and wear fine evening clothes at the film's conclusion.

Deleyto notes that romantic comedy employs debates about love, sexuality, gender and identity with a special atmosphere that allows the intimate, sexual, social and gender relationships between the characters 'to be expressed in a less inhibited way; it protects them from social pressure and repression and it may allow them to change their identity and mature'. The nature of these changes, however, is specific to each film, 'although obviously affected by cultural and historical determinations' (2009: 38). This is certainly the case with Power's work in the genre, and his career overall. Although he had shown a flair for comedy, Power's final film of the genre, *That Wonderful Urge* (discussed earlier) was made a decade before the end of his career, in the immediate post-war years. However, the film did seem to take his career in a backward direction instead of forwards, adding a sense of nostalgia for his earlier pre-war persona but also highlighting how his acting skills had developed and his physical frame had expanded. His youthful beauty of the 1930s had been replaced with a more mature handsomeness in his mid-thirties, but the immediate pre- and post-war years are perhaps Power's most physically magnificent era, his frame now broader and more muscular, and his beauty obvious without the need for too many lingering close-ups. Indeed, he is allowed to be dominant and active, while continuing to be presented as the object of the erotic gaze merely by his magnificent presence, and less through camerawork, framing and angles that force us to look. Power had honed his gift for comedy throughout the years, with elements of it surfacing in other genres, such as the war film *A Yank in the RAF*. However, as discussed in the next chapter, it is his characterisations in musicals that most strongly resemble his comedic characters, particularly in the films co-starring Sonja Henie.

Notes

1. Marshall also co-starred with Power as Maugham in *The Razor's Edge*.

Chapter 3

The musical star

Overview

Although Power's first musical was *Flirtation Walk* (1935), as discussed in the introduction, he had a minor, uncredited role in this film. However, despite his lack of singing and dancing ability, he was cast as the lead in five musicals between 1937 and 1939, although he made no more films in this genre after the decade ended. To compensate for his lack of musical talent, Power was cast opposite female stars who were skilled dancers and singers, being paired with ice-skating champion Sonja Henie twice (*Thin Ice* and *Second Fiddle* [Sidney Lanfield, 1939]) and singer Alice Faye three times (*In Old Chicago*, *Alexander's Ragtime Band* and *Rose of Washington Square*). This move by Twentieth Century-Fox demonstrates the actor's appeal to contemporary audiences at a time when musicals were extremely popular, and its plans for his maximum exposure. A similar pattern emerged at MGM, where non-singers Robert Taylor and James Stewart sang in *Broadway Melody of 1936* (Roy Del Ruth, 1935) and *Born to Dance* (Roy Del Ruth, 1936), respectively, and non-dancer Clark Gable danced in *Idiot's Delight* (Clarence Brown, 1939). Thus, like Bette Davis posing for obligatory swimsuit pin-ups in her early career and originally being moulded into a platinum blonde, these ill-fitting roles suggest the tension between genres and stars on the one hand and studios' attempts to find suitable roles for their young performers on the other. Aside from *Rose of Washington Square*, Power's musicals were all nominated for Academy Awards, with *In Old Chicago* and *Alexander's Ragtime Band* both receiving six nominations and winning two and one respectively, thus proving their importance to the industry.

Power's characterisations in all five musicals are slightly different, some building on his already established screen image and others advancing it either slightly or significantly. Indeed, while his films with Henie have many similarities to his comedic pairings with Young, Faye provides his most sensual screen pairing to date, suggesting a new sexual maturity to his image at the end of the 1930s.

Making and masking the star

In his first musical, *Thin Ice*, Power's character is similar to his comedic roles of the time; some might say they are interchangeable. The film's alternative title, *Lovely to Look At*, appears to have a deliberate double meaning, which the viewer may assume refers to Henie's ice-skating numbers but could just as easily be used to describe Power and the development of his star image at this time. Although his stardom was being strongly built around his recognisable looks and beauty, and the fact that he is obviously 'lovely to look at', he is unusually repeatedly concealed and disguised throughout the film, thus making the alternative title more playful. But when his looks are revealed they are exquisite; perhaps no more so than when sitting by a log fire in a white sweater, the firelight shining on his tanned face giving him an ethereal glow while correspondingly highlighting his newly forming manly features as he starts to fill out and becomes less boyish (Figure 3.1).

Figure 3.1   Power's face lit by firelight in *Thin Ice* (1937)

The film acts almost like a reversal of *Café Metropole*, since Power plays a prince pretending to be a commoner and not the other way around. He makes his entrance after most of the principals, including Henie, have been introduced, with a brass band playing what appears to be a national anthem and several men standing to attention. Those in military dress salute as Prince Rudolph (Power) is lifted from a train carriage in a wheelchair. Fully concealed by a hat, heavy overcoat, gloves and scarf, he looks up and sneezes before the scene fades out. Arriving at the hotel, several older men fuss over Rudolph while he remains silent, rolls his eyes and looks annoyed before sneezing in one man's face. After his manservant closes the hotel room doors, Power utters his first words: 'Are they locked?' before throwing off his blanket, jumping up and removing several layers, showing that Rudolph is not actually sick. This initial scene introduces him as important, while delaying the reveal of the beautiful Power for the audience.

This initial reveal is brief, however, and when Rudolph meets skating instructor Lili Heiser (Henie) on the ski slope shortly afterwards, his body is again concealed by a ski suit, scarf and mittens, his face beneath a cap and half-covered by large goggles. Stopping for coffee, Lili stares at him and wonders out loud what he looks like behind the disguise; although we know, we too desire to see his beautiful face again, and Lili acts as a surrogate for us. Informing her that he is with the conference at the hotel, she immediately jumps to the conclusion that he is a reporter and he does not correct her, introducing himself as Rudy Miller. The plot of *Love is News* is almost reversed here, since he is the celebrity and Lili is suddenly thrust into the limelight and put on the front pages of newspapers in a concocted romance. While Lili spends time with 'Rudy the reporter', she is unaware that he is Prince Rudolph; in fact, it never seems to occur to anyone that 'Rudy' and Rudolph are the same person.

Arriving for dinner at the hotel, Rudolph adopts his fourth and most ludicrous disguise yet. Power is almost unrecognisable in a curly wig, glasses, moustache and fake nose resembling Groucho Marx, therefore providing a comic moment since this is far removed from the beautiful Power we are used to seeing. Asking for a ginger beer, he corrects his voice by lowering it to make him sound older, thus revealing the construction of his performance and his self-flexibility. Watching Lili perform, he removes the glasses before realising the nose is still attached, panics and replaces it as the scene fades out. Returning to the hotel in an almost identical disguise, but this time the wig and moustache are white, he again attempts to order a ginger beer before altering his voice mid-sentence. This time Rudolph claps so hard for Lili that his glasses and fake nose fall off and he must quickly replace them. Calling the waiter for another drink, his dark hair is showing from under the wig, and as the waiter stares, he simply clears his throat like an old man would, oblivious to his predicament. As with Alexander Brown, Power must act well in order to depict Rudolph's poor acting. 'Rudy' wears this disguise again to reveal to Lili that he is Prince Rudolph, although this time the youthful voice clearly belongs to Power and contrasts with the image. The film ends with Lili performing in the dining room once more; a brief cut to Power shows him wearing a now familiar tuxedo and white tie, thereby looking like himself (both character and actor) for the first time in this location.

Music, maturity and Alice Faye

Power's musicals with Alice Faye were instrumental in expanding his characterisations and adding another layer to his screen image. In their pairings, he is both charming ladies' man and somewhat of a heel. Since Faye was Twentieth Century-Fox's top female singing star her musical performances compensate for Power's lack of skill in this area. Although Power and Faye were being built up as a new romantic team, just as Power and Loretta Young had been, they only worked together in three films between 1938 and 1939.

Peter Lev argues that Twentieth Century-Fox lacked a fully formed identity until 1938, when the studio began to establish its own house style. Combining Zanuck's Warner Bros influence and Fox Films' premerger interest in 'Americana', the studio produced 'nostalgic stories from the nineteenth and early twentieth century, often set in the Midwest or West' (2013: 26). This is how *In Old Chicago* begins, its title card reading 'A Mid-western Prairie in 1854' over a Western sunrise. Although costing $1.55 million, it was a huge success and earned $2.5 million in domestic rentals alone upon its initial release (Lev 2013: 26). Lev calls the film a 'one-of-a-kind roadshow attraction' blending several genres, thus making it 'a historical fiction, a drama, a comedy, a love story, a family melodrama, a disaster film, an epic (the fire becoming the "founding story" of Chicago), and a musical' (2013: 27). This interweaving of genres is characteristic of many films and explains their wide appeal, but due to Faye's musical numbers scattered throughout, it is in the genre of musical that I place the film.

Lev suggests that 'the most thematically striking aspect' of the film is that 'the main character is not the straight-arrow Jack ... but his scoundrel of a brother Dion' (Power), who 'lies, cheats, fixes elections, and treats women roughly and yet he is the hero of the film' (2013: 27–8). However, I would argue that Jack (Don Ameche) is deliberately depicted as too strait-laced to be a truly interesting character, whereas Power's portrayal of Dion created depth and human failure in the protagonist who is redeemed at the end. As is discussed, the film repeatedly sets Power up as the film's main star through characterisation, lighting, framing and so forth.

As several of Power's films do, the narrative begins when his character, Dion O'Leary, is a child (portrayed by Gene Reynolds). Like Power, Dion is of Irish descent, and the initial scene shows the O'Leary family arriving in America from Ireland. As they reach Chicago, tragedy strikes when their father is thrown from their wagon and fatally injured. As he dies, he tells his three sons that one day they will grow into fine, strong men who will be a credit to his name, with everyone speaking with respect of the O'Learys and how they made their mark.

The film then moves forward to 1867, where the brothers are reintroduced as adults. First is youngest brother Bob, played by Tom Brown, who was the star of *Tom Brown of Culver*, the film in which Power made his screen debut in a minor role.[1] While Brown's career never really took off, and he receives eighth billing here, Power's flourished. Next is eldest brother Jack (Don Ameche), an honest lawyer who helps the poor without taking a fee, set up as the caring brother and the opposite of Dion. Finally, Power's Dion makes his spectacular entrance, which sets him up as the film's star, emerging from the back of a police van with sirens blazing. Handing the guard a cigar, Dion bids him farewell with a wide grin and enters the house. Greeting his mother (played by Alice Brady), he immediately walks towards the camera and begins to undress while the others remain in the background. Picking out a shirt from the pile his mother has washed for customers of her laundry business, he measures it against his body by extending his arm towards the camera, drawing the viewer's eye and emphasising his at-tractiveness. Positioned in the centre of the frame, he unbuttons his shirt and stands with an exposed chest as he discusses the money he has won from gambling, a seemingly regular pastime of Dion's. Continuing to preen himself, he announces his plan to build a saloon, and when his mother looks outraged, he hugs her and says in an Irish accent, 'And free beers to you, Mrs O'Leary'. While the family talk, Power continues to dress, and our attention is focused on him as the best-looking brother as well as the most animated. Thus, this introduction constructs Jack as the sensible and serious brother and Dion as the reverse; their personalities demonstrated by the difference in Power's and Ameche's body language, gestures, facial expressions and vocal intonations, which echoes their pairing in *Love is News*.

Dion enters the local saloon run by Gil Warren (Brian Donlevy), and Belle Fawcett (Faye) is introduced when she begins to sing. Standing directly in front of the stage, Power does a double take at her, much like women did with him in previous films. Thus, he is placed firmly as the bearer of the gaze as she performs in a revealing outfit; his eyes widening, he grins before whistling and announcing, 'What a woman!', his mouth gaping as he blinks repeatedly. She begins a charity auction, and he waves his hand in the air in order to get her attention. Belle then takes some power back, objectifying him too and highlighting his looks by repeatedly referring to him merely as 'handsome'. When Dion is thrown out of the saloon, he waits in Belle's carriage before physically overpowering her by holding her arms down when she enters. She struggles but cannot break free as he tells her he loves her. Later appearing at her bedroom door, she sees his reflection in the mirror and demands he leave, she throws ornaments and perfume bottles, which he dodges, until one breaks on his head. Entering the room, he again grabs her by the wrists and wrestles her to the floor. Faye falls on her back while Power lies on his stomach, his longish curly hair falling down the right side of his face as he kisses her cheek twice while she struggles. Turning her head towards him and really looking at him for the first time she releases an 'oh', as if overcome by his physical appearance, and stops struggling as he kisses her on the lips. Afterwards it is her turn to grin widely, his virility evidently demonstrated and compensating for his beauty and her earlier objectification of him. He smiles too as he repeats, 'What a woman!', and she offers him her lips. This second kiss is much more sensual and, as they remain in a horizontal position on the floor, she reaches around his neck and pulls herself slightly off the floor and into the kiss as he places a hand on her back, on top of her flimsy negligee, and leans down into the kiss. This rather rough foreplay is repeated later when Belle throws objects at him before he restrains her against a wall. A close-up of Power in profile accompanies his whispered words of affection, with bright lighting emphasising his long dark eyelashes, shiny hair and upturned nose and confirming that he is as beautiful in profile as he is in full face (Figure 3.2).

Figure 3.2   Dion (Power) restrains Belle (Alice Faye) in *In Old Chicago* (1938)

Dion and Belle open their own saloon and he greets the guests in white tie and tails, which emphasise his manly frame and handsome face. Senator's daughter Ann Colby (Phyllis Brooks) remarks, 'He's nice looking, isn't he?', before looking him up and down; and he watches Belle perform, thus unaware of her gaze. When he turns to whisper something to her, a look of delight comes over her face and he does his own looking at her, regaining some of his masculine power as the bearer of the gaze. Belle and Dion then retire to the backroom and she leans against a table, emphasising her curves, and calls him a 'dirty dog' in a pun that refers to his politics and sexual morals. Taking her stance as an invitation, he moves in, grabs her around the waist and pulls her into him. Telling her to say she loves him 'before I break your back', he nuzzles her neck and bites her as she squeals with delight before they kiss and the scene fades out on a now sexually mature Power.

Jack is elected mayor and vows to clear the town of undesirables, requesting Belle's help in exposing Dion's criminality. After marrying Belle in a ceremony conducted by Jack, Dion laughs as he cockily declares that Belle can no longer testify against him because she is his wife, and the brothers engage in a physical fight, which Jack unusually wins. These events make Dion Power's first really unscrupulous character, much more scheming than Steve Layton or Alexander Brown, although Dion is not as heartless as Barton Dewitt Clinton in *Rose of Washington Square*. There are, though, hints of Jesse James and Johnny Apollo that would follow shortly. However, the film ends with the great Chicago fire and an injured Dion, in ragged clothes and covered in dirt and blood, searching for Belle and his mother. Finally locating his mother, he cries out and rushes towards her before she cradles him to her breast as if he were a child again. Trying to tell her Jack is dead, he cannot get the words out and merely nods before turning to Belle. A final close-up of Power and Faye's dirty faces staring into the distance as the fire rages is what audiences would take away with them. It is a powerful ending and one that redeems Dion in the eyes of his family and the audience. Following the film's success, that same year Power, Faye and Ameche were paired in *Alexander's Ragtime Band*, which was also nominated for six Oscars, including Best Picture and Best Music, winning for the latter.

Alexander's Ragtime Band is the only musical in which Power plays a musician. To compensate for his lack of skill in this area, he portrays a bandleader, but plays the violin on occasion. The film opens with Roger Grant (Power) playing at a concert, his face slightly obscured by his violin, therefore allowing another slow reveal of Power's face for the anticipating audience, as well as providing the immediate opportunity for him to wear evening clothes. At the concert's conclusion, three women rush over, grab his arms and beg him to attend a party. He smiles widely but politely excuses himself as they disappointedly watch him leave.

Attending an audition at a downtown dive, Power's dark, formal eveningwear contrasts with that of the other band members, who are all in lightly coloured street clothes. Singer Stella Kirby (Faye) is also auditioning and she is dressed rather commonly in excessive make-up, accessories and a feather boa. Although she has brought her own sheet music, it is handed to Roger for the band to play and as the furious Stella begins to sing the lyrics, the song is revealed to be 'Alexander's Ragtime Band'. Although the manager hires them as a team, Stella initially refuses to work with them after surveying Roger and mockingly calling him 'fancy pants' in his 'monkey suit'. Power, the object to be studied by both Stella and the audience, stands erect and formal throughout her barrage, before bowing and sarcastically replying, 'It's always nice to meet a lady', as he looks at her indignantly. Based on the music, and given his position as the bandleader, the manager calls Roger 'Alexander', and it is this name that he is known by for the rest of the film, even by his bandmates.

Roger's second interaction with Stella occurs in her dressing room before going on stage. Criticising her costume, he tells her he wants his band to have class and distinction. Power's stance and tone are formal, the most formal he had ever been on-screen, and he uncommonly remains unsmiling throughout. Analysing her outfit, he removes her feather boa, then a large corsage, ruffles around her waist and an elaborate headpiece, explaining why he is discarding each item as he does so. They shout at each other and he walks out, but when she arrives on stage all the accessories are back. He makes a face while continuing to conduct the band. Following the performance, pianist Charlie Dwyer (Ameche) locks Stella and Roger together in her dressing room to try and stop their fighting. Standing stationary just inside the door, Power holds the violin case at his side. When she bellows, 'Well?!', he smiles and moves towards her. While she is animated and loud, he stands aloof and speaks quietly and with perfect diction. Their conflicting vocal intonations and gestures are reinforced by their contrasting looks, Power with jet-black hair and a simple tailored suit and Faye with platinum blonde hair and a busy, cheap-looking outfit.

Stella enters the next scene in understated make-up, sophisticated clothing and more natural blonde hair, and Charlie sings 'Now It Can Be Told', a love song he has written for her. The next time the song is heard, the band is playing it in a spacious nightclub. Power is dressed in white tie and tails, and Faye wears a complementary white evening gown, carries a white feather fan and has her hair in a simple wave. As she sings, she turns towards Power, who briefly looks over his shoulder at her, his face more relaxed now as he looks her up and down. With these shots, the audience is given a brightly lit close-up of Power's face that emphasises his beauty but also allows him to remain an active male, since he is both conducting and returning her gaze (Figure 3.3). Although his back is to the diegetic and non-diegetic audiences while conducting, he turns slightly to look in Faye's direction as she sings, a brief smile visible as his profile is revealed. Continuing to sing, she looks at him again before there is a cut to another close-up of Power. This time, however, he does a double take as if Roger is seeing Stella for the first time, momentarily stopping conducting as he turns slightly and blinks when she directs the words 'every other tale of boy meets girl is just an imitation' towards him. He stares at her, and his eyes widen and dart to the side before returning to her. Opening his

Figure 3.3 A close-up while conducting in *Alexander's Ragtime Band* (1938)

mouth, he looks confused as if Roger is just realising his feelings for Stella for the first time, before catching himself, licking his lips and turning back to the band. It is a brief exchange of glances and well-rehearsed words but Charlie, who has been grinning from the piano, notices this intimate exchange between the two, his smile fading since he is in love with Stella and wrote the song for her.

While Faye finishes the song, Power remains in profile, conducting the band but keeping his eyes on her throughout. After the song ends he continues to stare, holding his bow in mid-air as she turns around and they lock eyes before she runs out the room. He chases after her and they kiss on the balcony before he stands back and looks her over, announcing, 'Let me look at you, for the first time', before moving in and kissing her softly. Telling her, 'That's for tonight', he then moves in more forcefully, twisting her body around and kissing her passionately before adding, 'That's for all the times I've wanted to break your neck', suggesting that their quarrelling has made him more passionate. She then kisses him and says, 'And that's for all the times I've wanted to slap your ears down'. Although presented as opposites, Roger and Stella learn a lot from each other; she is more refined and he is less stuffy. But when a talent agent wants to make Stella a star, without the band, they argue again and he walks out.

Years pass, and their stubbornness gets in the way of them getting back together; he joins the army and Stella marries Charlie. When Roger returns from the war he tries to pick up where they left off, but when he learns of her marriage he becomes detached and cold. Charlie realises they are still in love and gives Stella a divorce, which Roger is unaware of. They are finally reunited at the film's conclusion as Roger is playing a sold-out concert at Carnegie Hall, and Stella arrives to sing the final number, 'Alexander's Ragtime Band', meaning the narrative has come full circle. While Faye is dressed in ordinary street clothes, Power wears white tie and tails, is brightly lit and occupies the centre of the frame in front of the orchestra. With Stella's help, Roger has become much less uptight and Power is extremely animated in this final scene, almost dancing as he conducts, now with a familiar grin on his face which was a major part of Power's star image.

Rose of Washington Square was Power's third, and final, pairing with Faye. Her character, Rose Sargent, is singing in an inn where she first meets Power's Barton Dewitt Clinton. Swaggering in, Barton asks to use the telephone before briefly glancing at Rose and her friends. Leaning on the desk and chewing gum, he grins widely as he addresses the man on the telephone as 'cowboy', a recurring greeting he uses throughout the film. While talking, he stops chewing, his smile fades and he stares forward before a point-of-view shot shows Faye smiling and singing at a piano. Sensing him staring, she looks back, her face mirroring his as Faye's character once again returns Power's gaze. He continues his conversation while observing her from the side of his eye, before hanging up slowly and continuing to stare. Later, he has removed his overcoat and hat and integrated himself into the group, playing the piano while she sings at his side. Continuing to chew arrogantly, he joins in the singing on occasion and when the song is over, he stands up, leans over the piano and tells her, 'I wish you were in some sort of trouble', and when she asks why, he replies, 'So that I could get you out of it'. This foreshadows the trouble that Barton will soon get Rose into.

Barton's taking Rose to a house party provides another excuse for Power to wear evening clothes. As they dance, however, the wide grin, witty talk and gum-chewing are gone as he stares intensely at her before he stops dancing. Looking at her seriously, he pulls her to a dark corner of the garden and kisses her passionately twice before the scene cuts to them walking hand in hand in the inn's lobby. He kisses her on the cheek as she turns to enter her room, pulling her back towards him for a more passionate kiss. As with Carroll in *Lloyds of London*, Faye then exits the scene and we remain with Power. Smiling, he takes some sort of candy or peanut from his pocket, throws it in the air and catches it in his mouth (another of the film's recurring tropes). As he enters his room across the hall, he looks back and grins at her closed door, but two men are waiting for him inside. One is a detective, and we discover that Barton is well known to the police and is being threatened with jail. Although he tries to charm the men and feign innocence, by the next morning he has checked out.

Next seen heading to a club, Barton tosses a coin into a sidewalk Santa's pot, still as cocky as ever as he quips, 'Here you are cowboy, buy yourself a reindeer'. Dressed in a tuxedo, he checks his coat and hat before again catching a snack in his mouth; but as he lifts his shot glass to his mouth, he freezes when recognising the voice of the club's singer as Rose's. Letting the glass slowly descend towards the bar, he turns around abruptly, smiles and excuses himself before walking over to her. Leaning on the doorframe out of her view, he grins and chews as he watches her. The camera films Power from a low angle, making him appear particularly dominant here, while correspondingly breathtakingly beautiful in his formal attire. When the club is raided, Barton refrains from calling the police officer cowboy, but greets him with 'Top of the evening to you Captain' in a semi-Irish accent before arrogantly saluting and tapping the man on the chin.

When gangsters try to collect money that Barton owes their boss, Lefty, he is dressed in a smart pinstriped suit and sips on champagne while trying to fob them off with feigned nonchalance. Taking a snack from his pocket, he plays with it for a while this time, placing it in his mouth rather than throwing it up; nor does he chew as vigorously as before, letting it sit in his mouth to reflect his nervousness. Although he looks fearful as they walk away, he soon drains his glass and tells the bartender to 'fill it up again, cowboy', before falsely informing agent Harry Long (William Frawley) that he represents Rose and 'selling' him her contract for the sum he owes Lefty. But when Rose's singing partner Ted Cotter (Al Jolson) confronts him, Barton lies and says the money is for Rose. When Ted leaves, he takes another snack from his pocket and throws it up out of habit, but this time he catches it in his hand and looks down at it, tossing it around as if to show he is thinking. Walking towards the piano, he leans on it and looks back at his hand before throwing the food on the floor and turning away abruptly. Quickly turning back to the piano, he opens the lid and smiles before rushing to the telephone and asking for the classified ads. Although it is a friend's apartment, Barton sells all the furniture while ironically describing the buyer's offer as 'a crime'. Although we are asked to be shocked by this behaviour, we are also not surprised at this act, although there is a hint of remorse in his eyes before he casts them downwards at the cheque.

Barton and Rose are married, and when they return from their honeymoon his friend threatens to call the police unless Barton repays him immediately for the furniture, leading Barton to borrow from Lefty again. Saying he is trying to avoid dragging Rose into a scandal now that she is a famous singer, the following day the headlines reveal that Lefty's gang have been targeted by the police, with 'Follies' star's husband' arrested as a member. As the men sit in court, Power is seen with a bandage on his head, slumped in a chair and looking down as a man announces that they are 'all desperate criminals' and, except for Barton, have long police records. Ted bails him out and Barton tells Rose about his situation. A plaster on his forehead now, he lights a cigarette and moves around the room as he speaks. Less cocky than before, Barton's actions show desperation and shame as he rushes over to her, grabs her hands and desperately explains why he needed the money. Although Rose refuses to leave him, the reality of the situation is just sinking in for Barton. Staring forward, he describes his fear of prison: 'stone walls', he pauses, his voice slightly breaking, 'iron doors for years and years'. He stops, shakes his head slightly and shudders before adding, 'I'd rather be dead', without moving or blinking as if he is already dead inside.

Skipping bail the day before the trial, Barton is seen much later looking in a music shop window that is advertising Rose's song 'My Man'. Attending her show, Power is almost unrecognisable with his large beard and longer, wavy hair as he sits in the audience. Watching her emotional performance of the gut-wrenching song about him, he begins to cry, twists his hat with both hands and lets a tear fall down his cheek. Barton in redeemed by the fact that he feels remorse and truly does love Rose. He rushes out of the theatre and down a dark city street with his head down before he throws down his cigarette and walks into the police station. Approaching the officer, he repeats his oft-uttered, 'Hello, cowboy', without any arrogance this time, before a headline discloses that he has surrendered and faces five years in jail. Cleaned up at the end of the film, he bids Rose farewell as he is led away, his voice cracking as he shouts back. Barton shows a progression in Power's screen image as a suave heel who is somewhat of a precursor to Stanton Carlisle, only less unscrupulous and willing to take his punishment in the knowledge that they can start again, much like Johnny Apollo does.

The final musical

Although doing nothing to advance his screen image, Power's final musical *Second Fiddle* did help cement his likeable but cocky persona, which would re-emerge shortly in the comedy *Day-Time Wife* (1939) and the war film *A Yank in the RAF* (1941). The film's title describes the position that Power's film studio publicist Jimmy Sutton has within the film and, even though Power was an international star at this point, Henie received top billing and the actor played 'second fiddle' to her too. As Davis notes, studios normally followed a film's premiere with a national tour by the film's stars, 'while the publicists looked after the stars and handled the press' (1993: 152). Here, Power (who was a star, and therefore receiving this sort of publicity) plays publicist to rising star Trudi Hovland (Henie), thus playing another dual role: Power (the star) as Jimmy (the publicist). Unusually for a character playing opposite Power, Trudi is not in love with Jimmy and takes very little notice of him; her sights instead are set on Roger (Rudy Vallee) and the phoney romance that both she and the public buy into.

Released the same year as *Gone with the Wind*, *Second Fiddle* plays on MGM's famously extensive casting for the role of Scarlett O'Hara. Jimmy is a publicity man for major film company Consolidated Pictures, which is testing hundreds of girls for the coveted role of Violet Jansen in *Girl of the North*, a screen adaptation of a fictional best-selling novel. Power makes his entrance first, rushing through the door of a newspaper office and beaming at an older female reporter while exclaiming, 'Hello honey'. He stops smiling when she scowls at him, removes his hat and leans on her desk. Looking directly into her face, he grins as he tries to sweet talk her into running his 'exclusive scoop'. Patting her on the back and then on the cheek, he tells her she is getting the story 'because I love ya', before she informs him that his last exclusive was 'bunk'. His smile fades again and he slowly stands upright as she thrusts his hat at him. Fiddling with the hatband, he tells her that if she was not an old friend he would go out and 'give that story to ...', hesitating as he points left then right before comically adding, 'erm, somebody else'. A close-up shows Power slightly raising an eyebrow before he turns away and back again, rubbing his hand across his mouth and feigning a casual demeanour as he asks about vacancies at the newspaper. Producing a telegram signed by his boss, he announces that he will be fired if he does not generate publicity, bids her farewell and slowly and deliberately walks towards the door, waiting to be called back. She reluctantly agrees to run the story and his wide grin reappears as he animatedly rushes back with outstretched arms. Grabbing her face in both hands, he kisses her forehead three times and calls her 'a pal' before racing out the door shouting 'Bye'. Power hardly stands still for a moment in this introductory scene, which establishes Jimmy as another sneaky character, but also a loveable rogue that people cannot help liking. This is verified in the following scene when Roger refuses to do an interview because he has a date with girlfriend Jean (Mary Healy). Jimmy produces the same telegram, repeats the claim about losing his job and tells them he will find work somewhere before giving Roger a friendly pat on the arm and slowly walking away. When Roger calls him, he rushes back, declares them both 'a pal' and hurries off with a wide grin and a 'goodbye', in almost a repeat performance.

When schoolteacher Trudi is chosen for a screen test, her boyfriend Willie Hogger (Lyle Talbot) notes his disapproval of Jimmy accompanying her to Hollywood, obviously jealous of his good looks. When a group of locals gather to congratulate Trudi, she informs them that Jimmy is from Hollywood and they immediately crowd around him, talking over each other as he tries to escape. One asks him if he has ever seen Joan Crawford, while another enquires as to who Don Ameche really loves; he replies, in a deadpan voice, 'Mrs Ameche'. When a man asks him if the Ritz Brothers are really brothers, he quips back, 'No, they're the fathers of the Dead End Kids'. A woman holds her child, who is singing 'The Good Ship Lollipop' in the style of Shirley Temple, and he comically cringes. This scene ironises Power's stardom since Twentieth Century-Fox's biggest star is mobbed here not because he is a star but because his character works with the likes of Ameche, who played second fiddle to Power several times on-screen, thus it is a self-reflexive jokiness that makes Power seem more approachable while also consolidating his stardom. Later when Trudi prepares for her screen test, Jimmy tells her George Arliss was nervous the first time he made a picture too, 'he told me so himself'. Another in-joke: Arliss was a predecessor to Power at the studio. There is also a fake column by Louella Parsons, a gossip writer who wrote plenty about Power and Henie's off-screen relationship; the pair were even parodied in the Warner Bros short *Hollywood Steps Out* (Tex Avery, 1941), dancing in the famous Ciro's nightclub, he in a tuxedo and she wearing ice skates.

When Trudi informs Jimmy that she is not going to Hollywood he attempts to use the telegram trick on her. The camera is placed in front of him as he walks across a frozen lake, expecting her to call him back. He starts off by grinning, but it soon fades when she remains silent. We see his face changing from arrogance to confusion and then to panic as he frantically looks around and thinks his scheme has failed. When she eventually does call him, he stops abruptly, slips on the ice and turns around with a confident 'Yes?' before rushing back, sliding comically as he goes. When she wins the lead, he helps construct a backstory for her 'real life' biography, pacing as he repeats the occupation of her family over and over with disdain, waving his hands and declaring there is 'no romance in the fish business, we've got to get you some ancestors', before deciding she comes from a long line of 'explorers, Vikings, pirates', smiling with pride at his own imagination and demonstrating the constructed nature of Hollywood stars' backstories.

When Jimmy is ordered to get Roger some well-needed publicity, he creates a phoney romance between Roger and Trudi, but does not inform her. Believing that Roger's feelings are genuine, she falls for him while Jimmy, who is behind the romantic gestures attributed to Roger, finds himself falling for Trudi while thrusting her into the arms of another man. As Trudi practices facial expressions in front of a full-length mirror, she gushes about the lovely poetry that Roger has written for her (which was actually written by Jimmy). In a self-reflexive scene, she critiques Jimmy's appearance, an ironic subversion of the relative fame and attractiveness of Power and Vallee. The scene also parallels the grooming of stars since, ironically, it is ingénue Trudi, being taught how to be a star, who tells her publicist (who is really a star, and a beautiful one) how to be more attractive. She tells Jimmy, 'It wouldn't hurt you to look in the mirror once in a while yourself'. His smile fades as she says, 'Look at your hair, look at your tie', flicking his tie before pushing his nose up and patting his cheek, concluding, 'You may be handsome if you took a little care of yourself', before walking off, paralleling his trait of walking away after showing people the fake telegram. Silently smiling as he watches her leave, Power blinks a few times as if Jimmy is letting her words sink in. Looking down, he lowers his eyebrows and lets the grin fade. Slowly bringing his hand up to touch his cheek, he puts a pinkie finger briefly on his lip before reaching for his tie and looking towards the door again. Turning towards the mirror, he fixes his tie and pulls down his sweater before looking up at his hair and pushing it back. Glancing down and back at the door, this scene shows Jimmy at his most vulnerable, with no one there to perform for. It is also the first time he is seen without a grin as he calmly examines himself in the mirror, allowing the audience to see his attractiveness reflected in it and to disagree with Trudi's observations. As with the exchange with Faye during the song in *Alexander's Ragtime Band*, this is also a turning point for Jimmy who suddenly thinks romantically about Trudi for the first time, his confusion played out through Power's facial expressions while he fixes his clothes and hair.

The next scene opens on a close-up of a piece of sheet music, the handwritten title 'I Poured My Love into a Song' at the top of the page as someone whistles and draws in musical notes before scoring out 'love' and replacing it with 'heart'. It is a man's hand, and a cut to Power at a piano reveals it to be Jimmy who is writing the song. His hair is messy and he wears a casual tank top and open-necked shirt. Popping the pencil behind his right ear, he begins to play the notes he has just written with one hand, looking between the paper and the keys as he does so. Raising an eyebrow to suggest he is impressed by his creation, he takes the pencil again, nods and smiles as he leans forward to add several more notes. Pushing his hair back, he mumbles, 'Yeah' before replacing the pencil and sitting with both hands on the piano, starting to play and sing. Looking at the music as he plays, Power leans forward and then looks up, singing the chorus and humming the rest, suggesting that Jimmy has a melody without all the lyrics yet. As he plays and hums, a pan to the door shows his boss walking in without Jimmy noticing. He adds a few more lines of lyrics while his boss stands directly at his side undetected, staring at him in disbelief. Starting to casually play a middle eight, he looks down and sees a pair of feet, before freezing and stopping playing instantly. Scowling and embarrassed at being caught, he turns to the man with a curt, 'Well, what are you doing here?', before explaining that he has run out of ways to help Roger romance Trudi so he is writing a love song for Roger to perform. As the man picks up the music and reads the title, Power stiffens his body, his hands on his knees and his eyes cast down at the keys, before violently grabbing the sheet music and throwing it down. Reading between the lines, his boss taps him on the shoulder, saying, 'Too bad, Jimmy', but the frustrated and humiliated Jimmy dismissively tells him to leave. An image of published sheet music for the song fades over the top, featuring a photograph of Trudi and Roger embracing, reading 'words and music by Roger Maxwell', even though we have just witnessed Jimmy emotionally composing the song. A complete version is then performed in a nightclub by Vallee, a professional singer. During this number, there is a cut to Power reclining in a chair and staring at the ceiling. A close-up of his face, with a ribbon of bright light across the top half, highlights his beauty, which strongly contrasts with the plainer Vallee. But while Vallee is active, Power sits stationary in a pose resembling that of a passive pin-up, indeed we might see this very pose as a glossy studio publicity shot or a full-page portrait in a fan magazine. As he looks towards a radio set it becomes apparent that the song is being broadcast live and is therefore a diegetic sound that Jimmy is also hearing. He sighs and looks back towards the ceiling with a melancholy look on his face.

When Trudi finds out about the concocted romance she goes home to marry Willie, whom she does not love. Jimmy follows, confesses his feelings and tells her that she loves neither Willie nor Roger but the man who wrote the song, therefore she must love him. Although he kisses her, there is a lack of chemistry and it appears that Trudi has never considered Jimmy romantically. Indeed, apart from his efforts to chat up a brunette early in the film, Jimmy is surrounded by women (the female reporter, Trudi, Jean, Trudi's aunt) yet does not romance any of them, which is unusual for his characters, particularly at this stage in his career, and almost queers him.

Power's work in musicals allowed him to expand the range of genres he was appearing in during the first decade of his career and, despite his own musical limitations, he both cemented the star persona he developed in his early comedic roles and advanced his screen image by portraying more ruthless and sexually dangerous characters. This mix of brutal and heroic screen image would be developed even further when he moved into his first male-driven genre: the Western, when he was cast in the title role of *Jesse James*.

Notes

1. Tom Brown was born on 3 January 1913 and Power on 5 May 1914.

Chapter 4

The tough Westerner

Overview

As noted, during the first few years of his career, Power starred in a range of dramas, comedies and musicals predominantly aimed at female audiences. These genres helped develop Power's recognisable and popular star image as a cocky ladies' man, while highlighting his exquisite looks through cinematic techniques such as framing, brightly lit close-ups and a range of historical costumes and contemporary evening clothes. Perhaps surprisingly, then, Power's first major career curve came in 1939 when he was cast in the title role of Hollywood's first 'A' Western of the 1930s: *Jesse James* (Coyne 1997: 17). Marking Power's initial venture into a genre described by Deleyto as 'the quintessential male genre, with its narratives of violence and conquest' (2009: 16), it was the first time Power had appeared in a film predominantly aimed at male audiences. Furthermore, it became Twentieth Century-Fox's biggest hit of the year (Belafonte 1979: 85), proving that audiences were ready to accept Power in more masculine roles at the close of the decade.

Released in the period directly preceding America's entry into World War II, the film was integral in developing a much-needed shift in Power's screen masculinity, appearance and performance style, reflecting the shifting industrial and social context in which it was made. In advancing his star image away from that of a womaniser, and instead placing it within an overtly homosocial environment, Power was able to convincingly demonstrate male bonding and leadership through a tougher masculinity, which was essential for both the historical timeframe and Power's own upcoming real-life war service.

Despite the huge success of *Jesse James* for both the studio and Power's career development, he would make no more Westerns for twelve years, thereafter appearing in just three more during the early 1950s. While still under contract to his home studio, he made *Rawhide* (1951) and *Pony Soldier* (Joseph M. Newman, 1952); subsequently, his first film after becoming an independent agent was *The Mississippi Gambler* (Rudolph Maté, 1953).

Moreover, no discernible Western image was created for Power after *Jesse James*, his portrayal of the outlaw being the one that has endured, while the other three films are almost forgotten. In contrast to Jesse as a ruthless outlaw, *Rawhide*'s Tom Owens is an ordinary man held captive by bandits for most of the film; *Pony Soldier*'s Duncan MacDonald is a Canadian Mountie and *The Mississippi Gambler*'s Mark Fallon is a tough but honest riverboat gambler.

Although I am less concerned with the components of the Western itself and more with the presentation and performances of Power within the genre, how it advanced his star image and the place these films occupy within his career trajectory, I begin by stating the importance of the Western for Hollywood in general and Power's career more specifically. The Western and American cinema evolved concurrently, the Western being 'without question the richest and most enduring genre of Hollywood's repertoire', with a lifespan as long and varied as Hollywood's own (Schatz 1981: 45). Noting how the genre generated the basic framework for Hollywood's studio production system, Schatz calls *The Great Train Robbery* (1903) not only the birth of the Western film but of America's commercial narrative film (1981: 45). According to Dyer, the genre's textual pleasures lie in its visceral qualities, including chases on horseback, 'surging' through the land, exciting music and stunning landscapes (1997: 33). To this list can be added the visual spectacle not only of the distinctly masculine (and American) figure of the cowboy, but of erotically charged stars, such as Power, embodying these cowboys.

A new direction

Although Hollywood's major studios produced a steady flow of Westerns throughout the 1930s, big-budget sound-era or 'A' Westerns were extremely rare before 1930 (Coyne 1997: 17). One exception to the 'low-budget rule' was *The Big Trail* (1930), marking not only John Wayne's first starring role but the only sound film Power's father, Tyrone Power Sr, ever made. Although the resurgence of 'A' Westerns was an important industrial development, which demonstrated that Hollywood was turning towards subjects from American history while the prospect of war loomed, it actually involved a very limited number of films (Schatz 1997: 108). During 1939, Hollywood's eight major studios released 378 films, and while forty-eight of these were Westerns, only nine were 'A' Westerns. The first to be produced by any studio was *Jesse James* starring Power in the title role (Coyne 1997: 17). Several other still famous 'A' Westerns were also released in 1939, including *Destry Rides Again* (George Marshall) and *Stagecoach* (John Ford), perhaps the most famous Western of all. As Stephen McVeigh suggests, the Depression era marked 'a significant fault line of the United States and the cinematic Western' since, during this 'traumatic time ... the resolute, certain hero of the Western practically disappeared from the Hollywood landscape' with a new kind of cinematic hero, or rather anti-hero, emerging instead (2007: 69). Power's Jesse and Wayne's Ringo Kid in *Stagecoach* 'invigorated the genre' by modifying the 1930s gangster into an American hero (McVeigh 2007: 70). Tim Pulleine calls Power 'sympathetic, if slightly stolid' as Jesse, and highlights that the extensive literature on Jesse and Frank James usually depicts them as authentic American heroes, which is how cinema also portrayed them, at least until the 1960s (1993: 377).

However, as Pulleine notes, the James brothers were slow to achieve the cinematic status they had acquired in literature. Between 1908 and 1927, five film versions of their story were produced: *The James Boys in Missouri* (Gilbert M. Anderson, 1908), *The Near Capture of Jesse James* (director unknown, 1915), *Jesse James Under the Black Flag* (Franklin B. Coates, 1921) and *Jesse James as the Outlaw* (Coates, 1921), the latter two starring Jesse James Jr as his father, before *Jesse James* (Lloyd Ingraham) was released in 1927. Thus, the 1939 film was the first to be made in twelve years, as well as the earliest sound film on the subject and Power's first film to be shot in colour. Due to its great success, Pulleine suggests that the film ensured that Jesse became 'the most popular of all cinematic outlaws' (1993: 162). His counterpart Robert Taylor made his Western debut two years later as *Billy the Kid* (David Miller, 1941), the West's other most notorious outlaw. Since Power was now a leading star with a much more accessible and disseminated image, audiences would have expectations of Jesse looking like Power, rather than the other way around; the same is true of Taylor as Billy. Although photographs of these two historical men exist, neither possessed the actors' good looks, but filmmakers are asking audiences to suspend their disbelief and allow the performers to 'become' their character for the film's duration. As Gill Plain notes, 'the actor's value lies in the extent to which he or she can be imagined as the character, and in this context the corporeality of the performer is integral to the construction of the role' (2006: 9), which is certainly the case here.

Power's playing Jesse James means that he is first and foremost Power, the actor and film star, who adapts his costume (Western gear), actions (killing, robbing, holding up banks, riding a horse) and appearance (moustache, unshaven, dirty) in order to play the infamous outlaw, but throughout the film he still remains fully recognisable as Power. His looks, voice and mannerisms are particularly familiar at the start as the wide-grinning, clean-shaven farm boy dressed in a clean blue checked shirt. This is perhaps why, when he later becomes a humourless, vicious outlaw it is a particularly shocking change (unlike Stanton in *Nightmare Alley*, for example, who is an egotistical schemer from the start). Despite Power adopting a southern drawl – though not to the extent of Henry Fonda as Frank – and repeatedly using terms such as 'I'll be doggone', 'ain't' and 'I reckon', it cannot fully disguise the richness of tone and vocal control that Power had developed by this point. Thus, we still identify it as Power's voice, just Power with a twang.

As with many Westerns, the railroad is a motif for power, corruption and progression, and can be read as a metaphor for the government. When the railroad indirectly causes the death of the boys' mother (Jane Darwell), it leads them into a life of crime that audiences are asked to see as justifiable. Those running the railroad are depicted as brutes and bullies, while the 'outlaws' are shown as heroes, and this is how the townspeople see them, having lost their land, homes and livelihood to the railroad. Jesse is initially depicted as an ordinary farmer led into robbing and killing without wanting to at first, until it becomes a habit and finally a compulsion with him. His jobs get bigger and more dangerous as he becomes colder and more brutal. Furthermore, Jesse is not present when wife Zee (Nancy Kelly) gives birth, meeting his namesake son for the first time when the boy is five years old. When Jesse eventually returns home and tries to readjust to domestic life, he cannot. Wearing his guns at home, he is constantly jumpy and lives under a false name, but death finally releases him.

Jesse is introduced to audiences while working on his mother's farm, politely answering questions the railroad men ask him. When Frank informs their leader, Barshee (Brian Donlevy), that his mother does not want to sign a deed to her land, Barshee attacks Frank but Jesse reappears with a gun to assist his brother. Jesse holds the gun on the men while kneeling beside his mother to ensure her safety, while Frank engages in a physical fight with Barshee. When Barshee picks up a scythe ready for attack, Jesse skilfully and calmly shoots it out of his hand. This shows the importance of family to Jesse, while demonstrating he is no pushover, despite his appearance. With a warrant out for their arrest, the brothers make their escape as one man comments that 'two little farmer boys' have no chance against the authorities. Believing the boys to be home, Barshee has explosives sent into their house that kill their elderly mother. As she dies, local newspaper editor Major Rufus Cobb (Henry Hull) comments that he is 'so sorry'. When Barshee grudgingly replies that he too is sorry, Cobb rather chillingly adds, 'It's you I'm sorry for', as the scene fades out. This foreshadows the revenge that the James brothers will seek, and when Zee arrives at their hideout to inform them of the news, Jesse immediately saddles up and heads to town.

Standing at the opposite end of a bar from Donlevy, the calm and unsmiling figure Power embodies here is already a very different Jesse from the one we met less than fifteen minutes earlier, as well as far removed from the familiar Power screen image of previous films. Dressed in the same plaid shirt, but now stern and with a glint of hatred in his eyes, he slowly walks into the bar, where all laughter and talking ceases and everyone looks at him. In a monotone voice, he menacingly warns Barshee he will shoot him on the count of three, and when one of Barshee's men tries to kill Jesse, he shoots him first before immediately turning to Barshee and killing him too. Quickly leaving the saloon through the swinging door as calmly as he entered, Power had played his toughest scene to date.

The scene that follows begins with a disembodied hand pinning up a poster requesting information on the whereabouts of Jesse and offering a $1,000 reward. This is a recurring motif, with the sum of the reward increasing each time. The poster notes that he is wanted for murder and, even though it was an act of revenge, the next time we see Jesse he is standing in shadow which suggests the darker persona he now exemplifies. With staring eyes, Power covers his face with a red bandana while he waits on horseback for a train to arrive, the ultimate symbol of Jesse's troubles. Remaining a shadowy figure, Jesse gallops alongside the approaching train before jumping on its roof, his outline visible against the night sky as he makes his way across the carriages to the engine room. Although the bandana covers most of Power's face and a Stetson covers his hair, the dark eyes and heavy brows are irrefutably still Power's, along with the familiar voice firmly informing the staff that he is holding up the train. Demanding the driver stop around the bend, there is a cut to Frank and his gang on horseback, also covering their faces with bandanas. While Frank and the other men wear dark blue and black bandanas, those worn by Jesse and Bob Ford (John Carradine) are red. A vibrant colour connoting blood and death, it links them together in their murderous ways while subtly foreshadowing Jesse's death at the hands of Ford. While the others take money from the passengers, Power stands stationary with an unblinking stare and a gun in either hand before shooting out the lights and terrifying the passengers as they make their escape (Figure 4.1).

Another wanted poster follows, which looks much more professional than the first, and now offers a reward of $5,000 for the capture of Jesse dead or alive and $2,500 for Frank. With each subsequent poster, the reward for Jesse is always much higher than for Frank, and Jesse's name in bigger letters not only reflects the importance of their characters but also the actors and their billing. Someone off-screen, whom we assume to be Jesse, shoots the poster several times, an act that was reimagined the following year in *The Mark of Zorro* in which Power's off-screen protagonist carves a 'Z' on his own wanted posters.

Returning to town to visit Zee, Jesse's broad smile echoes the character from the start, but now he wears a moustache and discusses his hatred for the railroad, evidently showing that he is no longer the cheerful farmer

Figure 4.1 Power in bandana: the enduring image from *Jesse James* (1939)

he once was, but now a bitter outlaw and killer. The moustache is gone in the next scene as he proposes to Zee and kisses her by a stream; this is the closest Jesse comes to embodying Power's established persona as a romantic lead.

As with films like *Johnny Apollo*, the strength of many scenes depends almost entirely on Power's facial expressions, rather than dialogue, and his ability to convey Jesse's inner feelings this way. After marrying Zee, Jesse is promised a pardon and gives himself up. Accepting his fate and the opportunity to become a free man, he bids Zee farewell and turns towards his jailer. Walking into the small cell, he looks around before throwing his hat on the bed. Looking up, Power lifts an eyebrow and cocks his head before removing his coat, showing that Jesse has resigned himself to the fact that he will be here for a while. As he begins to remove his waistcoat, the cunning railroad owner McCoy (Donald Meek), who has issued the pardon, approaches the cell. With the camera placed behind the extremely short Meek, Power looks particularly tall and dominant, with McCoy's cowardice emphasised, since he will only approach Jesse now that he is behind bars. The scene resembles a child taunting a caged lion at the zoo, safe in the knowledge that the metal bars prevent the animal from tearing him apart. Jesse talks civilly, even respectfully, to McCoy and uses open body language while giving the man his full attention. Power repeatedly nods his head as the older man tells him, 'I just want to welcome you and tell you how glad I am to see you', pausing before adding, 'here in jail' with a smirk before walking away and leaving Jesse alone. Merely staring after Meek at first, the camera focuses in on Power as he effectively demonstrates the conflicting emotions Jesse is feeling upon realising that he has been tricked into giving himself up. Widening his eyes, Power opens his mouth slightly before clenching his jaw. Raising both hands to grip the bars at shoulder height, he looks towards the jailhouse door and then to the other side of the cell (presumably at a window, therefore the outside world) before looking back at the door, much like a caged animal. Finally, his face comes to rest where Meek had been standing and where the camera has remained throughout. Although the vertical metal bars obscure both sides of his face, Power's features remain visible between the bars while he portrays Jesse's initial shock and panic. With his body motionless and his hands still gripping the bars, Power moves his eyes across the frame, furrows his brows and slightly grimaces, before closing his mouth and allowing his expression to harden, his eyes filling with hatred as the scene fades out. Without uttering a word, we fully understand the conflicting emotions Jesse is going through in just a few seconds of screen time through Power's subtly changing facial expressions.

Power uses a similar technique later to convey a contrasting set of emotions. After being shot in a botched bank robbery, Jesse stumbles home, where Zee discovers him unconscious on the bed. Dirty, unshaven and bleeding, he awakens dazed and confused to find her standing over him. Unable to move through sheer exhaustion, and breathing hard due to his injury, he closes his eyes again before Zee shouts, 'Jesse, hurry baby, hurry'. The camera then focuses in on Power's face as he looks at the ceiling and blinks in confusion. Pulling himself onto his elbows, he squints his eyes and looks forward, his mouth moving without any words coming out as he stares forward. The camera cuts to a small boy, who has clearly been asleep, rubbing his eyes and staring back. The camera returns to Power as he continues to stare, his mouth opening and closing as he exhales three times but unable to form any words; his eyes fill with tears until he is finally able to mutter 'I'll be doggone', as Jesse sees his son for the first time. He continues to stare with his mouth gaping, before blinking back the tears, closing his eyes and falling onto the pillow, Jesse's strength gone. As Zee and Jesse Jr rest their heads on his chest at either side, it is an extremely poignant image which shows a human and tender side to Jesse, the family man, but is juxtaposed with his appearance and gunshot wound depicting his other self: the outlaw and heartless killer, which he will never truly escape.

The film's concluding scene is particularly effective, and one that audiences may be anticipating if they are familiar with Jesse's story. Recovered and living as Thomas Howard, Jesse receives a visit from his old friend Bob Ford and his brother Charlie (Charles Tannen), who ask him to do one more job, which he refuses since he is taking his family to California to start a respectable new life. Despite his new name and cleaned-up appearance, Jesse's outlaw past is still a part of him since he continues to wear his guns, even in the family home. While he is packing for California, sitting with Zee on his lap and receiving the two men, his guns remain ever prominent in the frame. When Jesse opens the door to retrieve his son, who is playing outside, Charlie asks if he is 'gonna walk around outside with them guns'. Despite their bulk, Jesse has obviously been wearing them for so long at this point that he does not even notice them anymore, although others do. Jesse mutters, 'You're right', and removes them. Placing them on a small table positioned between the Fords and himself, he leaves the house, for once unarmed. His son has been playing with a group of friends who are pretending the boy is Jesse James (not knowing that he is in fact Jesse James Jr and that his father is Jesse). In an effective piece of foreshadowing, the boy's friends gather around him with sticks, pretending they are guns; when Jesse chastises them for being rough on 'such a little fella', one boy tells him that is how you play outlaw and that 'even Jesse James has gotta die'. Again, using a complex set of facial expressions, Power, who has been brushing down the boy's clothes, snaps his neck up to face the speaker before looking back at the small boy, his eyes wide. As he glances around the group nervously, the boys shout, 'Bang, bang' and 'You're Jesse James, you're dead', and the small boy lies down, closes his eyes and mutters, 'I'm dead', as Jesse looks on, silently and horrified. A close-up of Power follows, his brows furrowed and mouth open as he breathes heavily to demonstrate Jesse's panic, as the truth begins to sink in – that he will die violently because of his outlaw past. Looking around, his eyes come to rest on the boy on the ground; with hurt in his voice and without looking up he monotonously says, 'Go home, boys', before picking his son up and carrying him indoors. Giving his apologies, Jesse then walks the Fords to the door past the guns, which Charlie glances at while picking up his hat.

The play scene is played out for real almost immediately when Bob returns to shoot Jesse for the reward money and a pardon. The camera slowly pans back from Power, who is standing on a wicker chair removing Zee's 'God Bless our Home' tapestry from the wall with his back to Bob and us. Bob peeks back through the open door, his hand shaking as he aims his gun at the oblivious Jesse, before firing twice. The first shot goes through Jesse's back, near his heart, and Power spins around, clutching his chest and grimacing as his foot almost goes through the chair. The second shot hits him in the chest, which he grabs with both hands before falling off the chair and onto the floor, rolling between his stomach and his back, before finally coming to rest on his side. Zee runs downstairs and cradles his face, but he is already dead.

A brief glimpse of Jesse's funeral follows, with Cobb giving a speech about his being an outlaw, but 'we ain't ashamed of him . . . I don't think even America is ashamed of Jesse James', and that 'maybe it was because he was bold and lawless, like we all of us like to be sometimes . . . he wasn't altogether to blame for what his times made him'. The final fadeout reveals Jesse's headstone, which states that he was 'murdered by a traitor and coward whose name is not worthy to appear here'. Thus Jesse is presented as an outlaw but one that America is proud of. Viewers are asked to excuse at least some of Jesse's actions, since family circumstances led him to criminality, as with *Johnny Apollo*. Given that *Jesse James* was made so early in Power's career, and at the peak of his beauty and popularity, it is obvious that Twentieth Century-Fox wanted to add a more masculine, darker side to Power's screen persona, without completely alienating his established fanbase by having the character deviate too far from previous screen incarnations. It was a gamble that paid off, both for the studio and the development of Power's star persona.

As Murray Pomerance notes, although performances are 'of the body and from the body, expressed by way of the body', a recognisable face is central 'not only for our appreciations of feeling and identity but also for Hollywood's business machine' (2019: xvi). This is particularly pertinent to the star machine and recognisable star images, particularly leading performers like Power who were known for their looks. Thus, although Power uses his body more in *Jesse James* than in any previous film (riding, shooting, holding up a bank, moving across the top of a train), he is still recognisable as Power, a performer audiences had come to know, despite his portraying a historical figure in a genre he had never appeared in before. Thus even when donning a moustache, Western clothing or a bandana over his face, he is still identifiable as Power, and yet we simultaneously accept him as Jesse James. Moreover, despite Power being marketed as a star to be looked at, the most enduring image from the film, and the one featured most readily on contemporary promotional material such as posters, programmes and lobby cards as well as more recently on DVD and Blu-ray covers and the sole image on the front of Larry C. Bradley's book *Jesse James: The Making of a Legend* (1980), is Power with the bandana obscuring part of his face.

The film's sequel, *The Return of Frank James* (Fritz Lang, 1940), begins by replaying Jesse's death, followed by newspaper headlines reporting on it as would happen with a modern celebrity. Continuing from this point in the narrative, when Frank is informed that Jesse is dead, he immediately seeks revenge on Ford. Thus despite not appearing in the film, Jesse/Power remains ever-present due to the words and actions of the characters. After Ford is killed, the film ends on the close-up of a reward poster offering $10,000 for Jesse's capture or death, it is old, faded and torn but still readable. Just like Power, Jesse has left his mark. Undeniably, despite Power's beauty and star image being cemented through his appearance in historical dramas like *Lloyds of London* and *Marie Antoinette, Jesse James* remains one of the few films that Power is remembered for today.

The post-war Westerns

Power's second Western, *Rawhide*, was not made until twelve years after *Jesse James*, his Tom Owens being an extremely different character from his portrayal of the tough outlaw. A hired hand at a stagecoach stop, Tom is held captive along with passenger Vinnie (Susan Hayward) and her young niece Cally, by four bandits planning to rob the incoming stagecoach carrying a large shipment of gold. Mistaking Vinnie for Owens's wife and Cally their daughter, the bandits lock them up in Owens's bedroom and tensions mount as they all wait for the scheduled stagecoach to arrive.

Rawhide opens with a familiar Power, shirtless and shaving in front of a mirror, looking as handsome as ever. But a comic effect is soon added which hints at slight incompetence that Power would expand on later in *The Long Gray Line*. Learning the business, as he puts it, Tom is unable to properly blow the bugle that alerts incoming stagecoaches to proceed, perhaps hinting at his impotency. Later when he carries Vinnie's luggage into the house, the camera is placed inside the building, and as he approaches it soon becomes apparent to the viewer that he is not going to fit through the doorframe. Hitting the sides, Power stumbles backwards, dropping several bags in a physical comedy sketch reminiscent of Jerry Lewis or Charlie Chaplin. Much like Lewis's screen image, despite being the protagonist played by a major romantic star, Owens is depicted as being lower than those around him, the older men repeatedly calling him 'boy', which emasculates him and makes him appear younger than he is (Power was thirty-seven at the time). Almost dehumanising him, or making him appear simple, Vinnie refers to him as 'mule boy' and takes his gun, thus taking charge of the phallus and further rendering him metaphorically impotent (unlike in *The Sun Also Rises*, where Power's Jake Barnes is physically impotent).

Rawhide highlights Power's extremely expressive face, which he uses to great effect throughout. This is particularly vital since most of this psychological Western takes place in a constrained physical space. His gestural performance is predominantly revealed in scenes involving a kitchen knife that Tom acquires after asking to fill a pitcher with water. Walking to the open kitchen area, he takes a small metal cup in his right hand and starts filling the pitcher from a bucket of water. As he does so, his eyes dart around, glancing at the bandits and his surroundings before he does a double take when he notices the large bread knife unattended on a low table positioned near his right thigh. The men watch in silence as he fills the pitcher painfully slowly, Power using his eyes to silently demonstrate Owens's nervousness and his consideration of how he can obtain the knife undetected. Shifting the metal cup to his left hand, he extends his right hand back and feels for the knife while keeping the rest of his body stationary and forward facing. The camera's placement inside the kitchen area allows us the privileged position of observing Power's movements while also being able to see the men watching him. The low angle of the camera further makes it clear that the knife is just out of the bandits' eye view, given the position of the table behind a wooden counter. Reaching for the knife, Power moves his body just a fraction in order to block their view, placing the knife inside the pitcher just as ringleader Rafe Zimmerman (Hugh Marlowe) approaches and tells him to pour it in. Picking up the bucket, Power fills the pitcher, the knife's black handle showing slightly above the rim. Placing his thumb over it, he walks past the men and safely enters the bedroom. The whole scene lasts two-and-a-half minutes, with us (and Tom) repeatedly wondering if he will get away with it, and with Power expertly portraying Tom's fear and panic.

In an action resembling an attempted prison escape, Tom uses the knife in an effort to break through the building's outer brick wall. Power lies on his stomach under the bed, his gritted teeth, messy hair and sweat-beaded face suggesting the gruelling nature of the task, but Tom's desperation makes him persist. Vinnie also takes turns, and they eventually create a small hole. Later, as Tom works on expanding this hole, the knife becomes embedded in the brick. Straining to pull it out, a dull snap is followed by the knife pinging onto the path outside. At first he pauses, a stunned reaction on his face as he looks out at the knife; pulling himself towards the hole, he looks out with his mouth open. The camera is then placed outside with the knife, filming Power through the opening as it captures his horrified silent expression while he slightly jerks back and forth with wide eyes and an open mouth, resembling a rat caught in a hole. Grimacing, he reaches out, before a close-up shows his hand frantically grasping for the knife just outside his reach. Returning to the room, the camera shoots Power in close-up, his face half in darkness since his arm is blocking the light, as he continues to grab for the knife with his eyes screwed up and teeth clenched. No words are spoken throughout this harrowing scene, Power's gestures alone portraying Tom's anguish and frustration at the hopeless situation.

In Alfred Hitchcock's *The Birds* (1963), Tippi Hedren's Melanie Daniels wears the same outfit (a green suit) for the duration of the film, its 'progressively dishevelled look reading into her persona's fall into disorganization' (Pomerance 2016: 105). Here, Power's black shirt receives similar treatment, its shade reversing the Western stereotype since Tom, the hero, wears black for the film's duration. After shaving at the start, he puts on the clean shirt, which slowly becomes dustier and more soiled as the film progresses. He wears the sleeves up or down depending on the task he is undertaking, and as the hole he is digging expands, brick dust slowly builds up on his shirtfront. Attempting to fight with, but getting knocked out by, Zimmerman on the dusty ground outside, a bullet penetrates the now ragged shirt and enters his arm in the final shootout. The outward state of the shirt reflects not only Tom's inner turmoil, but his progression from young, pristine greenhorn to a more rugged, mature man.

While McVeigh discusses the links between gangster films and Westerns, Belafonte suggests that *Rawhide* closely resembles Twentieth Century-Fox's 1935 gangster film *Show Them No Mercy* (George Marshall), although it was never identified as a remake. Belafonte feels that *Rawhide* 'holds up surprisingly well' despite failing at the box office upon its initial release (1979: 168), perhaps due to Power's unusual characterisation. As Schatz suggests, in the post-war period Hollywood had a newfound maturity evident even in traditional genres like Westerns (1997: 4). *Rawhide* was an unusual film for the genre at this time since, although it features outlaws, Western apparel and a final shootout, it is by no means a traditional Western. Likewise, Tom is a very different character from Jesse James and the series of virile heroes and heels Power had portrayed thus far. He is not brave, is afraid of gunfire, is uncomfortable handling a gun and admits that he followed the bandits' demands because he was 'scared. Scared stiff.' Indeed, Tom Owens is an unassuming, ordinary man who is thrown into extraordinary circumstances outwith his control. Furthermore, although we may think that during the final shootout Tom will victoriously kill the remaining bandit, thus proving his masculinity, it is Vinnie armed with a shotgun, who does so while Tom walks towards him unarmed. There is little action in this tense psychological Western, with facial expressions and understated gestures marking the true strength of Power's performance. Furthermore, there is unusually no real romance for his character, and although an obvious chemistry is formed between Tom and Vinnie, their only kiss is demanded by Zimmerman and not through their own choice. They oblige, perhaps to keep up the pretence that they are married, however they do play the scene more tenderly than if their characters were completely acting, and it appears to be a genuine kiss that hints at feelings they have developed for each other. Moreover, after all the bandits are dead, thus there is no longer a need for them to act, he places his arm tenderly around her shoulders as they walk, while they stand and sit in close proximity like a real couple would. Therefore, we are led to believe that Tom, Vinnie and Cally will become a family; Tom taking on the conventional role of the patriarchal figure in a nuclear family, even if it is a readymade one.

Pony Soldier, also known as *MacDonald of the Canadian Mounties*, was released the following year. Beginning with a voiceover delivered by Power, he speaks to a modern audience but does so as the historical protagonist. He informs us that we will learn about the Royal Canadian Mounted Police of 1876, when the service was in its infancy and attempting to enforce the law in scattered areas across Canada. His words are accompanied by a montage of images before we see him momentarily riding a horse while introducing himself as 'Constable Duncan MacDonald, at your service'. Visually, Power stands out against the muted natural landscape, the Technicolor film exhibiting his bright red coat and white gloves to their best advantage and plainly making him the focal point.

When Duncan enters the narrative and speaks for the first time he is reporting to his superior. The combination of a helmet that comes down to Power's eyes, a heavy five o'clock shadow on his chin, a high-collared coat, dark surroundings and a low camera angle results in much of Power's face being disguised in this introductory scene, thus he is identifiable mostly through his familiar voice. Sitting down, he removes the hat and gloves, revealing a mop of shiny black hair and a more familiar image. He is consistently paired with a short, stout comical figure, the Native American guide Natayo Smith (Thomas Gomez), whose heaviness emphasises Power's slender, toned physique in his fitted Mountie outfit, and his overt attractiveness. The only time Power is seen without the red coat occurs when he emerges from his tent in a tight white short-sleeved t-shirt, his expansive chest and arms shown to their best potential through clothing and camera angle and hinting back to his presentation in earlier films *Nightmare Alley* and *Son of Fury*, thus demonstrating that he is still as muscular and highly desirable in the 1950s.

Unlike Tom, MacDonald is a skilled fighter who signifies his masculinity by engaging in a physical fight and shootout, in both of which he is victorious. He also overpowers a man who attacks him with a knife, further proving his strength and virility. As with his shirt in *Rawhide*, Power's pristine red coat becomes more ragged and dirtier as this scene progresses, his slicked back hair becoming messy and stuck to his forehead in the process. Like Tom, Duncan has no wife or children, but adopts a native boy whom he also names Duncan, a traditional family name that was also his father's. Highlighting its Gaelic connections, the name not only creates a link to Power's important off-screen heritage, but again connects him to Britain, this time specifically Scotland. Also like Tom, Duncan has no love interest, but the ending hints that he may end up with Penny Edwards's Emerald Neeley, although the characters have very little interaction, and what conversations they do have are formal and brief. While the pair are never alone and make no attempts to become romantic, the film ends with Edwards standing just behind Power, the small boy by his side, suggesting that they too may become a family unit after the narrative ends. Similar to *Diplomatic Courier*, many of the film's official posters present a very different version of the story with an illustration of Power wearing the red coat and holding a gun, poised for action, while a scantily clad Edwards grips his shoulder and looks lovingly into his face.

Given its lack of plot and character development and no advancement for Power's screen image, *Pony Soldier* was not only Power's poorest Western, but one of his weakest films overall. The role did not challenge him in any way, if anything it was a step back. The film's lack of quality was commented on by Romina Power, although it was clearly so forgettable that she incorrectly calls it *Pony Express*. Calling it 'probably the worst treatment that Fox had handed out to its leading actor', Romina notes that the director was Joseph M. Newman, 'who only worked in "B" movies' (2014: 190). Romina feels that Power's being handed this lesser role meant that Twentieth Century-Fox no longer viewed him as one of its top stars. Likewise, co-star Edwards was somewhat of an unknown actress, Power being the only star name carrying this routine film.

Pulleine calls Power's post-war Westerns 'not among his most rewarding' (1993: 377). This is particularly true of *Pony Soldier*, which Belafonte refers to as 'a "B" movie given "A" trappings', claiming that it 'demonstrated the Fox front office's waning interest in its foremost star' (1979: 177). *Pony Soldier* was, in fact, the last film Power made under contract to Twentieth Century-Fox, a sad reflection of how the studio now viewed its top leading man almost twenty years after first signing him. Power's next film, *The Mississippi Gambler* (1953) was also a Western, and an important film in his career trajectory since it was his first venture as an independent agent.

An independent Westerner

Power is not only the sole player billed above the title of the Technicolor spectacle *The Mississippi Gambler* (1953), but his title card reads 'Universal-International Presents Tyrone Power', highlighting his importance to the production and Universal's pride at being able to use the star for the first time after he left his home studio. As with *Blood and Sand*, his female co-stars, Piper Laurie and Julia Adams,[1] receive joint credit after the film's title.

Although Power enters the film immediately, it is with his back to the camera, which follows him as he walks through a boat dock, his riverboat gambler Mark Fallon having just arrived in a small town. Reminiscent of the opening of *Nightmare Alley*, as he walks past three women they turn to look him up and down approvingly, their eyes remaining fixed on him as they walk out of frame. While he remains oblivious to their glances, this interaction asks the audience to remember how extremely desirable and attractive to women Power still is and indicates that his face shall be revealed to us shortly as well. This exchange also highlights Power's masculine frame with his dark suit and hat contrasting with their lightly coloured, extremely feminine frilled dresses, bonnets and parasols. As he slowly turns towards Kansas John Polly (John McIntire), Power is also turning towards the camera and thus towards us. Polly's comment that Fallon is 'a decent looking young fella', in relation to his getting mixed up in the crooked life of gambling, could also act as an in-joke concerning Power's appearance.

Almost immediately saving the life of the ungrateful Angelique Dureau (Laurie) after her horses are spooked by a train whistle and bolt, Fallon tells her, 'Sometimes horses and . . . beautiful women are upset by whistles', pausing before the words 'beautiful women' and openly directing the statement at her. When she glibly questions, 'And you're an expert on both?', he stares at her and replies, 'I'm interested in both', while leaning into her carriage. Although Angelique pretends indifference towards Mark for much of the film, he has obviously aroused feelings that are new to her; her curt attitude and attempts to avoid him signal that her desire scares her. When Polly remarks that Mark does not know women, Mark bets him that Angelique will look back as she ascends the stairs of the riverboat; she does, and the surprised Polly admits that maybe Mark does know women after all. Not only does he know women, but, like many of Power's characters, two women are in love with him: Angelique (although she will not admit it) and Ann Conant (Adams) whose unrequited love leads to her turning down a marriage proposal from Angelique's brother Laurent (John Baer). Baer's blond, insipid appearance and slight frame contrast strongly with Power's dark good looks and large physique, but unlike Laurent, Mark is also kind and considerate, so we can easily understand why Ann would fall for him. When Mark discovers how Ann feels about him, he tactfully discourages her until she realises it is hopeless; but she continues to look at him longingly, even though he does not return her gaze, and we understand and sympathise with her situation. While Mark is fond of Ann, he is in love with Angelique, and the last time we see Ann he hugs her and kisses her once on the lips before walking off. Adams turns towards the camera, wide mouthed and breathing heavily before beginning to cry, showing that Mark makes an impactful and lasting impression on the women around him and, given that he is portrayed by Power, this is fully believable.

A particularly sexually charged scene occurs between Mark and Angelique, despite their being at opposite sides of the screen and neither speaking nor touching. Instead, their magnetism for each other is projected through glances. Watching native dancers, the frigid and restrained Angelique is mesmerised by the unbridled sexuality of the female dancer with bare feet and shoulders, her body freely moving to the music and her hips and breast shaking as she dances suggestively with several men. Angelique's mouth is slightly open and she breathes rapidly while watching this display, which obviously excites her, as she searches the room for Mark. Looking away as if disinterested, she regularly steals looks back at him while he stares and smiles at her, fully aware of how she feels about him. When a woman moves forward and grabs his arm, Angelique turns to suitor George Elwood (Ron Randell), whom she does not love but eventually marries, (falsely) flirting with Elwood in an attempt to make Mark jealous. When her father (Paul Cavanagh) enquires about her interest in Mark, she becomes flustered and asks why he would ask that, to which he replies that Mark's name 'seems to arouse more emotion than most', as she fusses with her hair as a way of avoidance.

Their romance comes to a head when Laurent challenges Mark to a duel over Ann, and Angelique visits Mark's room the night before the scheduled duel on the pretence of discussing her brother. As he takes a step towards her she turns away, but as romantic non-diegetic music plays he grabs her arm and forcefully turns her back around to face him. He kisses her but after a few seconds she breaks away, and then turns back around with wide eyes but breathing heavily. Holding her by the arms, his face close to hers, he gives a speech that horrifies her since it reveals her innermost thoughts and fears. Releasing herself from his grasp, she replies, 'I hope he kills you', before walking out.

In the duel that follows, Laurent turns around and fires at Mark too early, attempting to shoot him in the back but missing, thus giving Mark the right to fire in his own time. With knitted brows, Power shifts his stance, grimaces, squints his eyes and slowly aims the gun. With Laurent in his sights, his face loses its intenseness, his eyes widen slightly and he withdraws the gun. Looking at the gun and Laurent with the same disgust, Mark throws the pistol down and walks away, sparing Laurent's life while proving his masculinity.

As with previous Power characters, Mark engages in fist fights and overpowers a man with a knife. As an honest riverboat gambler, he is an unusual figure and, like Tom Owens, has a good heart; unlike Tom though, Mark is extremely tough and virile, having a manly aura about him without the need to try too hard or prove himself. As in *The Mark of Zorro*, Power's physical prowess and swordsmanship are displayed when he engages in several (victorious) fencing matches. However, after one match Power engages in a conversation with his bare torso on display, noticeably contrasting with the fully clothed and much older Cavanagh. Furthermore, as in *Blood and Sand*, he is fitted for a suit while several men surround him and observe his body as he dresses; the placement of the camera inviting us to join in with the erotic spectacle of Power's form. Moreover, this is the only Western in which he dances, a ballroom scene presenting the opportunity for him to wear (historical) evening clothes, while exhibiting his allure since several women gather around him and beg him to dance with them. Wearing white gloves, white tie and a coat with tails, Power's hair is slightly longer in this film and is curled to fit with the time period; he cuts a dashingly handsome masculine figure indeed.

At the film's close, Angelique finally realises she must act on her feelings for Mark before he leaves. Standing on the deck of the riverboat as it prepares to sail, Mark absentmindedly stares into the crowd when a sudden movement captures his attention. A close-up of Power with a cigar (an overtly masculine symbol) in his mouth shows a furrowed brow as he blinks several times and looks perplexed (Figure 4.2). Removing the cigar from his mouth, he leans forward as though Mark is trying to get a better view, before a long shot shows Laurie running towards the boat. A cut back to Power shows that Mark realises Angelique has finally come to him and a shocked but delighted look comes across his face, his

Figure 4.2   Power as tough riverboat gambler Mark Fallon at the end of *The Mississippi Gambler* (1953)

eyebrows go up and a brief, excited smile plays around the corners of his lips before he turns, buttons his jacket and rushes down the stairs to meet her. Reaching the lower deck, he puts out his arms and she runs towards him for an embrace. Although she begins to talk, he interrupts her with a kiss and this time she kisses him back passionately. The final shot from over Laurie's shoulder shows Power tenderly stroking her hair, his eyes gleaming as he smiles upwards with a look of contentment on his face.

This final scene of Power's last Western sums up his work in the genre and his career development over time by proving that his characters could be depicted as more mature, virile and manly while remaining irresistible to women. However, while his Westerns allowed him to develop his performance skills in a more male-driven genre, he continued to be presented as a desirable and attractive figure for audiences and, at times, female characters. Unusually perhaps, given his dominant screen image as a ladies' man, except for *The Mississippi Gambler*, Power's romantic scenes in Westerns were either incidental (*Jesse James*) or non-existent (*Rawhide*, *Pony Soldier*). The next chapter explores another genre in which Power only made four films, but which also allowed him to show a tougher, more masculine side. It is also the genre that created the most noticeable connection between his on- and off-screen personas: the war film.

Notes

1. The actress Julia Adams was often billed as Julie Adams, and Julie is the name used on her official Facebook page and autobiography *The Lucky Southern Star: Reflections from the Black Lagoon* (2011).

Chapter 5

The war hero

Overview

As Robert Eberwein suggests, war films can be particularly effective vehicles for remarking on the period in which they were made as well as the period they depict (2005: 4). Power starred in four war films between 1941 and 1950, and they can be categorised under the three historical timeframes of World War II for America: pre-war (*A Yank in the RAF*), wartime (*This Above All* [Anatole Litvak, 1942] and *Crash Dive*) and post-war (*American Guerrilla in the Philippines*), yet all are directly concerned with World War II.

Schatz sees the war as cinema's defining event of the 1940s, calling Hollywood's production between 1942 and 1945 the industry's finest hour 'as a social institution and a cultural force' (1997: 1). Robert Fyne notes that the volume of propaganda films released by Hollywood during World War II is incomparable to any other period of cinematic history. As a result, the industry heightened the nation's morale 'by capitalizing on America's love affair with the movies' (1994: 13). The American public also had a love affair with Power and his established screen persona at this time; thus even his war-themed films included elements that had made him a recognisable star image, only now these were positioned within a wartime setting. His familiar witty dialogue, wide grins and charm with the ladies from earlier comedies and musicals are still overtly displayed in *A Yank in the RAF* and *Crash Dive*, despite much of the latter taking place onboard a submarine with a crew made up exclusively of men. Although Power's closest contemporary Robert Taylor had also built a strong on-screen persona as a ladies' man throughout the 1930s, in his war films *Flight Command* (Frank Borzage, 1940), *Stand by for Action* (Robert Z. Leonard, 1942) and *Bataan* (Tay Garnett, 1943) he has a distinct lack of love interest. This is particularly apparent in the latter, an overtly homosocial and brutal combat film following the wartime struggles of a battalion of men stationed on the Bataan Peninsula. Power, on the other hand, has a love interest in all his war films and his characters meet and romance women in a variety of ways.

In *A Yank in the RAF* Power's Tim Barker is reunited with former girlfriend Carol Brown (Betty Grable) while stationed in London; in *This Above All*, his deserter Clive Briggs falls for aristocratic WAAF Prudence Cathaway (Joan Fontaine) after they meet on a blind date in the dark. In *Crash Dive* his Lieutenant Ward Stewart attempts to pick up schoolteacher Jean Hewlett (Anne Baxter) on a train, unaware that she is engaged to his superior officer (Dana Andrews), and in *American Guerrilla in the Philippines* his Ensign Chuck Palmer meets Jeanne Martinez (Micheline Presle) and her husband Juan (Juan Torena) while stranded in the Philippines. Given her marital status, Chuck hides his desire for her, but the two begin a romance after Juan is killed. However, although each of his characters has a love interest, it is only the courtships with Carol and Jean that hint at Power's pre-war screen image as a confident charmer with a wide grin who finds himself irresistible to women. Clive's relationship with Prudence develops out of a sense of need and the deep love that grows between them as they become more serious; with Chuck, duty and honour come first and his romance with Jeanne only begins after she instigates it. Similarly, examining these films in chronological order illustrates the development of a newfound masculinity and maturity in Power's screen image, which advances greatly from Tim's cocky self-assuredness and incessant womanising (even when engaged to Carol) to Chuck's more stable and understanding relationship with Jeanne. To Susan Jeffords, the term masculinity describes 'images, values, interests, and activities' important for successfully achieving male adulthood in American cultures (Jeffords 1989: xii; Eberwein 2005: 10). Thus the advancement of masculinity in Power's star image throughout his work in war films helped him create a tougher, more mature persona than even his Westerns did, while also allowing him to retain the elements of his recognisable star image that had made and kept him a top leading man.

The pre-war and war years not only had a profound effect on how the Hollywood film industry operated, and on Power's screen image more specifically, but also directly impacted the actor's off-screen life. Schatz notes that by late 1942 the war claimed around four thousand (22 per cent of) studio employees to the armed forces, this included 1,500 actors, most notably popular leading men Robert Taylor, Clark Gable, James Stewart, Robert Montgomery and Power (1997: 2). While these stars were at war and therefore off cinema screens, new talent was brought in to replace them. Schatz lists these new male leads as including Alan Ladd, Van Johnson, Roy Rogers, Gregory Peck, and Ray Milland (1997: 106) (in fact Milland, a contract player at Paramount, had already made sixty films by 1943).

A Yank in Britain

Power's first war film, *A Yank in the RAF*, was released in 1941, the year Colin Shindler refers to as 'the start of the financial boom years that took Hollywood to its remarkable peak of 1946' (1979: 28). Writing about Hollywood's World War II propaganda of this same year, Fyne notes how *Dive Bomber* (Michael Curtiz), starring Errol Flynn and Fred MacMurray, and *I Wanted Wings* (Mitchell Leisen), with Milland and William Holden, 'stressed military preparedness by glamorizing the elaborate training for both flight surgeon and aviators', while also reiterating the enduring theme that successfully completing a mission requires a group effort (1994: 23). These themes were not dissimilar to those displayed in *Flight Command* the previous year. Indeed, *A Yank in the RAF* could be seen as a hybridisation of the aforementioned films, with Power's Tim a fusion of Taylor's cocky all-American flier Alan Drake of *Flight Command* and his brash American student Lee Sheridan from *A Yank at Oxford* (1938), the ultimate pre-war embodiment of the 'yank' in Britain and a blueprint for future 'yank' films, *A Yank in the RAF* placing him within a wartime sensibility.

To put the film into its historical context, having declared war on Germany on 3 September 1939, Britain (and France) had been at war for a little over two years when *A Yank in the RAF* was released. The film made its US debut on 26 September 1941, slightly more than a month before the Japanese bombing of Pearl Harbor, which resulted in America joining the war (Dixon 2006: xi). Directly after the attack, President Roosevelt called cinema the most effective medium in keeping the nation informed, emphasising the vital role Hollywood could play in wartime. Calling for the regular production of films that would keep the public abreast of events, Roosevelt promised the studios that there would be no governmental censorship (Fyne 1994: 9). As Mark Glancy notes, unlike the earlier *Foreign Correspondent* (Alfred Hitchcock, 1940) which starred Joel McCrea as the 'yank', Tim's transformation is achieved without 'a final reel speech', and the film avoids any direct references to Nazi Germany. Glancy feels the film's propaganda value lay in part with its depiction of the 'collective British war effort', but mostly because stars

Power and Grable were part of the production (1999: 120). Indeed, their only on-screen pairing helped the film earn around $2.5 million in the US alone, making it the fourth most popular production of 1941. Similarly, the British publication *Kinematograph Weekly* named it the second most popular film in February 1942 (Glancy 1999: 122).

Glancy proposes that the fact that American studios produced 150 'British' films between 1930 and 1945 proves that this was a time when 'Hollywood loved Britain' (1999: 1). Essentially American films, and not to be confused with actual British films, they 'celebrated the most famous aspects of Britain's culture and history'. Among his examples are Power's star-making film *Lloyds of London*, along with *A Yank in the RAF* and *This Above All*. Made between 1939 and 1945, the last two also fall under Glancy's heading of 'British' films that portrayed 'the British war effort in the most heroic terms' (1999: 1). According to Glancy, these films are 'compellingly significant', since 'no other foreign country was portrayed by Hollywood so often and with such admiration' as Britain (1999: 1). Made by American companies, the films either came from British source material or were set in Britain. *A Yank in the RAF* is set in Britain and centres around the British war effort, even though principal players Power and Grable and the writers of the original screenplay were American. Zanuck created the outline of the story, initially titled *Eagle Squadron*, in October 1940; this original title suggesting the more collaborative and comradery nature of wartime films, whereas the film's final title concentrates on Tim Baker as an individual. Glancy notes that Zanuck based his story on America's first war hero, Billy Fiske, who was an RAF volunteer killed in August 1940 after shooting down three German planes over England; in Zanuck's version Power's character died at the end (1999: 117). However, for the final film, a wartime reimagining of *A Yank at Oxford*, Zanuck wanted a 'cock-sure know-it-all' who 'never knew how to take orders . . . [and] doesn't know how to play team ball' (1999: 117–18). Like Taylor's Lee Sheridan in the earlier film, Tim learns that 'fighting is more than personal gain, they are fighting for freedom, for a cause they believe in and he becomes part of the *esprit de corps*, willing to die for it' (Glancy 1999: 118). As Glancy notes, the film worked as propaganda, with the US audience expecting to go through the same transition as the character (1999: 118).

Schatz suggests that 'perhaps the most significant and complex development in pre-war Hollywood was the on-screen treatment of the war' (1997: 116). Between 1940 and 1941, war featured in romantic comedy, slapstick, melodramas and suspense thrillers, but 'noticeably lacking ... were the combat films and home-front melodramas that would typify Hollywood's war-film production during and after the war' (1997: 116). Although *A Yank in the RAF* is classed primarily as a war film, it contains strong elements of comedy and drama, as well as musical numbers performed by Grable, whose Carol is a WAAF by day and a nightclub entertainer at night. Schatz adds that at this time, 'Hollywood's treatment of the war had been remarkably tentative', but changed with the bombing of Pearl Harbor (1997: 2). Both this film and *This Above All* are set in England; in the former, Power plays an American who enlists in Britain's Royal Air Force, and in the latter a British deserter with psychological issues. Although *A Yank in the RAF* features some aerial combat near the end, *This Above All* is devoid of any combat scenes and Power's co-star Fontaine wears military uniform while Power is dressed in a tweed suit and flat cap for most of the film.

In *A Yank in the RAF*, Power is first seen emerging from the cockpit of a small plane, wearing aviator sunglasses, a leather jacket and sporting windswept hair he resembles the handsome cocky young American of the era. Grinning widely, he offers some wisecracks to the stuffy military personnel greeting him while arrogantly chewing gum (a habit he continues throughout the film, although the reduction of his chewing and cockiness are simultaneous). Taking a job as a flier for the RAF in order to earn $1,000 a mission, Tim arrives in London and immediately chases after a beautiful woman leaving a hotel. Left despondent when her husband picks her up, he soon notices a group of women undertaking an air raid drill, one of whom he realises is his old girlfriend, Carol. This scene sets Tim up as a ladies' man and, as his subsequent conversation with Carol shows, he is well known for his philandering. In fact, Carol repeatedly calls him a worm despite being in love with him, and he even calls himself one in the film's last line after flirting with a nurse despite now being engaged to Carol. Thus although Tim goes through professional and personal changes, he has still not given up his womanising ways. Like Lee in *A Yank at Oxford*, Tim becomes integrated into the group but, given the wartime sentiment, there is less Anglo-American conflict than in the earlier film. Tim does not mock the British customs as much as Lee, and he even adopts elements of the language, such as using the term 'bloody'. Along with the closer proximity of war in the US, Power's off-screen connection to Britain may also have been a factor in how the actors played their respective 'yanks'.

After ten minutes, Power adopts the military uniform he will be seen in for the majority of the film as Tim is pitted against two Brits in the same outfit: the comical Roger Pillby (Reginald Gardiner) and Wing Commander Morley (John Sutton), as all three vie for Carol's affections. Power is clean-shaven, while both Brits wear moustaches, and are significantly older than Power (Gardiner was born in 1903 and Sutton in 1908). They also have average looks, strongly contrasting with the tall, dark, broad-shouldered and exceedingly handsome Power. There are even times when it is hard to distinguish between the two British men, which is never an issue when Power is on the screen, even when he dresses identically to the other men in the group. Likewise, the characters' personalities are very different since the Brits are presented as stereotypically more serious and stuffier, while Tim is chatty and breezy.

During the nineteenth century, new concepts of masculinity and male beauty emerged that still influence today's thought. At this time, masculinity's new status was most obviously expressed through uniforms, 'which shaped the male body and mind' (Hackspiel-Mikosch 2009: 117). As Elisabeth Hackspiel-Mikosch notes, uniforms are frequently depicted as masculinity at its highest potency and enquires as to what makes uniforms so sexually appealing (2009: 117). She suggests that it might be because the uniformed body is 'closely connected with power, politics, and the military', and that it is this 'eroticism of power' that is most appealing (2009: 125–6). This could have a dualistic meaning here when considering power (the military ranking) and Power (the actor), both of which are highly desirable. David H. J. Morgan proposes that of all the sites where masculinities are constructed, reproduced and deployed, those relating to war and the military are among the most direct since the warrior remains the key symbol of masculinity; suggesting that uniforms absorb individuals 'into a generalized and timeless masculinity' (2006: 444). However, although Power is dressed identically to other men around him, his physique and striking looks enable him to stand out and remain an individual, even within a group situation. Yet this association with war added a new layer to Power's masculinity since his body remained an object of erotic spectacle as well as becoming a site of control and discipline. As Morgan explains, one of the major ways in which direct links between hegemonic masculinities and men's bodies are forged is through war and the military, 'insofar as masculinity continues to be identified with physicality . . . there are strong reasons for continuing to view military life as an important site in the shaping and making of masculinities' (2006: 446). Similarly, J. C. Flugel feels that the military uniform stands out from any other type of uniform because of its unique social and historical importance, along with the way it reveals 'an extreme development of the hierarchal features of dress', not only in terms of nationality, but its clear indication of ranking, each successive rank signified by an increase in decorativeness of the corresponding costume' (1971: 131).

Near the end of the film, a standout moment occurs, which contains no dialogue and little movement by either Power or the camera. Having undertaken a physically taxing and dangerous mission, the men are seen in long shot heading for a small boat as the enemy shoot at them. There is then a dissolve to an extreme close-up of Power's face as Tim lies sleeping, the diegetic sound of the previous scene still audible, as though we are hearing the noises inside Tim's head. Power moves restlessly until he is facing the camera, which shoots him from above. Lingering on his face, the audience is able to view Power's long dark eyelashes, thick brows and unshaven chin, the latter adding a layer of rugged masculinity to his otherwise beautiful face, before his eyes spring open in fear and the diegetic noise immediately ceases as he stares at the ceiling. Continuing to stare, Power squints without moving any other part of his face or body, before moving his eyes from side to side to take in the surroundings. With a confused look on his face, he lowers his brows slightly and looks down to suggest Tim's inward panic, before directing his eyes back to the ceiling, screwing them up once more before lifting his head from the pillow. A cut to a long shot shows that he is in a hospital ward with nurses rushing around, which acts in extreme contrast to the intimate close-up of Power's face. The scene is similar to, but even more intense than, the ending of *Lloyds of London* since, although Power's face still fills the whole screen from forehead to chin (and for historical audiences watching it on a theatre screen it would have been a large and imposing image indeed), unlike in the earlier film he is lying down and we also get to see the tip of his jet-black hair contrasting with the pristine white pillowcase (Figure 5.1). Furthermore, by this point he was a leading man with a very recognisable star image.

This extreme close-up lasts thirty seconds, an extraordinarily long stretch of screen time since the camera is so close to the actor's face and the sequence has no dialogue or non-diegetic sounds and very little diegetic sound, only a soft rumbling in the background that makes it hard for Tim to determine where he is. He is shortly back to his old ways, however, when he attempts to flirt with the nurse attending him, looking her up

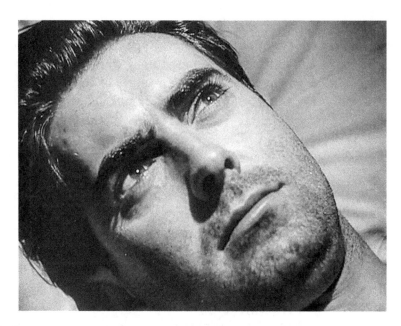

Figure 5.1 An extreme close-up as Tim (Power) wakes up in hospital in *A Yank in the RAF* (1941)

and down and telling her she is cute, and thus reinforcing his masculinity and making him the active possessor of the gaze, no longer the passive recipient he was for audiences. Furthermore, since this scene follows those of intense masculine strength and courage in perilous wartime situations, the longevity of his passivity and the focus on Power's face can be excused, and reduce the feminisation that may have occurred had he not been previously involved in aerial and ground combat. Except for his earliest roles, Power's beauty was always implicated with his masculinity, evident here since Tim is temporarily passive because he has been injured in combat. Without question Power possessed extreme male beauty, but he was able to appeal to heterosexual men as well as (heterosexual) women, particularly in his war films, his beauty not holding him back from being active on screen as well as an object of the erotic gaze.

The wartime war films

Power's next two war films, *This Above All* and *Crash Dive*, were made while America was at war, therefore were even more reflective of the time than *A Yank in the RAF*. The former made its US debut on 12 May 1942, around six months after the US joined the war, and the latter almost a year later on 28 April 1943, just prior to Power going off to war for the duration. *This Above All* presents a much grimmer picture of Britain in wartime; gone is the cocksure flier, replaced by the mentally tortured army deserter Clive Briggs, who rarely smiles and lacks confidence in both himself and his country. An adaptation of Eric Knight's best-selling 1941 novel of the same name, Roger Manvell suggests that 'efforts to sift truth and actuality from fiction' during the war emerged with this film (1974: 116). Knight, originally from Yorkshire, England, grew up in poverty before emigrating to the US at the age of fifteen; as the novel and film show, he retained a longing for Britain. An advocate of Anglo-American understanding, Knight joined the US Army but was killed at the age of forty-five in January 1943, two years after the publication of his novel and just over a year after the film's release (Manvell 1974: 119).

'British' films in the early war years became more self-conscious in their depiction of class relations (Glancy 1999: 131). Released at the same time as *Mrs Miniver* (William Wyler) in the summer of 1942, Glancy suggests that although these films came from very different source material and were produced by rival studios (Twentieth Century-Fox and MGM respectively), they nonetheless share some 'striking similarities' (1999: 131). The most obvious is their fore-grounding of class issues in a way that was unusual for 'British' films at the time. Both address America's 'disdain for the "old school tie" England with assurances that a new and more egalitarian England is emerging from the rubble of the Blitz' (1999: 131). However, Glancy adds, even the films portraying 'the new England' do not 'stray very far from the characters and settings of the old England' (1999: 131). Power is once more linked to Britain, his American identity and British legacy creating a bridge between countries and making him an obvious choice for the lead. As Manvell notes, the film emphasises the distinctions of class in Britain, 'and the need for the "working class" to win a higher place in the society which they form by far the greatest part'; but Manvell feels that the film oversimplifies the arguments, with Clive's 'return to duty . . . too facile' (1974: 119). However, Clive gives himself up because he is tired of hiding out like a criminal and more so because of his love for Prue and her belief in Britain. Moreover, he is not actually seen returning to duty, just briefly giving a statement before ending up in the hospital for the remainder of the film.

Manvell quotes a friend of Knight's professing that *This Above All* did more to cement the US's Anglo-American understanding 'than any piece of conscious propaganda', because it showed the American people that Britain was able to 'examine her own faults and virtues with equal objectivity' (1974: 119). This is embodied through the characterisations of Clive (faults) and Prue (virtues). Clayton R. Koppes and Gregory D. Black call it the film that dealt most directly with the theme of Britain as a class-ridden society, with Power's 'young, embittered, lower-class Englishman' contrasting with Fontaine's upper-class WAAF (1988: 233). They quote Philip Hartung of *The Commonweal* who, writing at the time of the film's release, declared it 'the most interesting movie that Hollywood had made about this war' (1988: 233). Clive is a soldier of the British army who fought in France and was a hero at Dunkirk. Upon returning to England he becomes a deserter because he feels the British army is 'inefficient, unprepared, and run by upper-class snobs', and since the country will not treat him as an equal, he sees no reason why he should fight for it (Koppes and Black 1988: 233). Koppes and Black suggest, however, that by the film's conclusion 'one assumes that the war will not only defeat fascism but bring down the class structure' (1988: 233).

Shindler calls the casting of Power 'powerful and daring' but also Zanuck's first step in 'cleansing' the property (1979: 48), while Fyne dismisses Power as 'Adonis-like' and 'too wholesome to portray this down-and-out limey' (1994: 213). Although there is much more to Clive than being 'down-and-out', Fyne dismisses Power's performance merely as a result of his appearance, suggesting that his good looks mean he cannot give a convincing performance. Coming thirty-six years after Power's death and fifty-two years after the film's release, Fyne's words are the kind of counterproductive assumption that journalists were making during Power's career that undermined his skills as a performer. Moreover, Fyne does not explicitly state why he sees Power as 'too wholesome', thus overlooking his previous roles as outlaw killer (*Jesse James*), historical heel (*In Old Chicago, Rose of Washington Square*) and modern-day scoundrel (*Ladies in Love, Love is News, Café Metropole, Day-Time Wife, Johnny Apollo, Blood and Sand, A Yank in the RAF*). Several of his characters had cheated on their wives or girlfriends, got into physical fights, lied and schemed for self-gain, stolen, were imprisoned and had committed murder. Therefore Power's screen image up to this point could hardly be deemed 'wholesome', even if his looks may be read as such. Although mentioned by neither Shindler nor Fyne, perhaps the least convincing component of Power's portrayal is his playing an Englishman, whose speeches about Britain are delivered in his American accent (albeit in Power's familiar intonation). This is most apparent when Fontaine's obnoxiously upper-class vocals recount Prue's extensive monologue about what Britain means to her, which is directed at fellow Brit Clive.

Belafonte calls the film a 'beautifully-realized version' of Knight's novel, which gave Power 'a then-rare chance to do some serious acting and he managed to match ... Fontaine's magnificent performance'. Belafonte adds that 'unfortunately, Power discovered that his fans preferred to see him in costume, sword-in-hand' (1979: 22), but he had only made one 'sword-in-hand' film by this point: *The Mark of Zorro*, and swords had featured to a limited degree in *Blood and Sand*. However, the film did extremely well at the box office, taking $2.4 million during its initial release, which is not an unsubstantial amount.

Unusually, both Prue and the audience are introduced to Clive during a blackout, and are therefore unable to see his face. Although the outline of a peaked cap is the only thing visible, the voice is undeniably Power's, only here it is low and sombre, a very different tone from that used by the happy-go-lucky Tim. Power is on-screen in complete or almost complete darkness for a full three minutes before he lights a cigarette, the flame from the match momentarily illuminating his face for the audience, but not for Prue, before it goes out (Figure 5.2).

Figure 5.2   Power's face is briefly revealed to the audience in *This Above All* (1942)

After meeting in the dark, Prue and Clive arrange a date for the next day so they can see what each other looks like and, as they shelter from the rain in a haystack, Prue tells him she knew exactly what he looked like. When Clive enquires, 'What do I look like?', she sits up to face him as he lies back on the hay, propped up on one elbow. Laughing, she reflects his body language by leaning back on her elbow and replying, 'Oh, you're rather good looking really', before analysing Clive's face in precise detail, thus also analysing Power's face. Cocking her head to one side she continues, 'A nice sort of face. Nose a little on the fine side, mouth a little too big. One of your ears sticks out a little more than the other. Did you know your face is slightly lopsided?' After he interrupts her with a smile, a pointed finger and a 'Now wait just a minute', she laughs and adds, 'But your eyes are good. Nice deep brown. A little tired looking, late hours perhaps.' Although Clive seems amused by Prue's assessment of his features, the words appear to have been written for Power since his nose is very fine for a man's, especially in profile, and his deep brown eyes were a major part of both his visual appeal and expressionistic acting. When she lies down on the haystack, he suddenly kisses her and although she looks startled at first, a look of delight soon comes over her face and she asks him to kiss her again, his virility again proven as another woman begs him to kiss her.

Along with their speech, clothing helps to highlight the contrast between the characters. In a reversal of traditional roles, she is in uniform while he is not. While travelling by train, Clive asks Prue to change her clothes so they can forget the war for a few days since her uniform acts as a constant reminder. As she dresses, he looks out of the window and discusses the idle rich, which she takes with good humour. When he indignantly asks why she would want five gardeners, Prue laughs and replies, 'We didn't want them, our garden did'. When he turns around, she is dressed in an elegant black dress, silk stockings, high heels and a string of pearls, her hair in a decorative low bun. Clipping a large belt around her waist she asks, 'Well?' twice, but he remains silent. This time it is his turn to analyse her, although not to the same degree. Power stares at Fontaine in an unsettled manner, his eyes wide as if Clive is seeing Prue for the first time. In a monotone voice, he says, 'You're very pretty. Taller. Slimmer. Cooler. And a stranger.' His face hardens and he adds, 'I met a WAAF in the dark, and I haven't a gardener to my name'. Although he never wears a uniform in the film, her uniform, which is worn by women of all classes, helps to put them on an even keel, but when she changes she suddenly appears to him as the upper-class woman she really is. Power wears a loose-fitting blazer and trousers for most of the film, often with a flat cap, which evokes the British working-class male of the time, and reminiscent of Cary Grant's working-class Brit Ernie Mott in *None but the Lonely Heart* (Clifford Odets, 1944).

Clive's fragile mental state is revealed to both Prue and the audience after they go off to a hotel together. He talks in his sleep but denies it, snatches a telegram and reads it fearfully before stuffing it in his pocket, and is irritated and uptight by any mention of war before his heroic past and status as a deserter are revealed. Given Clive's views on the class system, and Prue belonging to the upper echelons, they are an unlikely couple and yet they have much to teach each other about their respective classes, their union representing the war more generally, with men and women fighting together for a greater cause: the freedom of their country, no matter their social position. Prue's dramatic and emotional speech about what England means to her leads to Clive leaving the hotel while she sleeps. Hiding out like a criminal, he is unshaven, dirty and edgy, resembling Jesse James at his worst. Clive lives in fear until his love for Prue and a priest with one arm convince him to give himself up.

However, Clive wakes up in the hospital with a head injury sustained after a burning building collapsed on him as he tried to save a woman and her children trapped inside. He and Prue are married while he lies with bandages on his head. A fellow soldier brings a gift that he says shows Clive to be really highbrow, despite the social position he was born into: a book of Shakespeare. The book is revealed as *Hamlet* when a nurse reads to him from it in the next scene. Quoting from Act I, Scene III, she reads Polonius's speech that states 'This above all: to thine own self be true/ And it must follow, as the night the day/Thou canst not then be false to any man/Farewell, my blessing season this in thee'. Power repeats the first line, 'This above all: to thine own self be true' in a weak voice. In the final concluding minute, Clive, who is still bandaged and immobile in the hospital bed tells Prue (and the audience):

> It's going to be a different world when all of this is over. Someday we're going to fight for what I believe in, but first we've got to fight for what you believe in. You were right. We've got to win this war. We've got to.

He gets more desperate and animated as he talks. Prue replies, 'We will', and a close-up of her hand squeezing his is followed by one of Power's face as he looks up and repeats, 'This above all, to thine own self be true' as the film fades out and non-diegetic music resembling a church choir swells. The image we are left with is a less-than-glamorous Power, with bandages around his head and chin, but it is a powerful statement about country, class and patriotism, which were particularly prevalent during the war. Much has been written about the psychological issues that men faced in the post-war period, both in film studies and other disciplines, not least social and cultural studies (see Epstein 1994; Bruzzi 2005; Chopra-Gant 2006), but Clive is the study of a man who suffers from these issues amid war. It is a more mature and complex characterisation for Power, but Clive keeps his feelings bottled up, releasing them only in occasional bouts of anger. He is also far removed from the cocky all-American charmer from *A Yank in the RAF* who sees war as a bit of a lark and a way to make some money.

Power's Lieutenant Ward Stewart in *Crash Dive* can be read as a combination of Tim and Clive, but more grounded than either. *Crash Dive* was also Power's final film for three years since, in August 1942, during the making of the film, he enlisted in the United States Marine Corps. Combining his already established screen persona as a persistent ladies' man with a new wartime sensibility, sense of duty and pride in America, the film allowed an important development for both Power's on- and off-screen personae. Not only did he receive top billing above co-stars Anne Baxter and Dana Andrews, but is credited as 'Tyrone Power USMCR',[1] the first deviation since 1936 when he was billed as Tyrone Power Jr. This alteration suggests a wartime advancement for Power's image: a military ranking instead of a younger incarnation of his father. The decision to bill him as such would also have boosted Twentieth Century-Fox's sense of patriotism and pride in their top leading man, as well as alerting audiences that they were losing him for the duration. Overall, the studio lost 755 actors, writers and directors to the service and was therefore required to find new talent (Schatz 1997: 142). Among the studio's new breed of leading men was Dana Andrews, who plays Power's commanding officer Dewey Connors, thus providing a way for Power to hand over the reins.

As Wheeler Winston Dixon notes, 'one can look at the films from early 1942 to 1945 as a sort of frenzied and successful effort to keep the country's eye on victory, while simultaneously distracting it with light entertainment' (2006: 7). In *A Yank in the RAF* and *Crash Dive* these contrasting elements occur within the same film. In the former the beautiful Power and Grable engage in an on-and-off romance while she sings in nightclubs and he flies a bomber, and in the latter Power and Andrews fight together on a submarine while unknowingly sharing romantic interludes with the same girl onshore. Thus, despite the wartime setting and combat scenes, Power's characters are still allowed opportunities for romance. Like Tim, Ward's grandmother (Dame May Whitty) lets slip that he is a bit of a womaniser when she asks Jean (Baxter) how she is and he whispers, 'You don't know this one'. The old lady gives him a disapproving look before calling him a 'scoundrel' and telling Jean he will 'charm the shirt off your back'. Like *Johnny Apollo*, we are presented with a framed photograph of Power in the hallway, only this time in military uniform. Additionally, a close-up of a photograph showing Ward as a child is an authentic photograph of Power as a youngster, further blurring the lines of his on- and off-screen lives. Despite the strong military theme throughout, the opportunity still arises for Power to dance with a woman, only this time at a military event, wearing a formal white uniform rather than the modern tuxedos or historical evening clothes of previous films.

Crash Dive was also Power's first war film to be shot in colour, as well as only his fourth colour film of any genre. Ward is introduced leading a rescue mission on a torpedo boat, and we are immediately presented with an active and masculine authoritative figure in a homosocial situation. Looking through binoculars, a look of concentration on his face, he locates a small boat of survivors of a U-boat attack and immediately gives orders for the crew to head towards it. As he helps the passengers onboard, he notices an enemy submarine approaching and successfully destroys it before going back for them. Following a huge explosion, the tanned and healthy-looking actor grins widely and winks, the wind blowing through his dark hair as he steers the craft with ease. Dressed in a utilitarian outfit of beige shirt, trousers, tie and bomber jacket, the outfit helps highlight Power's handsome, bronzed features and jet-black hair, thus aligning with his recognisable star persona, while simultaneously reinforcing an active wartime element in his image through this costume. Furthermore, while his pre-war characters would no doubt have winked at a woman, here the wink is directed towards his fellow military personnel as a way of signalling a job well done.

After an almost documentary-style montage showing work being done at the submarine base, Power re-enters the film dressed in a more formal, form-fitting dark naval uniform with gold trim. His lieutenant stripes are clearly visible as he arrives at the office of his superior officer, who also happens to be his uncle. Power is filmed in full body as he walks across the room, sits down and grins widely before excitedly talking about how much he loved working on PT boats, battleships, cruisers and destroyers. When his uncle mentions submarines, however, he becomes silent, his smile fades and he looks down at the desk before glancing back up at him indignantly, squinting his eyes as if he knows what the man is about to say. Ward makes his feelings clear when he declares that submarines are 'no life for a dog, even a seadog', and that he would rather 'sink 'em than sail 'em'. He stares at the older man who assigns him to submarine duty before stating that the Stewarts have been in the navy for three generations, much like Power's family and the acting tradition. Power looks down again before nodding to show that Ward has resigned himself to the assignment.

Ward and Dewey meet for the first time in the subsequent scene, the actors' physical differences remarkably apparent as they face each other in a two-shot. Probably best remembered for playing Detective Mark McPherson in *Laura* (Otto Preminger, 1944), Andrews only started making films in 1940. Although he had portrayed a tough gangster in *Ball of Fire* (Howard Hawks, 1941), he was able to look manly when juxtaposed with the soft spoken, bumbling professor played by the tall and gangly Gary Cooper. Here he plays opposite the taller, broader and physically more imposing Power whose dark hair and striking looks stand out against Andrews's lighter hair and less impactful features. Likewise, Power's dark, fitted uniform stands out while Andrews's beige shirt and trousers almost blend into the background (Figure 5.3). While Carl Rollyson feels that Andrews's 'leading man looks' were hidden away in 'too many costume epics and uniforms' before finally being shown off in a tailored suit in *Laura* (2012: 165), it was just such films that emphasised Power's looks. The actors' looks are also reflected in their characterisations and how other characters view them. For example, Jean refers to the ever-proper Dewey as stable, safe and 'the rock' while trying to dissuade the cocksure and devastatingly handsome Ward from any romantic entanglement, distressed by her strong sexual attraction to him. Looking uninspired at a photograph of Dewey, Jean tells a friend, 'The rock's the one you marry', and describes her initial meeting with Ward as merely 'an episode', despite the audience being asked to encourage their union.

Figure 5.3   Dana Andrews and Power as military personnel in *Crash Dive* (1943)

During a particularly suspenseful scene, Dewey is knocked unconscious and Ward finds himself in charge as their submarine is repeatedly blasted by a German Q-boat. Looking through the periscope, Ward calmly orders the release of torpedoes, which successfully destroy the enemy vessel, and Power once again grins widely and winks at the crew. This action-packed scene is juxtaposed with the next, in which the two men lie shirtless under sunlamps to counteract their having been underwater for a prolonged period. Andrews faces away from the camera, lying on his stomach as a topless woman would when sunbathing, resulting in the pose feminising him. Contrastingly, Power lies on his back, the positioning of the camera allowing his ample chest to fill the screen and provides us with a central focus. Thus, despite his beautiful face (partially hidden by protective goggles), Power's manly physique presents him as the male to Andrews's female. This is reflected in how Jean considers them, since she is frightened and disturbed by her desire for Ward, and runs from him to the safety and security (read impotence) of Dewey. Although Jean kisses Dewey before boarding the train where she will meet Ward, it appears staged and almost for show since lovers are expected to embrace when parting at a railway station. Baxter stands on a step ready to board the train while Andrews is positioned on the platform below. He does not touch her when kissing her, his arms remaining at his side, and it is certainly not the passionate, all-enveloping kiss that Power later delivers when they wrap their arms around each other, causing Baxter's coat to fall off her shoulders before she looks at him and sighs. When the spinster who runs the school approaches, Jean rushes off and Ward affectionately kisses the older lady on the cheek. As he drives away, her poker face instantly transforms into an excitedly girlish grin, she bites her lip and her monocle drops from her eye in response to his evident virility.

Ward and Jean meet rather awkwardly in a train berth that they both claim to be theirs. Power lies in the berth wearing beige pyjamas reminiscent of his military uniform, a small piece of hair falling on his forehead making him look both relaxed and sexy. Reading a magazine, Ward looks surprised when Jean gets into the berth. With an amused look on his face, he silently observes as she buttons the curtain with her back to him, unaware of his presence. He slightly moves to give her more room, grinning while leaning a hand on his chin and a forefinger on his head. He brazenly fixes her pillow as she leans forward to retrieve the cover, before pulling it further up over himself. She lies down before discovering his presence and sitting up in a panic while he continues to stare silently. Arguing over whose berth it is, Ward realises he is wrong but attempts to flirt as he leaves. Embarrassed and angry, Jean is now the one who remains silent, continuing to be so the following morning when he seats himself behind her in the dining car, grinning widely and chatting. Ward schemes to get Jean to go out with him, thus Power performs Ward performing, smiling towards the camera without her seeing. Accordingly, Power must act well when playing Ward, who is acting poorly. He perseveres until she finally agrees to go out with him, although he does so through blackmail and scheming until she comments, 'That's not gold on your uniform, it's brass'. Jean soon falls for Ward, although he is unaware that she is engaged to Dewey.

Ward follows Jean to the school she teaches at, stands under her window and whistles, using his silver cigarette case to reflect light into her room. Jean panics when seeing him, but her friend looks out, smiles and asks, 'Why so frightened? He *is* a dream.' Jean asks what she should do, the friend quipping that she would 'probably break a leg rushing down the stairs'. Offering to get rid of Ward, the woman fluffs her hair and asks to borrow Jean's lipstick, which leads Jean to go herself. Again dressed in a dark naval outfit, he hands her a large red apple, the stereotypical teacher gift, while some passing schoolgirls giggle.

The next day, after Ward and Jean share their first kiss, he walks around Dewey's quarters with an unusually wide grin, failing to notice two framed photographs of Jean on the bureau. Sitting his glass of milk down in front of them, he carries on their light-hearted conversation before turning to stub out his cigarette and finally seeing them. Stopping dead, his smile fades before Dewey gestures to them and points Jean out as his fiancée. The shocked Ward excuses himself, his wide grin and joking now replaced by a deadpan voice and grave seriousness. When Ward asks Jean for an explanation, Dewy catches them together and animosity has developed between the men when they return to the submarine. After Ward saves Dewey's life, he resigns himself to the fact that Ward and Jean are in love and steps aside, since Ward has proven himself capable of great strength and has a clear devotion to Dewey and Jean.

Ward can be read as a manifestation of Tim in a submarine, the action scenes allowing him to be active and advancing his masculinity being intercut with more familiar romantic interludes with Jean. Combined, these components remind audiences that despite its being wartime it is not all doom and gloom. The decision to make the film in colour helps lift the mood, with Baxter's bright outfits and red lipstick particularly striking. Moreover, Power being shot in colour and dressed in military uniforms for the duration help to emphasise both his beautiful face, of which there are ample close-ups, and his manly physique, which combined present him at perhaps his most handsome.

The film concludes with a montage of different branches of the service accompanied by rousing music and a voiceover by Power, which could easily be part of a documentary or recruitment reel. Although Ward was unsure about taking up his post, he realises he was wrong and that each branch of the US Navy is of equal importance, each having its own part to play in the war.

Crash Dive would have to satisfy audiences until 1946, when the war was over and Power returned to Hollywood. Offered a commission, Power refused and enlisted as a private, working as an aviator and aiding at both Iwo Jima and Okinawa. He was promoted to second lieutenant in June 1943, and awarded the American Campaign Medal, the Asiatic-Pacific Campaign Medal (with two bronze stars), and the World War II Victory Medal. Remaining in the military long after the war ended, at the time of his death Power was ranked a major and was buried with full military honours, thus blurring his on- and off-screen images.

When Roosevelt died on 12 April 1945 while still in office, he was succeeded by Harry S. Truman. Less than a month later, on 8 May, Germany surrendered before a US B29 dropped the first atomic bomb on Hiroshima on 6 August, killing over seventy thousand people. A second bomb dropped on Nagasaki three days later killed an additional thirty-five thousand people and led to Japan's surrender, which officially ended World War II (Dixon 2006: xii; Shindler 1979: 83).

The post-war war film

Although Schatz suggests that Hollywood's output of war-related features 'simply stopped soon after the war' (1997: 4), Power's most brutal and combat-fuelled film, *American Guerrilla in the Philippines*, was released in 1950. Set in 1942, thus depicting events from World War II, Power's performance has a sense of authenticity and nostalgia attached to it since it was the only war film he made following his own active duty. Furthermore, it features a slightly older Power with a short military haircut and a more rugged manliness that separates his Ensign Chuck Palmer from the inexperienced flier Tim Barker of nearly a decade earlier.

As Shindler notes, the Japanese had made successful landings in the Philippines and elsewhere by 1 January 1942, with General Douglas MacArthur forced to retreat on the Bataan Peninsula. This becomes a recurring trope throughout this film, particularly through MacArthur's quotation on American cigarette packages that says he will return (1979: 38). Although it might seem counterproductive to readdress the war in 1950, given the volume of war films already produced during the conflict, it was also a decade of much political unrest, with threats of communism and the Cold War still very real. Therefore, perhaps looking back at a battle the country had won helped to alleviate some of the fear Americans were experiencing.

Writings on the film have tended to be negative, including that of its director Fritz Lang, but perhaps none more so than Reynold Humphries, who notes in the preface to a study of Lang's American films that '*American Guerrilla in the Philippines* is best forgotten', making no further mention of it (1989: xv). Belafonte calls the film 'too episodic and rambling in its loosely-constructed sequences', but notes that Power 'did his best' (1979: 29). In his faint praise, Paul M. Jensen claims that Lang 'has made far worse films', while signalling its importance as the first Hollywood film to be entirely shot on an actual battle locale: Luzon Island (1969: 174). Jensen concludes that although parts of the film and its concept are noteworthy, its overall direction and the script's looseness resulted in it being little more than adequate (1969: 174), although he does not expand on which parts he found noteworthy. Nevertheless the film, based on Ira Wolfert's novel of the same name, made $2.275 million at the US box office upon its release.

Several voice-overs by Power are interwoven throughout; his description of the soldiers' experiences and activities often being accompanied by montages of their treacherous journey. They include a light-hearted voiceover about how they created a radio station from junk on the island, as well as darker ones about the brutality of the Japanese soldiers. The film opens as numerous bombers fly low over a military vessel that has just been destroyed, black smoke still billowing from it. The low-flying bombers shoot at a group of soldiers in the water who have clearly been forced to bail out and are heading for shore. Power's Ensign Chuck Palmer is among them, and we see him helping a man on a stretcher reach shelter below a tree. The film is put into its historical context when Power's voiceover tells us that this is the Philippines in 1942, and that the men we are seeing are the last of Torpedo Squadron 3. He announces that they hid out in an abandoned lighthouse to tend their wounds, and we join the narrative as the men hear a chilling radio announcement that Bataan has fallen. Deciding that it is safer for the men to travel alone or in pairs, the captain orders Chuck to be the first to leave, and Jim Mitchell (Tom Ewell) decides to go along with him. Best known for starring opposite Marilyn Monroe in *The Seven Year Itch* (Billy Wilder, 1955), Ewell's appearance contrasts even more strongly with Power's than Dana Andrews's did, the small blond man looking almost childlike beside Power despite being five years his senior.

When Chuck suddenly finds himself in charge of a group of military personnel from different branches of the service, including the air corps and the army, he suggests they attempt to sail to Australia in a bunker (a small boat), but they capsize within seventy-two hours. Chuck shows his virility, physical strength and masculine power by relentlessly swimming across eight miles of open sea, while also saving Jim from drowning. Reaching shore, but in rather a bad state, like Tim and Clive, he wakes up in a strange bed. As he is fed soup by some locals, Power is once again shirtless throughout the scene while the others around him remain fully clothed.

Chuck's romantic life is different from his other wartime characters since Jeanne Martinez (Micheline Presle) is not only married but is married to a respectable man whom Chuck also likes. Not knowing anything about her, he helps her when they first meet because he finds her attractive. Later, hiding his growing feelings for her, they dance on the island while he is dressed in military uniform. When her husband Juan, an older man who is slightly jealous of Chuck, comments that he (and, by extension, Power) is 'a very attractive young man', Jeanne stares after him and smiles before replying, 'Yes. Very.' When Juan is killed, Jeanne arrives at Chuck's wooden hut to spend Christmas with him, and as they fall into each other's arms in a passionate kiss the scene fades out. The audience is asked to draw its own conclusions as to what occurred before the next scene begins with the two sitting together on a foldout bed.

US nationality is a key element of the film, the American cigarette package that carries MacArthur's promise 'I shall return' repeatedly acting as a metaphor for the courage, faith and determination of the American people. The longer the men are stuck on the island, however, the more disillusioned they become by MacArthur's claims. The Americans and native islanders are constantly in danger from Japanese soldiers, and this comes to a head in the film's ultimate, and rather brutal, combat scene set in and around a church. Just as it looks hopeless for the Americans, MacArthur does indeed arrive at precisely the right moment to save them, which not even their virile leader Chuck can do, although he does make a good job of keeping his men alive before the general appears.

Overall, Power's work in the war genre advanced his screen image by allowing him to exhibit a new-but-different version of his previously constructed star persona. As with his pre-war characterisations, all four military figures have a love interest, while each film presents a different version of the wartime military male embodied by Power. Tim is a flier, as Power would become off-screen, while Clive is an accomplished soldier suffering from mental health issues. Ward is a cocky but skilled naval officer stationed on a submarine, and Chuck is also navy personnel, but is stranded on a small island in the Philippines. Despite this being a male-driven genre, Power is again repeatedly displayed as an object of erotic desire while dressed in military outfits, particularly in *A Yank in the RAF* and *Crash Dive* where his body in form-fitting uniforms is displayed from a number of angles in both black and white and colour. Although Clive is never seen in uniform, several close-ups of Power's beautiful face are included throughout, while Clive's military record and bravery at

Dunkirk confirm his masculinity. Lastly, although Chuck mostly wears more realistically dirty and ragged uniforms, this does not stop him being highly desirable to audiences and the women around him, as was frequently the case with Power's characters in any decade and any genre.

Notes

1. United States Marine Corps Reserve.

Chapter 6

The rugged adventurer

Overview

This chapter explores the final genre with which Power was associated and perhaps best remembered for: action-adventure. Second only to his output in drama, Power starred in eleven action-adventure films between 1939 and 1957. While *The Rains Came* (1939) was his only action-adventure film of the 1930s, he made six in the 1940s: four in the pre-war years (*Brigham Young: Frontiersman* [Henry Hathaway, 1940], *The Mark of Zorro*, *Son of Fury: The Story of Benjamin Blake* and *The Black Swan*) and two in the post-war period (*Captain from Castile* and *Prince of Foxes*). Subsequently, he made a further four in the 1950s (*The Black Rose*, *King of the Khyber Rifles* [Henry King, 1953], *Untamed* [Henry King, 1955] and *Abandon Ship!* [Richard Sale, 1957]).

With large budgets and an emphasis on aesthetics, action-adventure films present audiences with visual spectacles, both in the *mise en scène* and the star images within them. Within his work in this genre, audiences are asked to focus on Power's physical prowess, agility and masculine strength alongside his beauty and position as erotic spectacle. There are moments when the action slows down or even stops to allow the viewer to gaze at Power's beautiful face and impressive (exposed) body. Casper calls knights, pirates and explorers of the late Middle Ages to the nineteenth century 'the extraordinary male type' (2007: 163), a type that Power embodied in this genre. As Cohan notes, within the Hollywood star system a male star may play manly roles, 'but the apparatus of stardom turns him into a spectacle, valuing him for his whole body as well as his good looks even more than for his impersonation of agency' (1997: xvi). Jeffery P. Dennis asserts that 'the adult male body was strictly censored' in the 1930s and 1940s, with only Johnny Weissmuller's Tarzan, Buster Crabbe as Buck Rogers and 'the occasional boxer' appearing shirtless on screen (2008: 87–8), while Dyer suggests that until the 1980s, 'it was rare to see a white man's semi-naked body in popular fictions' (1997: 146). Cohan calls the status of the male body on screen in the 1950s both exploited and problematised, with the 'spectacularity of the actors the central dimension of their stardom' (1997: xvi). Additionally, Dyer notes that the first major African-American star, Paul Robeson, appears shirtless for large sections of his films, which would be 'unimaginable' for white male stars, who may be 'glimpsed for a brief shot' getting out of a swimming pool or the sea (1997: 146). However, in *Son of Fury* and *The Black Swan* Power is frequently bare-chested and for long periods. Even when fully dressed in *Son of Fury*, it is in tight-fitting clothing that accentuates his muscular arms and broad chest, while his costumes in *The Mark of Zorro* are particularly revealing around the buttocks and crotch area. Thus, whatever the plot, setting or time period, audiences were repeatedly asked to look at and desire Power's body.

Early action

The Rains Came, Power's first action-adventure film, was nominated for six Academy Awards and won for Best Special Effects.[1] Power's Indian doctor, Major Rama Safti, was not only another non-American character but also his first non-Caucasian role. Furthermore, although Power wore a moustache intermittently in *Jesse James*, this was the first time he wore one for the duration of a film, and it was never part of his star image unlike contemporaries Clark Gable, William Powell, Robert Taylor and Errol Flynn. Additionally, his hair is covered by a turban for much of the film and his skin is darkened, making Power somewhat unrecognisable although the familiar nose and smile remain. Furthermore, his voice possesses the familiar Power lilt but is more rigid and pronounced, reflecting Rama's profession and cultural background.

In her study of the film's director Clarence Brown, Gwenda Young briefly discusses the origins of *The Rains Came* as a 1937 novel by Ohio-born Louis Bromfield, who based it on his recent travels to India (2018: 223). Although David O. Selznick had considered buying the rights when the novel was first published, the Production Code Administration (PCA) had warned that its 'risqué aspects and . . . critique of British rule in India' made it too contentious to bring to the screen (Young 2018: 224). Thus, while Selznick turned his attention to *Gone with the Wind*, Zanuck bought the rights for $52,000 in March 1938. According to Young, the main draw for both men was the earthquake and flood, along with the 'exotic setting, evocative prose, and portrayal of miscegenation' (2018: 224).

Young states that Zanuck considered several actors for the role of Rama, including Charles Boyer and Ramon Novarro, but opted for Power, 'then on the brink of box-office success' (2018: 225). However, Power was the studio's top leading man by this point, having already starred in the likes of *In Old Chicago, Alexander's Ragtime Band* and *Jesse James*. Young calls the casting of Power 'a canny commercial decision', while suggesting that it 'neutralized any concerns about miscegenation – Power had dark and smouldering good looks, but he was also "reassuringly" white' (2018: 225).

Rama is introduced visiting the home of Tom Ransome (George Brent), the characters immediately set up as close but very different. While Rama is a serious, career-driven doctor who sits erect in his chair, Tom is a free-spirited artist, known for drinking and womanising, who lounges with his feet up. Rama works incessantly and has no time for a personal life, noting that he may need to perform surgery later that day before attending a conference at the royal palace. However, Rama is also allowed to joke in this introductory scene, and behind the darkened skin, moustache and turban is a glimpse of the familiar Power smile, the recognisable gap in his teeth suddenly visible and working against his pronounced speech, with which he articulates all his words, unlike his comedic reporters and musical heels who use a lot of clipped speech.

Leading lady Myrna Loy was borrowed from MGM to play Lady Edwina Esketh, and while attempting to seduce ex-lover Tom, she suddenly notices Rama. Staring open-mouthed, she asks, 'Who's the pale copper Apollo?', a truly befitting name. Looking him over, she seductively adds, 'Not bad. Not bad at all.' Tom's informing her that Rama is a surgeon and scientist, so 'any interest he might have had in romance is purely biological', suggests that Rama is a very different role for Power. As Young notes, 'the expressionistic shadows and the exotic setting contribute to the sensual mood, and Loy's appraising gaze of desire conveys Lady Esketh's sexual voraciousness with no need for dialogue' (2018: 229). I would add that her appraising gaze is also shared by the audience, who are being asked to find Rama as exotic and exciting as she does.

In addition to the turban, Power wears a surgical gown, a military uniform and a much more familiar white dinner jacket with black bow tie; thus, even when portraying an Indian doctor he was permitted to wear evening dress on-screen. Although Edwina persistently tries to seduce him, Rama remains politely aloof until one evening she boldly announces, 'I've done everything but fall at your feet and you haven't even blinked'. He silently stares at her before they are interrupted by a major earthquake and flood, which kills many, including Edwina's elderly husband, and Rama must rush to the hospital. The spoiled Edwina volunteers for hospital duty where she is given menial tasks that she conducts without complaining, thus proving her feelings for Rama. He trains her in ward duty, and one evening they converse with surgical masks covering their faces. She tells him of being sick numerous times a day, to which he admirably answers, 'And yet you stayed'. Power removes his mask before asking why, but Loy just stares at him while he looks back, his mouth slightly open to show Rama detecting her unselfish love for him. Without breaking his gaze, and blinking only once, Power stands up and slowly walks towards her, gently reaches up and pulls her mask down, reminiscent of a groom with a bride's veil, as they continue to stare intensely at one another. A moment later Power lets his tense shoulders drop, softens his eyes and relaxes his face as he smiles and almost whispers, 'You don't have to answer', although he never lets his eyes leave hers. Breaking the intensity of the moment by telling her to use plenty of disinfectant since she is too valuable an asset, his smile fades and his face becomes hard before he abruptly turns and walks away, thus breaking the gaze for the first time. These subtle gestures, in bleak surroundings, make it both a tender and overtly sensual moment, devoid of any sexual incident and implied only by the understated and mostly internalised performances by the actors whose faces silently speak what their characters are thinking.

As they become more involved, Rama becomes gradually more Westernised. His turban is replaced by a cap and eventually he wears nothing on his head, revealing Power's familiar mass of dark hair; his clothing also evolves until his suits are similar to those worn by Brent. It is in this final incarnation that Rama reveals his feelings for Edwina, telling her he lives in 'torture every moment' because she is in danger. What the audience knows that Rama does not is that Edwina has drunk from the glass of a dying patient and is very sick. In the same positions as the previous scene, he confesses that when they first met he found her exciting and was tempted, but that it would have been like 'taking a counterfeit instead of waiting for the real coin', since he is now in love with the unselfish woman she has become and not the spoiled seductress she was. Walking towards her to kiss her, she stops him and asks him to just hold her. A shot from over Loy's shoulder reveals his reactions; smiling as they first embrace, when his face touches hers his smile fades and he looks forward in a panic. Reaching a hand up, he feels her face and pulls away as he realises she has a fever. Although Edwina denies being sick, she collapses and he picks her up and carries her from the ward.

Edwina knows she must give Rama up and he gets increasingly frustrated that she will not fight for her life, losing his composure for the first, and only, time. Leaving her hospital room, he walks across the corridor and looks out the window before Tom puts a friendly hand on his shoulder. Looking startled, as if unaware anyone was there, he turns slightly before saying 'I don't know what to do' twice. A third 'I don't know what to do' trails off, the 'do' hardly audible as Power turns towards Brent before sitting down and placing a hand on his head, running his fingers through his hair and covering his eyes. Giving a speech about being Indian, he claps his hands as if trying to find the right words before adding that he cannot be 'calm and unemotional'. Standing up, Power walks across the room with his hands on his head and his elbows raised, his back to both Brent and the camera. Abruptly, he drops to one knee, placing his elbows on a table and his head in his hands as he openly weeps, saying he has failed since he is unable to save Edwina. Sinking to both knees, he places his face directly onto the table before Brent walks over and pulls him to a standing position. Power's body remains limp, his legs buckling as Brent shakes him and tells him to think about his duty and his people who worship him. Power looks at Brent as the rain reflects off the windowpane and onto his face, looking down he pushes back his hair that had become unruly and is once again composed. In a steady voice, Power utters four short sentences: 'I'm sorry Tom. I'm alright now. It won't happen again. Thank you' – taking a slight break between each one, which suggests that Rama is trying to convince himself that this is true.

Rama sits by Edwina's bedside as she passes away, and although he looks shocked and says her name, he does not break down again. The final scene fades in on him once again wearing traditional Indian dress as the Queen gives him the authority to govern. Although wearing a turban for the first time since revealing his feelings for Edwina, this one is jewel-encrusted with an elaborate feather on the top, and his outfit is adorned with gold chains that look regal and expensive. Marching down the hallway and carrying a sword, he is flanked by guards and everyone he passes bows to him. Walking erect and unemotional, Rama embodies the strength and purity that Tom told him his people believed he represented. Their new leader, who must not see himself as a man with human desires, descends the stairs and towards the camera, fully ready to take on his new role as the film fades out.

Young sees the film as merely 'a slice of exotica designed to showcase beautiful stars and immerse viewers in a sumptuous spectacle that allowed them to escape their everyday woes' (2018: 231). Young also quotes Mary Harris of the *Washington Post*, who suggests the leads were miscast, Loy being '"not so much a siren as an elegant piece of deliberate wickedness", and Power simply "too handsome"' (2018: 231), although too handsome for what it is not made clear. Too handsome to be believable in the role? Too handsome to be a good actor? She does not say.

The following year *Brigham Young: Frontiersman* (1940) was released, and it is another unusual film in Power's career trajectory. Although his star power was demonstrated through his receiving top billing, Power is surprisingly relegated to a supporting player for much of the film with Dean Jagger taking on the title role as the American religious leader, politician and settler Brigham Young. Despite Power's top billing, Mary Astor, who played Brigham's wife, wrote, 'I had graduated from, I hoped, ever again just playing the "love interest": Linda Darnell and Tyrone Power, bless 'em, carried those dull honors' (1967: 148). George F. Custen notes that the serious subject matter concerned Zanuck, therefore he 'leavened it with romance and low comedy' (1992: 159). Power and Linda Darnell provided the romance, thus making the 'serious – and potentially controversial – subject matter' commercial through 'the usual biopic formulation of love, comedy, and just enough history to keep the audience entertained' (Custen 1992: 160).

Although the film did little to advance Power's screen image, one scene is particularly worthy of discussion here. As an unmarried young couple, Jonathan Kent (Power) and Zina Webb (Darnell) lie head to head in separate beds, a makeshift curtain separating them, the cinematography and *mise en scène* present the two beautiful stars very differently and fully favour Power over Darnell. Zina is unable to see Jonathan because of the curtain, giving audiences a prolonged and privileged view of the shirtless Power lying in bed and exhibited in a series of shots that underscore his attractiveness. The camera remains mostly stationary at Power's side, while the light shining on his face and torso highlight his glistening shoulders and dark eyes, making him look ethereal and drawing our attention to him and not Darnell. While the framing and lighting emphasise the delicate beauty that Power possessed at this time, not least his upturned nose and long eyelashes, his tousled black hair on the white pillowcase and masculine jawline also add a sense of manliness to his appearance. Failing to get a response to his proposal of marriage, Jonathan pulls the curtain back to

Figure 6.1 The brightly lit, shirtless Power is privileged over Linda Darnell in *Brigham Young: Frontiersman* (1940)

discover that Zina has fallen asleep. Power now lies on his stomach, facing the camera and the audience is given a prolonged shot of his muscular bare shoulders and beautiful face. Although the unmarried couple is sexually attracted to each other and in bed, any eroticism existing between them is shattered by the fact that his young siblings occupy the same room, his brother sniggering at the proposal. Yet the audience is allowed, in fact invited, to gaze at and appreciate Power's beauty whereas Zina cannot look because of the obstacles of the curtain and sleep (Figure 6.1). However, for much of the film he is an overtly active male, thereby escaping the trap of becoming emasculated.

Making his mark as Zorro

That same year, Power and Darnell were paired for the third time in one of his best known films: *The Mark of Zorro* (1940). In 2009, this became Power's only film added to the National Film Registry, a list of important films earmarked for preservation by the Library of Congress for their cultural, historical or aesthetic significance.² Tom Milne sees it as one of director Rouben Mamoulian's 'most elegant and intelligent films' (1969: 127), calling it 'one of the masterpieces of the genre, while at the same time escaping it' (1969: 121). As Power's first swashbuckler, it allowed an action-based component to be added to his screen image and meant that less emphasis was being placed on his beauty. Like *Thin Ice*, the film frequently reveals and conceals Power's face, but here almost to fetishised extremes through the eye mask he wears as Zorro. Likewise, Power's athletic body is repeatedly displayed in both action scenes and a range of tight-fitting costumes that highlight his toned and masculine form, while concurrently presenting him as an object of the erotic gaze.

The film opens in Madrid with Power's Diego Vega, nicknamed the California Corporal, demonstrating his impressive horsemanship and swordsmanship before being called home to California. Greeted by Captain Esteban Pasquale (Basil Rathbone), Diego discovers his father, Alejandro Vega (Montagu Love), has been replaced as Alcalde by the corrupt Luis Quintero (J. Edward Bromberg). While Pasquale waves around a naked sword, Diego pretends to know little about them, commenting that 'swordplay is such a violent business' as he takes a feminine-encoded frilled handkerchief from his breast pocket and delicately dabs his mouth as Pasquale laughs mockingly. The first woman to enter the film, Quintero's wife Inez (Gale Sondergaard), stares at Diego with bulging eyes and an open mouth before floating over to him, smiling and fanning herself as she attempts to flirt. He takes out the handkerchief before discussing his enjoyment of choosing materials for dresses and finding scents to pair with them, the two 'real' men groaning as Diego is depicted as homosexual. Reinforcing his heterosexuality for the audience, we are given a privileged view of Diego being captivated by Lolita (Darnell) through the window. As the women watch his carriage leave, Lolita asks the smitten Inez who he was and she replies, 'Someone new and very charming'; Lolita observes, 'Well he must be from the colour in your cheeks and the look in your eyes'.

When Diego arrives at his parents' house, local priest Friar Felipe (Eugene Pallette) grabs his forearm and says he can 'feel good muscle', while his mother (Janet Beecher) asks, 'Is he without a face? Can't you see he's even better looking than when he left?' She calls him a 'young angel', as all three stare at Power. When Alejandro says that he hopes Diego will fight for them, he keeps up his masquerade. Adopting a milder tone of voice, Power makes his eyes look heavy and blinks repeatedly while taking out a decorative fan, fanning himself and doing tricks with the object. Alejandro and Felipe watch in horror, the latter exclaiming that the boy he raised with a firm wrist has 'turned into a puppy' (read homosexual) before storming out.

Diego's curly hair and light-coloured, frilled and fussy clothes denote him as a fop or dandy, and Pasquale later calls him the alternative 'popinjay' as well as a 'fancy clown'. McDowell defines the fop as 'the over-fashionable man' who has been 'universally assumed to forfeit too much of his masculinity for the lure of the latest style' (1997: 40), while Peter McNeil and Vicki Karaminas add that fops were often seen as 'an unnatural hybrid, containing a mingling of male and female attributes' (2009: 6). McDowell suggests that the dandy likes to be on show, possessing 'an air of frigidity, heightened by his natural tendency to strike a pose' (1997: 23), while Roland Barthes, in his 1962 article 'Dandyism and Fashion', calls dandyism 'not only an ethos . . . but a technique', with the latter guaranteeing the former (2004: 67). Barthes further notes that the dandy must frequently devise idiosyncratic behaviours, which Power's Diego does by using the handkerchief and fan, while preening himself and fussing with his elaborate clothing. As Barthes suggests, the details on a dandy's clothes marks him as indefinitely 'other' (2004: 67), and Diego's clothing certainly makes him stand out from the plain-clothed men around him, his frilled shirts and sequinned trousers denoting him as 'other'. According to McDowell, however, 'dandy' is one of the most ambivalent words since it serves a 'multitude of purposes, including praise, blame, or mockery', which reflects an uncertainty of whether he is admirable or foolish, 'the high point of masculinity or merely another effeminate fop' (1997: 59). Ambivalence is a major element of Diego's dandyism or foppishness but is merely an act so that he is deemed homosexual, or at least cowardly, but this is only one layer of the complex persona Power builds for his character.

In her influential *Gender Trouble*, Judith Butler suggests that gender is historically and socially constructed in relation to cultural norms of masculinity and femininity rather than assigned at birth. Thus gender is performative and requires reaffirming and reinforcing by repeatedly being performed in public (1990: 32). Likewise, Seth Mirsky highlights the distinction between maleness and masculinity, one of the main focuses of men's studies, 'with a view towards diminishing the pervasive confusion which results from patriarchal society's confliction of the two' (1996: 29). Thus, Mirsky feels, masculinity may be usefully understood as 'a thoroughly contingent category which is politically implicated in the patriarchal structuring of the gender order' (1996: 31). He suggests that we can explore 'how (anatomical) men are gendered male within society', and perform masculinity according to social norms, thus 'this more nuanced, multidimensional approach displaces masculinity as the assumed category for men's studies analysis, and instead recognizes it as always a contested term within the larger context of gendered power relations' (1996: 31–2). Additionally, Deborah Cameron highlights the performative nature of speech, noting that men and women 'may use their awareness of gendered meanings that attach to particular ways of speaking and acting to produce a variety of effects' as 'active producers rather than massive reproducers of gendered behaviour' (2011: 252).

When a marriage is arranged between Diego and Lolita, to join the families, he 'reluctantly' agrees. Attending a dinner party at Quintero's house, the 'fake' Diego feigns indifference in Lolita, masquerading again as he looks at her through a monocle as if examining a specimen and not a woman, especially his future bride. Turning to the others, he bemoans his tepid bathwater and expresses the need for more to be carried and properly scented. Sniffing his handkerchief, he adds, 'Life can be trying, don't you think?' as Lolita looks horrified and Pasquale quips that her 'wedded life will be the same', suggesting that Diego will not satisfy her sexually. It is here that Diego wears his flashiest clothes yet: a silk shirt with frilled sleeves and ruffles down the front, a large bow around his neck, a bejewelled jacket and tight-fitting trousers with sequins down the sides, all in pale colours and almost merging with his skin tone. McDowell proposes that dandies supply 'perfect masculine elegance' through 'broad shoulders, narrow waist and immaculately figure-conscious pantaloons', with 'breeches in buff nankeen and silk stockinette, chamois and doeskin' producing the illusion of nudity and enhancing 'whatever masculinity the wearer might possess by exaggerating his male bulge' (1997: 54–5).

In *Undressing Cinema* (1997), Stella Bruzzi explores cinematic clothing and its relationship to sexuality and the body as primary signifiers, while Flugel suggests that decorative clothing draws attention to 'the genital organs of the body', since giving sexual attractiveness to their wearer is their 'overt and conscious purpose' (1971: 26). Writing about the male body in fine art, specifically Nancy Grossman's 'Male Figure' (1971), Andrew Campbell and Nathan Griffith declare that a well-defined torso and large arms and legs are 'evidence of the obsessive lengths to which men will go to create the perfect image, to pursue an ideal, to construct a specimen characteristic of that ideal', and suggest that it is through sculpturing that 'the male body is rendered beautiful' (1994: 160). Grossman's sculpture, with one leg forward and the other back, 'throws the buttocks upwards. A bountiful curve is effected. Ideal form comes alive.' This 'recalls the Grecian youth as a sign of perfection and grace. The body is rendered sexual. Thighs frame the genital region, articulating it, concentrating it, privileging the penis' (1994: 160). Similarly, Power's body is extremely sexualised as he engages in a Spanish dance with Darnell. The cut of his coat draws attention to the crotch, while his tight-fitting trousers emphasise both the curves of his buttocks and outline of his genitals, his movements and foot stamping leaving little to the imagination. Consequently, even when paired with the beautiful Darnell, it is hard to take one's eyes off Power's obvious assets and, as with *Blood and Sand* the following year, Darnell's dress is plainer than Power's highly decorative clothing. At the dance's conclusion, their faces almost touch and Lolita breathlessly exclaims that she has never dreamed dancing could be so wonderful. Although Diego almost blows his cover through a similar look of desire, he quickly regains his composure, takes out the handkerchief and announces that he found it 'rather fatiguing', as Lolita storms out.

Cohan's discussion of how costume is used in *A Streetcar Named Desire* to modify Marlon Brando's appearance and 'to underscore the performativity of his body as the setting for Stanley's masculine masquerade' (1997: 248), could just as easily be applied to Power here. Costume is used throughout to modify Power's appearance and characterisation, his effeminate actions as the 'fake' Diego particularly effective when juxtaposed with the terror he invokes as Zorro. Using make-up, lighting and costume, Cohan suggests that screen acting 'blows the cover of masculine ruggedness because the technology of performance makes virility just another masquerade' (1997: 187). Power's performative skills are complexly structured around cultural norms, both for the geographical and historical timeframes in which the film was set and made, requiring him to greatly vary his body language, facial gestures and speech accordingly throughout.

Jennifer Coates notes the metaphorical mask that men sometimes 'put on' in the form of 'an extreme kind of tough masculinity where the concealment of all traces of vulnerability is viewed as an essential part of men's self-presentation' (2011: 272). This involves a literal mask when Power/Diego portrays Zorro, becoming almost a caricature of extreme masculinity rather than 'real' masculinity. The opposite is true of the 'fake' Diego, whose metaphorical mask of extreme vulnerability allows him to remain above suspicion because of his lack of manliness. Dennis suggests that the body of a character engaged in an activity requiring or justifying physical display 'becomes a tool for practical use, and its aesthetic availability is minimized'. Equally, the 'aesthetic availability' of the body is maximised if a character is placed in 'an ornamental pose, with no physical task to interfere with the articulation of desire' (2008: 85). However, I would argue that physical fights draw attention to the strength and skill of the male body, while correspondingly highlighting its form. Power is presented in both active and ornamental poses during swordfights, thus is conversely pure spectacle and active male.

Although masculinity is often depicted as natural and monolithic, Michael Roper and John Tosh suggest that it is actually divergent, often competing and above all has changing forms (2006: 79). Indeed, masculinity not only changes historically and geographically, but also changes within the *same* body throughout a man's lifetime from adolescence to maturity and from middle age to old age, if the natural lifespan is completed. It also changes depending on his situation, since making love to a woman and fighting a battle present very different forms of masculinity. Roper and Tosh explore ways in which masculinity underpins social life and cultural representation, emphasising that masculinity has always been determined in relation to 'the other', such as differences between women and men, boys and men and heroes and fops (2006: 79). Conflicting levels of masculinity between hero and fop exist in the Zorro/'fake' Diego dichotomy. Adjusting these regarding their social roles, no single performance of masculinity exists, and the ideological binary opposites of masculinity and femininity are played out by Zorro's active, hard machoism and the 'fake' Diego's soft and weak passivity. This is further complicated since Power (the actor) masquerades as both the hypermasculine (Zorro) and the homosexual/camp (the 'fake' Diego), before becoming manly *enough* as the real Diego. Winning both physical fights and the love of Lolita, Diego is rendered safe as a 'real' man who exists between these two extremes and, therefore, is neither markedly hypermasculine nor homosexual.

When Diego masquerades as Zorro he rides a dark horse and dresses all in black, including long boots, wide-brimmed hat, leather gloves and eye mask. McDowell calls black the most flattering colour, connoting 'authority, intellectuality and probity' but simultaneously carrying associations of power and evil, which 'is what gives it its sexual allure. The black-clad figure is at once terrifying and seductive' (1997: 181), which is certainly the case here for audiences and Lolita. While Zorro carries and is highly skilled with a sword, symbolising the phallus and his sexual skills, the 'fake' Diego lacks the phallus, therefore is castrated/rendered homosexual. With echoes of Jesse James's train robbery the previous year, Zorro holds up Quintero's coach, a black bandana covering most of his face. Pointing his sword at the terrified man, Zorro retrieves the money Quintero stole from the villagers before carving a 'Z' in the upholstery and riding off.

Later, Quintero is in his study when a sword suddenly appears and snubs out a candle. One eye is visible in the darkness, followed by another before a wide-brimmed hat comes into view. Moving into the light, Power is again dressed as Zorro; leaning on a candlestick and pointing his sword at the older man, he speaks in a low, monotonous voice, using short sentences and rarely varying his tone (Figure 6.2). Despite his large frame, Power's movements are agile and quick, almost catlike, as he carves another 'Z' into the wall before exiting as silently as

Figure 6.2 The masked Zorro (Power) threatens Quintero (J. Edward Bromberg) in *The Mark of Zorro* (1940)

he entered. To escape detection on the grounds, he disguises himself as a priest and adopts an accent, although an encounter with Lolita almost makes him forget his latest masquerade. When she enquires whether it is a sin not to want to go to a convent, he seductively replies, 'The sin, I think, would be in sending you to one', and she is shocked when he compliments her beauty. Noticing a sword protruding beneath his cassock, she realises he is the escaped Zorro and smiles in delight while bidding him farewell.

Dressed as Zorro, Power rides into a bush and changes into the 'fake' Diego, in both clothing and posture. When soldiers ask Diego if he has seen Zorro, Power uses a camp, singsong voice to exclaim, 'Heaven spare me, my blood chills at the thought'. His flowery language and exaggerated tone result in Father Felipe again calling him a puppy, but when the soldiers leave Diego rushes to close the shutters. As he does so, Power completely alters his body language, denoting that he is now the 'real' Diego for the first time since returning to California. He also reverts to his own speaking voice, last heard in Madrid, which has a masculine authority to it and is neither as high-pitched and affected as Diego's nor as low and sombre as Zorro's. Giving the stolen money to Felipe to hide, he produces the black mask and places it in front of his face. Realising that Diego is Zorro, Felipe's face lights up and he repeats 'my boy' while laughing and hugging him, relieved that he is not actually the fop he has portrayed.

Given Power's previous screen image and his reputation as a ladies' man, when portraying the 'fake' Diego he must act against type by trying to 'change his social front (role) by changing his personal front (attributes)' (Peberdy 2011: 24). Donna Peberdy's discussion of Al Pacino adopting effeminate mannerisms and vocal inflections to perform homosexuality in *Cruising* (William Friedkin, 1980) almost parallels Power's camp performance here. The social and historical context must also be taken into account and, since *The Mark of Zorro* was released when war was raging in Europe but directly before America's involvement, the uncertainty of the time is reflected in the fluidity of male identity and the layers of masculinity embodied by Power, thus complicating where Diego's 'true' identity actually lies. The codes and conventions that Power uses to perform each version of masculinity are distinct, and even when he looks and dresses like Diego, his gestures, vocal intonations and interactions with others reveal to the audience whether he is portraying the real or the 'fake' Diego.

Exotic pre-war adventures

In *Son of Fury: The Story of Benjamin Blake* (1942) Power again has two leading ladies, this time played by Frances Farmer and Gene Tierney. As this film proves, despite the genre's name, these films do not always show the body in action. In fact, *Son of Fury* is the film that most frequently displays Power's exposed body as erotic spectacle across any genre.

The film begins in flashback when Power's Benjamin Blake is a child, the actor entering the film fourteen minutes later, with shirt sleeves rolled up and unruly hair, shoeing a horse. Power's interactions with Farmer and Tierney are erotically charged, depicting different facets of his personality and equally as passionate. The first romantic encounter occurs in this introductory scene, as sexually frustrated rich girl Isabel (Farmer) makes a play for Benjamin while he works in the stable. Feigning indifference and resisting her advances at first, when he bends down she pulls him up by the hair and he responds by pushing her into the wall with the ease of swatting a fly. When she attempts to attack him with a horsewhip, he easily overpowers her, forcing her to drop the whip and staring at her relentlessly. He then kisses her passionately three times as she breathes heavily and looks up at him.

Longing to be near Isabel, Benjamin attends a masquerade ball uninvited. In fine clothes, neat hair and a mask reminiscent of Zorro's covering the top half of his face, Power's beautiful eyes and masculine chin are accentuated, and he looks particularly seductive and sensual while smiling at Farmer. Thus, even in an action-adventure film, this scene allows Power the opportunity to dance with a woman before taking her into the garden and kissing her in the shadows. He slowly lies her down on a bench as she strokes the back of his head, her chest heaving as he presses his manly frame onto her. When Isabel's father, Arthur (George Sanders), catches them he challenges Benjamin to a duel before beating him unconscious with a whip. Benjamin awakes shirtless and bloody while Arthur's wife tends his wounds.

As Benjamin and his friend Caleb Green (John Carradine) sail to the South Seas, Power's muscular chest and arms are exposed in a tight-fitting, short sleeved t-shirt that contrasts with Carradine's rake-thin frame in a shapeless, long-sleeved top. Standing together and both wearing stripes, the contrast in their bodies is made particularly obvious (Figure 6.3). A few minutes later Power has removed his shirt and reaches up to pull on some ropes, further drawing attention to his manly arms and torso as he flexes his muscles. Swimming to an island, his mussed-up hair and the wet

Figure 6.3 Power and John Carradine's contrasting bodies in *Son of Fury: The Story of Benjamin Blake* (1942)

shirt clinging to his body are erotically charged. After drying off, he hands his pistol to the island's leader before ripping open his shirt, exposing his broad back and shoulders and bravely allowing the man the opportunity to shoot him. When the man refuses, he turns back around, his chest now fully exposed to the camera. When Eve (Tierney) first meets Benjamin, she follows him around. Later, he smiles while watching her perform a native dance, wearing only trunks and with his skin glistening in the moonlight, as with *Brigham Young*. Grabbing her as she passes, he kisses her and she touches her mouth, but when he tries to kiss her again, she runs away giggling.

Semiotics, the study of signs, can be used to explore the 'associative, culturally specific meanings' of clothing in film (Street 2001: 107). While residing on the island, Power wears only trunks, first seen in a full body shot as he dives for pearls. Thus, we could read this outfit as Benjamin's attempt to blend in with the natives, or as the result of a lack of materials available for clothing. Furthermore, it could reflect the island's climate, the costume's functionality and so forth. However, while on the island Carradine remains fully covered by his

Western clothing, thus making the near-naked Power stand out even more. As Paglia states, 'For three hundred years, Greek art is filled with beautiful boys, in stone and bronze', none of whose names we know, but whose 'nudity was polemical. The kouros stands heroically bare in Apollonian externality and visibility. Unlike two-dimensional pharaonic sculptures, he invites the strolling spectator to admire him in the round' (1990: 111). In cinema, the camera does this for the spectator, and not only do we know Power's name due to the more modern medium of cinema, but can view his body from various angles and through different types of shots, his lack of clothing allowing the camera to take in his whole body. This repeated display of Power's exposed body results in a sense of scopophilia in the viewer, which Sarah Street calls 'pleasure in looking; a fascination with the human form' (2001: 107). Thomas Doherty notes that women were 'classical Hollywood's prime movers, the audience most fervently courted and catered to', since, according to *Variety*, they were '"shopping chiefly for men stars and they prefer them with plenty of oomph in all the right places"', which is why *Son of Fury* 'was "such a stick of dynamite at the box office" because the ads "featured Tyrone Power showing off his manly form in a loin cloth"' (1993: 153).

But clothing is also important for Benjamin's character development. Beginning as a stable boy dressed in ragged clothes, he works his way up to the high status where he belongs, as reflected in his clothing. Leaving the island and returning to London to take up his birthright, he dresses like a gentleman and no longer wears the simple working-class clothing that he wore at the beginning. Finding that Isabel has betrayed him and that he truly loves Eve and the simple life on the island, he returns to both at the end. Thus, although Power's body is clothed for the location and his standing at any given time, it is consistently Power's body that is eroticised throughout.

Street notes that scholarship on cinema and costume was only recognised as a legitimate and fruitful area of study at the turn of the century, helping to challenge previously held negative views and opening up new approaches in exploring how costume links to wider debates about film form, *mise en scène*, the costume designer's role and the complex ways of 'reading' film costumes as intertexts and how these representations impacted on audiences (2001: 1). According to Street, many feminists within the academy felt that fashion was one of the chief ways in which women were trapped into gratifying the male gaze (2001: 1). But this can also be applied to men, and in Power's case how his clothing, or lack of, worked within his films and for the cinematic audience's gaze, and this is also overtly true of his next action-adventure film *The Black Swan*.

In Power's third colour film *The Black Swan*, his English pirate Captain Jamie Waring is very different from Benjamin Blake. Although there are several scenes in which Power's bare chest is on display, in the majority of these Jamie is depicted as hypermasculine: desirable, dangerous and active rather than a passive erotic spectacle. It is the most action-filled of all Power's films, with one reviewer calling the concluding fight scene 'as spectacular a sea battle as has been filmed since the birth of the motion picture' (Anon 1943c: 5). It was nominated for three Academy Awards, winning for Best Color Cinematography, and earned $3.5 million in domestic rentals, which made it not only Twentieth Century-Fox's highest earner of 1942, but the first of the studio's films to make over $3 million (Solomon 1988).[3]

Although Power portrays a lusty pirate, the film still includes several lingering shots of his bare torso that give us 'cultural permission to be a voyeur', to borrow a phrase from Susan Bordo's 'Beauty (re)discovers the male body' (2000: 114). In fact, there are times when, unless we divert our eyes from the screen completely, there is nowhere else to look but at Power's face, chest or between the two since nothing else is on-screen to avert our gaze to. Thus, for the most part, Power's lack of clothing here is as important as what he wears in other films. Although entering the film immediately, he is almost unrecognisable with a dirty, unshaven face, hoop earrings and a red bandana covering his head as Jamie and his shipmates engage in a swordfight, pilferer jewels and kidnap women. As he drinks wine from a stolen goblet, it spills down his chin and shirt, and he wipes it off with the back of his hand before refilling the goblet from a barrel. Jamie is gruff, rough and has no respect for women, truly a man's man and, although he also has an eye for the ladies, he has no idea how to romance a woman, unlike many of Power's earlier characters.

The next scene opens with a shirtless Power sweating and being tortured on a rack, several medium shots focusing on his exposed chest while his hands are tied above his head (Figure 6.4). Thus, while Bordo suggests that in the mid-1950s cinematic heroes were 'undressed, racked, whipped, and stripped of their dignity' but 'in a highly eroticized way' (1999: 127), these elements were already present in Power's films of the early 1940s. Jamie's shipmates rescue him, and when Tommy Blue (Thomas Mitchell) cuts him down, Power flexes his muscles to show how long Jamie has been strung

Figure 6.4 Power's bare torso in *The Black Swan* (1942)

up, his body both stiff and painful, but the action also reveals the actor's impressive muscular back and arms to the audience, particularly since his frame fills the screen and it is therefore not just an incidental action. In a two-shot with Mitchell, the young and muscular Power drinks thirstily from a bottle of wine as the older, stouter and plainer man looks on, the contrast particularly noticeable here.

When Lady Margaret Denby (Maureen O'Hara) descends the castle stairs, Jamie immediately walks towards her, takes her by the wrists and holds her forcefully against the wall with brute strength. Attempting to kiss her he says, 'I always sample a bottle of wine before I buy it. Let's have a sip. See if you're worth taking along', and she bites him. He responds by knocking her unconscious with one blow before throwing her over his shoulder with ease. When Captain Henry Morgan (Laird Cregar) arrives, Power comically drops O'Hara on the ground. Cregar's long curls, feathered hat and head-to-toe silks and ruffles draw attention to Power's exposed torso, Morgan telling Jamie to put a shirt on since he looks 'much too naked for a decent Englishman'. However, he is soon shirtless again (and repeatedly thereafter) after returning to the ship.

The pirates inhabit the castle and Jamie takes possession of Margaret's bedroom. Opening her locket containing a photograph of her fiancé Roger Ingram (Edward Ashley), a dandy whose elegant dress stands in direct contrast to Jamie's outfits, Power makes a face and sticks his tongue out comically before blowing a raspberry. When Jamie meets Roger, he knocks him out with one punch and without missing a beat asks Margaret, 'Now tell me, what the devil do you see in this weasel?' as Roger lies prostrate on the ground. The role allows Power a degree of character acting, and he is far more animated and freer on screen than he has been before. Unlike Diego, Jamie's masculinity is never in question, although half an hour into the film, we are given the privileged position of seeing Jamie vulnerable for the first time as he lies alone in bed. Sniffing Margaret's pillow and without saying a word, Power's face reveals Jamie's genuine feelings for her, which he hides from both her and his shipmates, thereby keeping up his façade as a heartless, lusty pirate. During this scene, Power is filmed from below and as he inhales, his expanding chest fills the screen.

Jamie's desirability is underpinned by Tommy informing him that 'hundreds of wenches' are 'ready to leap into your arms if you give them a whistle'. The day before her wedding, Jamie tries to romance Margaret by telling her, 'Unfortunately I have a tender feeling for you. Oh, I'm as annoyed with the fact as you are' and calls her as 'arrogant and silly a wench as I've ever run afoul on', whom he wants to strangle one moment and marry the next. When she refuses to go with him, he takes her by force. Grabbing her arm, he puts his cape over her head, pushes her to the ground, sits on top of her and gags her with her own scarf. Telling her to lie still or he will break her skull, he throws her into his carriage and rides off, hardly the romantic gestures we are used to seeing in Hollywood cinema.

When Captain Billy Leech (George Sanders) boards their ship, Jamie introduces Margaret as his wife, and when Leech insists they sail with him they must share a cabin so as not to arouse suspicion, much to Margaret's protest. Jamie sets up a hammock to sleep in, but when he hears movement outside the door he jumps out, pulls it down and begins taking off his shirt. Margaret panics when he climbs into bed with her, but he covers her mouth and tells her to 'keep still or you'll get your throat cut'. Lying down, he puts his arm around her just as Leech creeps into their room. As the moonlight shines in on Power's shirtless form, his dark skin and large frame contrasts with O'Hara's porcelain skin and delicate body and makes him appear extremely manly. The scene is extremely erotically charged, particularly since the couple is not married.

Before killing Leech in the final sea battle, Jamie is stabbed in the stomach and Margaret sees him as more human and heroic than before. Although Morgan apologises for Jamie kidnapping her, she lies and says she came of her own free will, thus proving she has fallen for Jamie. At the film's close, Jamie stumbles onto the deck, clutching his stomach before Margaret chastises him for getting out of bed. Now standing as equals, she wears trousers, a shirt and her hair is loose, no longer in frilly dresses and elaborate hairstyles. Margaret uses Jamie's own line about sampling a bottle of wine when they first met, before she instigates their first real kiss. When he enquires, 'What, no bites?' she grabs him, throws her arms around his neck and moves in for a second kiss. Although she feigned disinterest at the start, his words evidently made an impression since she now recites them back perfectly to him.

Bordo suggests that the bodies of male stars of the 1950s, such as William Holden, Paul Newman and Burt Lancaster, were eroticised far more than those during the 'sexual revolution' of the 1960s and 1970s (1999: 110). Yet as shown, Power's body was repeatedly exposed in the 1940s with prolonged shots of his bare, glistening torso and attention being drawn to his crotch and buttocks in tight-fitting costumes in *Brigham Young*, *The Mark of Zorro*, *Blood and Sand*, *Son of Fury* and *The Black Swan*, the duration of time his body is on display increasing with each film. As the last of his pre-war action-adventure films, *The Black Swan* presents Power at his roughest and manliest, adding greater depth to his star image than any of his post-war action-adventure films would do, especially the three historical European films he made upon returning from the war: *Captain from Castile*, *Prince of Foxes* and *The Black Rose*.

European post-war adventures

Historical films present contemporary audiences with past models of masculinity, recreated by twentieth-century men and exploring how they measure up with the past. As Cohan notes, male sexual identity on screen is always the effect of an actor performing a historically specific version of masculinity (1997: xviii). Likewise, Ulrike Wiethaus suggests that examining men's past identities can aid in more easily understanding 'present gender roles as constructs and future definitions of gender as rich and open-ended'

(1996: 48). The masculine stereotypes that emerged in the Middle Ages 'abound in contemporary culture' through toys, comics and movies that are 'still powerful enough to subtly shape gender norms and expectations' (Wiethaus 1996: 48).

After the genre's 'past heydays' of 1920–30 and 1934–42, Casper calls 1945–62 the action-adventure film's third flourish and its climax when Gable, Flynn and Power emerged as 'end of career adventurers', and 'aging actors' Robert Taylor, John Wayne and Louis Hayward reinvented themselves as adventurers (2007: 161). Additionally, Casper suggests, 'a band of unlined faces and taut bodies . . . helped to keep the genre flying'; examples are Richard Widmark (born the same year as Power), Stewart Granger, Alan Ladd, Burt Lancaster and Victor Mature (all a year older than Power); and Cornel Wilde (two years older than Power). The only actor he lists who was born after the 1910s was Tony Curtis, thus making the others all around the same age as 'aging actor' Taylor (2007: 162).

Captain from Castile, based on Samuel Shellabarger's 1945 novel of the same name and set in Spain in 1518, was Power's first post-war action-adventure film. Although the budget was originally set at $2 million, bad weather in Mexico resulted in location shooting taking months longer than planned and the budget more than doubled to $4.4 million. Thus, even though it was the studio's second highest grossing film that year, it still made a loss (Solomon 1988: 66). As Zanuck highlights in a memo to director Henry King, it was not a failure because it was a bad film, 'our failure was that we spent more . . . than the market could afford' (Zanuck 1993: 164).

The film opens with Power's Pedro De Vargas on horseback in the distance, before he rides up to the camera and stops, allowing the audience to admire his finery. Coming to the aid of waitress Catana Perez (Jean Peters in her cinematic debut), who is being tormented by two men and large dogs, he gives her a ride to the inn where she works. Telling her to hold on to him as they go over a wall, she grips his chest for much longer than required, clearly enjoying the moment, and at the inn she stands behind his table and watches while he drinks and chats with Juan Garcia (Lee J. Cobb). While Pedro appears indifferent to Catana, she is obviously smitten, watching him as he leaves. Pedro's betrothed is the refined and elegantly dressed Luisa De Carvajal (Barbara Lawrence), a very different character from Catana. As they sit in her garden, he moves to sit down on the bench beside her; his eyes tracing her face as he tenderly confesses his love, but she looks away. Although feigning aloofness, she starts breathing heavily as he moves in closer before a chaperon interrupts, informing him that a gentleman must keep his distance. Watching him leave, Lawrence's eyes are dreamy and she smiles widely as she excitedly asks, 'Did you notice how his eyes light up when he smiles?' The older lady replies, rather understatedly, 'Yes, he's not unattractive', while also watching him leave.

Like Jesse James, Pedro starts off as a kind and honourable man who is close to his family. When his family are falsely arrested and his twelve-year old sister dies under torture, his face takes on a hardened and murderous look, his eyes filling with hatred as he stares unblinking at the man responsible: Diego De Silva (John Sutton); moving his head only fractionally, Power ominously keeps his eyes locked on Sutton as guards lead him to a prison cell. When Juan learns of Pedro's predicament, he enters the cell, unties him and gives him weapons. When De Silva subsequently comes to gloat, a swordfight ensues in the tiny cell and Pedro overpowers De Silva. As De Silva begs for forgiveness, there is a close-up of the sweating, dirty and unshaven Power as Pedro informs him he has one minute left to live and to use it thinking about the girl he has killed. Pedro then relentlessly runs his sword through De Silva with no remorse.

Catana confesses her love for Pedro to an old professor who lends her a ring he claims is magical and will make Pedro love her back. In the following scene the pair engage in a sensual, almost animalistic Spanish dance by a campfire, which delights the diegetic audience. Throughout the dance, Power runs his hands over Peters's body, their faces almost touching repeatedly until the climax in which he bends her body backwards over his knee and kisses her passionately. Although Catana has long wished for this to happen, she pushes him away and runs into the woods, since she blames the ring and does not believe his feelings are true. Following her, he announces his love and wish to marry her. When she tells him about the ring, he ardently kisses her face, telling her he came of his own free will, before kissing her lips. Enforcing his virility, Peters lets her entire body melt and they passionately kiss again before the fadeout.

When it is revealed that De Silva did not die and has married Luisa, Pedro glares at him with the same hatred as before, time having alleviated none of his loathing. Power stands up and spits his words out to show Pedro's contempt for De Silva, pointing at him and calling him a 'fiend without honour. An assassin of infants.' When a shadowy figure murders De Silva as he sleeps, Pedro is accused and sentenced to death. Sitting in a jail cell with Catana, her arms around his neck, he speaks calmly showing he is resigned to the fact he is going to die. However, it is revealed that

Pedro did not kill De Silva when he notes in a steady and controlled voice that he is being hanged 'for a crime I didn't commit'. To save him the humiliation of being hanged, Catana stabs Pedro in the chest just before he is cleared of the crime. Pedro lives, however, and the film ends as they head to the New World where all men will be equal, Catana holding their new baby, a symbol of hope for the future.

Solomon suggests that, after the 'disastrous episode' with *Captain from Castile*, Zanuck did not want any more films costing more than $2 million. One way of doing this was to cut the budget on Power's next action-adventure film, *Prince of Foxes* (1949). By forgoing Technicolor and filming in black and white, Solomon suggests that this also limited the film's box office potential 'since audiences were growing accustomed to their period pictures in glorious, vivid, Technicolor' (1988: 73). Charles Higham and Joel Greenberg call 1949 'Hollywood's lowest point for some time' since only twenty-two features were in production, around half the usual output (1968: 17). This was also true of Power's creative output, since *Prince of Foxes* was his only release in 1949. Since 1936 he had made an average of three films a year, starring in an impressive five features in 1937 and 1939. Furthermore, aside from his absence from the screen during his active war duty, the only other years he made one film were in 1943 before his active war duty (*Crash Dive*), and 1946 after his active war duty (*The Razor's Edge*).

Set in 1500, and co-starring Orson Welles and Wanda Hendrix, the film did nothing to challenge Power's star image or career trajectory and can almost be seen as a backward step to *The Mark of Zorro* almost a decade earlier, or an inferior version of *Captain from Castile*. Once more Power's agility and athletic body are displayed in tight-fitting costumes that, along with the location shots, were key to the film's visual appeal but very little else. Furthermore, given the way that actors are required to deliver their lines in historical action-adventure films, Power appears more stilted in this genre than any other, but this was by no means a problem unique to him.

Higham and Greenberg suggest that the reduction in output reflected the fact that 'the old days of vast grosses, with Hollywood movies supplying most of the world's entertainment, was gone for good' (1968: 17). This dilemma can be applied to Power and his standing as a leading star, especially since he was now being cast in forgettable films making huge losses. It reflected the fact that Twentieth Century-Fox no longer saw him as their top money-making star, and he would soon leave the studio to become an independent actor and producer when he set up Copa Productions. Furthermore, Higham and Greenberg suggest that the 1940s can be viewed as 'the apotheosis of the US feature film, its last great show of confidence and skill before it virtually succumbed artistically to the paralysing effects of bigger and bigger screens' (1968: 18), which could also relate to Power. It was also around this time that the star system, in which Power had been a key player since the start of his career, collapsed.

Hollywood discovered Europe around 1950 which, along with the advent of television, was the result of increased international travel after World War II, meaning that cinematic audiences were no longer 'satisfied by studio replicas of foreign locales' (Davis 1993: 274). Ronald L. Davis notes that several studios had large sums of money frozen in Europe at this time, which they used up by making pictures there (1993: 274). Produced in Italy, *Prince of Foxes* was one such film (as was *The Black Rose*, which was filmed in Morocco and England), as part of Twentieth Century-Fox's 'steady production schedule in Europe', which invested blocked earnings and helped the studio deplete the money it had frozen in England, Italy and France (Steinhart 2019: 32). Daniel Steinhart points out that, in many of these productions, real locales are used as characters pursue their goals, the film's storylines of movement driving 'the visualization of authentic foreign locations', thus making the advancement through environments 'an integral part of a film's unfolding drama' (2019: 182). Steinhart notes that Cinecittà in Rome was Italian filmmaking's most important studio, and where Hollywood made its Italian-based productions. Benito Mussolini had opened the studio in 1937, and it became one of the largest in Europe before the German army used it as a shelter during World War II. It later served as a munitions depot and camp for displaced persons until 1947, when it began making films again; a year later *Prince of Foxes* was shot there (Steinhart 2019: 83).

Introduced wearing a similar hairstyle and clothing from *Captain from Castile*, Power utters his first two lines with an arrogant grin, making wisecracks that seem out of place at the funeral he is attending. Power's Andrea Orsini is conceited, is an outlaw like Jesse James and has adopted an alias, like Diego Vega, so that he can pass for a gentleman. He has two love interests, Angela Borgia (Marina Berti), cousin of Cesare Borgia (Welles), whom he kisses passionately before leaving behind, and Camilla Verano (Hendrix), whom he attempts to charm with a gift before discovering that she is married. Their brief initial meeting piques her interest, however, and she admits to finding him interesting before later telling him he would not be easy to forget. At this second meeting the pair stare at each other until they are interrupted by her much older husband, Count Marc Antonio Verano (Felix Aylmer). As Angela looks on jealously, Cesare demands that Andrea make Camilla fall in love with him before they dispose of her husband. Andrea really falls in love with Camilla and has a change of heart, joining sides with the Count against Borgia and his army. A bloody battle ensues, and the old man dies of his injuries, leaving the young couple free to come together.

Andrea's mother, who has not seen him for years, looks at him and calls him 'so beautiful', a common phrase used to describe Power by this point. After Cesare has Andrea imprisoned, his mother and Camilla are horrified to see him looking like a shell of his former beautiful, virile self. Dressed in filthy, tattered clothes, Andrea is barely able to walk or stand and unable to speak. With his hair over his face and a vacant stare, Power strongly resembles his incarnation as the geek at the end of *Nightmare Alley*. Cesare gloats and demands that Camilla look, informing her that this is Andrea 'out of masquerade, in the clothes proper to his station'. In the film's most disturbing scene, Andrea must pretend that his eyes are being gouged out, resulting in Power making inhumane noises, again like the geek. Later escaping from jail, and restored to his former glory, he engages in swordplay and physical fights, proving his strength and masculinity by taking on several men at once and being victorious.

Paul McDonald suggests that, while terms such as 'brand identity' and 'brand personality' are used in brand theory to link brands to people, 'movie stardom flips that relationship, making the person a brand, a collection of signs and meanings used to sell films' (2019: 3). Thus, even though a film like *Prince of Foxes* lacks uniqueness in its plot or delivery and is, by all accounts, a standard Hollywood film of the era, the 'Power brand' is being used to sell it. It is through the image of Power as swashbuckler and object of the erotic gaze, and therefore on the basis of his constructed and recognisable star image, that the film is marketed.

The Black Rose (1950), another European adventure co-starring Welles, directly followed *Prince of Foxes*, and Power's character, Walter of Gurnie, is another Englishman. An Oxford University student, Walter abandons his studies and talks of being disillusioned by his country, thus almost embodying a medieval version of Clive Briggs from *This Above All*. Receiving an Academy Award nomination for Best Color Costume Design, the film took $2.65 million at the US box office and performed well overseas, especially in Britain (Smith 2018: 122). Gary A. Smith notes that the film's director, Henry Hathaway, 'had only the highest praise for Power, whom he felt was a "perfect star" who never complained and was always prepared to give his best' (2018: 120).

By now, Power's beauty was evidently an in-joke, and although cinematic techniques like framing and lighting were often used to show off his good looks to audiences, his beauty is repeatedly mentioned in the dialogue of this film. Upon meeting Maryam (Cecile Aubry), she enquires if all English people are 'as beautiful as you are'. Looking annoyed, he points to his friend Tristram Griffith (Jack Hawkins) and says, 'Ask him, he's the beautiful one', but she laughs and replies, 'Oh no, I think you're much more beautiful than he is. You look just like ...' before he embarrassingly cuts her off as if his masculinity is being undermined by such discussions of his beauty, a word mostly reserved for describing women. Maryam later calls him a 'tall beautiful Englishman', and even Tristram calls him 'very beautiful' and recalls that 'he looked more beautiful than ever'. Like Annabella's Toni in *Suez*, Maryam throws herself at Walter from the start, eventually coming to him as he sleeps and asking him to pretend to love her. As she sits on the floor by his bed, he strokes her hair and they kiss, but again any eroticism of the moment is cut short when Tristram wakes up and begins talking to them.

Power's body is again repeatedly put on display, and in one scene a woman appears, examines him at close range by walking around him and then exits. While a group of men engage in conversation in their tent, each is fully dressed except for Power, who is shirtless and drying his wet chest with a towel. He then puts on a white shirt, but its extremely low neckline means a large area of his chest is still exposed. Similarly, when Walter is forced to walk across a thin rope with blades on either side, while men aim spears at him, Power is again bare-chested. His near-nakedness is particularly apparent since the other men mostly wear long coats and fur hats. Moreover, Power is most exposed in this film, and perhaps across his whole cinematic career, as he sits in a bath soaping his body, his chest and legs clearly visible through the water. Thus, while *The Black Rose* may not have advanced Power's screen image, it reinforced his position as an object of the erotic gaze and proved that he still 'had it' fifteen years into his career.

Independent adventurer

As Jackie Byars highlights, in the 1950s studios moved away from production and concentrated on distribution, with independent production decreasing costs by up to 50 per cent. All major studios, except MGM, drastically reduced their production activities, thereby 'eliminating the stock-company system and concentrating on aiding independent productions, which they would later distribute' (1991: 87). Although Power's first independent production away from Twentieth Century-Fox had been Universal's *The Mississippi Gambler*, his next feature, the action-adventure *King of the Khyber Rifles* (1953) was released by his old home studio.

Along with *Captain from Castile*, Casper calls *King of the Khyber Rifles* 'revisionist, undermining a long-standing, entrenched perspective about history, politics, societal issues, and cultures', in which characters 'voice their critique of colonialism, especially its inherent racism … or characters are shown to be victims of racism' (2007: 163). Set in India in 1857 during the 'hundredth year of British rule', Power's Captain Alan King (the 'King' of the title) is a soldier of mixed race who is fighting on the British side. When Alan opens his pocket watch and reveals photographs of his parents (the one of his 'father' being Power with a moustache), he informs his colleagues that his father was an English Protestant and his mother an Indian Muslim. The white British soldiers discriminate against him from this point forward, and one even moves out of their shared quarters. However, the Brigadier General's daughter, Susan Maitland (Terry Moore), falls for Alan and actively pursues him. In words almost identical to Edwina's in *The Rains Came* fourteen years previously when she told Rama, 'I've done everything but fall at your feet and you haven't even blinked', Susan informs Alan 'I've done everything in my power to make you aware of me, but you haven't even blinked'.

Barred from attending the Queen's birthday party because of his ethnicity, Susan leaves the party and goes to his quarters. Given the number of times Power has danced on-screen with women, it seems ironic when she asks, 'You do dance, don't you, captain?' and he replies, 'On occasion', and they dance outside, their silhouettes clear against the sky. Susan later follows Alan when he rides away from the base, but a storm approaches and they take shelter in ruins. As Alan tells a story about his childhood, depicted in Power's familiar steady and controlled tone, Moore turns towards him, staring into his face as she begins breathing quickly and touching his arm. The two almost kiss but he hears horses approaching and they are shot at, interrupting this tender moment.

Much later, Power lies in bed wearing a white t-shirt that emphasises his broad chest and darkened skin. His face depicts conflicting emotions in this private moment shared with audiences, just as with

Jamie in *The Black Swan*. Susan comes to his room to confess her love, and although he tries to send her away, she asks him to hold her and they share a kiss before he admits his love for her. The scene is shot mostly in medium close-up, moonlight shining in as Power's muscular arms engulf Moore, their size and age differences making him look particularly manly and mature here. In her autobiography, Moore calls Power 'the most gorgeous man in movies', but, reflecting Hathaway's words, she notes that there was 'more to him than a beautiful face' since he was an 'actors' actor' and the 'ultimate "giving actor"', who was always on time and always prepared (2008: 84).

Although Solomon notes that Zanuck did not want any more budgets going over $2 million, at $3.57 million *Untamed* had the highest budget of 1955 (1988: 117). Power again made this film for Twentieth Century-Fox, and his *Rawhide* co-star Susan Hayward was his leading lady. The film begins in Ireland in 1847 when Hayward's Katie O'Neill knocks Power's Paul Van Riebeck off his horse during a fox hunt. Power's bright red hunting jacket provides the main focal point, especially since Hayward is dressed in muted colours. Smiling, she looks him up and down and exclaims that she has finally got him to speak to her, but in anger he mounts her horse and rides off, leaving her to walk his lame horse back to the stable.

Attending a dance in her grand house, Hayward wears a green satin dress that reappears throughout the film, while Power is dressed in historical evening clothes comprising of a ruffled white shirt, fitted black jacket, white bow tie and white gloves. Following the dance, Katie ascends the staircase to find Paul at the top. He stares at her angrily before telling her, 'You're a killer', and slowly stepping towards her before adding, 'You're a beautiful, murderous killer', hardly finishing the last word before he grabs and kisses her passionately, his sexual desire for her proving stronger than his dislike. Paul is visiting Ireland to purchase horses from Katie's father, and when he prepares to return to South Africa she expresses her desire to go with him, but he tells her the land is too dangerous and untamed for her.

Despite Power's being the top-billed star, he exits the film in the first ten minutes and does not return until over twenty minutes later, when he is seen for less than two minutes sleeping outdoors and sporting a thick, dark beard and dirty clothes, contrasting with his immaculate presentation in Ireland. Paul returns only intermittently throughout the many years the film spans. This may be Katie's story, but it is also about her obsession with Paul and his being behind every decision she makes.

Hayward's voiceover tells of the blight that came to Ireland that killed many. She married Shawn Kildare (John Justin) and their child was born on the ship to South Africa, which they took to start a new life. Shawn is killed during a Zulu attack and Paul re-enters the film by riding in and stopping the attack. As a group gathers around Paul to thank him, Power stands nearest the camera, his hand on his hip as he dominates the frame. The sleeves of his white shirt are rolled up past his elbows, showing off his tanned skin, and he still wears a heavy beard. When an older lady shouts his name, he rushes over and embraces her with a wide grin, his white teeth suddenly shining through his dark beard. He squeezes her tightly before catching a glimpse of Katie, instantaneously letting the smile fade but continuing to loosely hold the woman's arm. An outdoor dance follows, and the newly widowed Katie puts on her green dress from Ireland. Clean shaven and wearing a crisp white shirt, Paul is dancing with a girl when Katie pulls him away. She tells him that she has only ever loved him and that everything she has ever done over the years was for him, despite their spending very little time together in Ireland. He admits his love for her too and they kiss, but when they emerge much later from the woods, suggestively laughing together and holding hands, Kurt Hout (Richard Egan) who is besotted by Katie, immediately attacks Paul with a whip. Paul pushes Katie to safety and a violent fight ensues in which both men are injured. Paul is the victor when he brutally strangles Kurt with his whip until he passes out. Power's white shirt is now ripped and bloodstained as he walks away with Hayward.

The pair share a much more passionate love affair than they did in *Rawhide* and are seen kissing repeatedly. One scene resembling a form of foreplay sees Power massage Hayward's neck with one hand, the other placed on her waist as she moans pleasurably and whispers that he has 'wonderful hands' with 'magic in them'. Asking him to say he is happy with her, Hayward lies down on the grass and adds, 'Say it'. Power looks down, runs his hand up her arm and says 'Alright. I'll say it', before forcefully kissing her as the scene fades out, suggesting that he will demonstrate his happiness without words. The couple lives together but are unmarried, with many fadeouts where they passionately embrace, pointedly indicating they are about to engage in sexual intercourse. When Power exits the film for another twenty minutes in screen time, but several years in the narrative, Katie has Paul's child out of wedlock.

Returning, Paul is shocked to see how much Katie's oldest son has grown, but he has never met her other son. The younger boy has a splinter in his finger, which Paul cheerfully removes with his knife before asking his name. When the boy replies 'Paul', Power gives his most emotive scene of the film. Kneeling down and smiling at the child, his elbow propped on his knee for support, as soon as he hears the name he knows the boy is his. Power takes him by the shoulders and looks into his face, taking the boy's face in both his hands and turning it up to get a better look before their nanny calls them. Watching them leave he immediately turns to Katie. His face is stony as he slowly stands up, blinks once and asks why she did not tell him. They argue and she tells him to get out, but they are reunited in the end after he saves her from bandits. Placing a ring on her finger, they ride off to begin a new life as a family, Paul's newly discovered son on his knee.

The last adventure: *Abandon Ship!*

The last action-adventure film Power made was *Abandon Ship!* (1957), produced by his own production company, Copa Productions, and distributed by Columbia. Released the year before he died, it was filmed in Shepperton Studios in Surrey, England, while Power was appearing on the British stage. Power portrays Alec Holmes, the executive officer of a luxury liner that sinks in mid-ocean after hitting a mine. Although there are twenty-six survivors, the only lifeboat holds twelve, and after the captain dies Holmes finds himself in charge of deciding who lives and who dies.

The film begins with an explosion and people screaming, a voiceover telling us that the luxury cruiser sank in seven minutes, and of the 1,156 onboard, 1,119 perished and thirty-seven initially survived. Close-ups of wreckage and a shark fin are shown before we see someone swimming towards the camera. Two men and a woman, looking in shock, sit on a piece of wood as the arm of the swimmer appears on screen. It is a man's arm, and as he pulls himself onto the wood it is revealed to be Power, who collapses face first onto the wood, his hair matted to his head and his dirty white t-shirt and trousers clinging to his body. Alec takes charge and tries to help them before rescuing a swimming dog. One of the men notices someone else swimming and, despite his own exhaustion, Alec dives in to rescue them. It is Mai Zetterling's Julie White, the ship's nurse, whom he obviously knows intimately, and although there are no romantic encounters between them in the boat, other than looks and an occasional touch, it is mentioned that they are in love. As he tries to avert a shark's path towards them, they are called over to an already full lifeboat with people in the water on either side and the fatally wounded captain inside, who puts Alec in charge before dying. Power puts on the captain's jacket and begins putting on his cap before stopping midway and slowly lowering it. Looking at the cap before touching the front delicately, he places it on the captain's covered body and takes a long look. After sliding the captain's body into the water, Power throws the hat in too before sliding over to take his place at the head of the boat. This is where he will remain for much of the film.

Alec appears calm and collected, taking charge and issuing orders since he believes an SOS call went through and they will be rescued in five or six hours. When 'Sparks' (John Stratton) informs him that no distress call went up, Alec grabs him by the throat before being restrained by Julie and some others. Sitting down, his head in his hands for a prolonged period, Power lets his whole body collapse in defeat before moving his hand down to cover his mouth as Sparks explains why he did not make the call. He repeats this action when the dying Kelly (Lloyd Nolan), his old friend, jumps overboard and cannot be saved. While a storm brews, Alec realises that for any of them to survive they must rid the boat of weaklings and the dying since they are a dead weight. Power's voice cracks with emotion as he gives orders for them to be passed over the side but must regulate it to stay firm since Alec cannot afford to show weakness.

Romina Power quotes Richard Sale, the film's writer and director, as saying that a journalist 'mentioned how "ugly" Ty was in that film', but noting that he 'was made up, and, for most of the film, he was playing the part of a man who was suffering', adding 'I think it was wonderful that he accepted looking so horrible. I don't know how many other Hollywood actors would have accepted it' (2014: 274). However, Power looks far from 'ugly' or 'horrible', and is still fully recognisable, especially at the start of the film. Indeed, he had looked far worse on screen, particularly near the end of *Nightmare Alley* and *Prince of Foxes*, and the other actors, including leading lady Zetterling could be deemed to be just as 'horrible' with their hair matted to their heads, sallow complexions and dark circles under their eyes to illustrate their characters' prolonged suffering, lack of sleep and starvation. Even so, passenger Edith Middleton (Moira Lister), who repeatedly refers to Alec sarcastically as 'brave captain', cannot take her eyes off him.

In a particularly shocking scene, Michael Faroni (Eddie Byrne) throws a knife at Alec's chest before being shot with a flare gun and screaming as he falls into the water. Severely injured, Alec reiterates that there are no exceptions to dead weight onboard before launching himself over the side, but is pulled back in just as a ship approaches. The passengers then turn against Alec, claiming he forced them to carry out his commands at gunpoint. Reaching the ship, Power climbs partially up the ladder, looks back at the lifeboat and winces to show Alec's agony from his wound. A voiceover states that the film was based on actual events and that Holmes was convicted of murder but given the minimum sentence of six months because of the 'unusual circumstances'. The audience is then directly addressed with, 'If you had been a member of the jury how would you have voted: guilty or innocent?' – the final three words appearing on-screen as Power climbs out of shot.

In an unusual cinematic trailer, Power stands in front of a plain wall and small window, dressed in a suit and tie, and introduces the film. Although initially noting that he 'portrays Alex Holmes', thus presenting himself as an actor discussing his role, he soon 'becomes' Holmes when he adds, 'it is my fearful responsibility to decide' who lives or dies. He notes that the film's theme 'created considerable controversy. Was Holmes justified in doing what he did or was he guilty of murder?', before requesting viewers to 'write and tell me what you think' once they have seen the film, with the writer of the winning letter receiving an all-expenses paid trip to Hollywood courtesy of Columbia. Power states that information about the competition is 'in the lobby of this theatre', and asks the audience to contact him personally, adding, 'Please let me hear from you soon'. Although it is doubtful that Power would actually read these letters, as one of the film's producers it is possible. With his hands in his pockets in a casual and friendly pose, he concludes with 'Thank you, goodbye', in the recognisable Power voice and with a familiar smile.[4]

Based on a real-life case from April 1842, *Abandon Ship!* is clearly set in contemporary times given the clothing and hairstyles of the cast. The Holmes trial took place in Pennsylvania more than a century earlier after an American ship, the *William Brown*, had left Liverpool, England, with eighty-two crew and passengers, thus much smaller than the film's cruiser. The trial's chief charge was manslaughter, with the court holding that self-preservation was not always a defence for homicide, and Holmes receiving a $20 fine (which, with inflation is $627.34 in 2020) and six months in jail. Oddly, the year before the trial, Power's famous great-grandfather William Grattan Tyrone Power, the Irish actor and comedian who was first to act professionally as 'Tyrone Power', had died at sea at the age of forty-three, the same age Power was when he made the film, which was the year before his own untimely death at forty-four.

Notes

1. Other nominations included Best Music for Alfred Newman's original score. Newman first won the award for *Alexander's Ragtime Band* and received another thirty-six nominations, three of which were for other Power action-adventure films (*The Mark of Zorro, The Black Swan* and *Captain from Castile*).
2. The Library of Congress 'Complete National Film Registry Listing' https://www.loc.gov/programs/national-film-preservation-board/film-registry/complete-national-film-registry-listing/ (accessed 6 June 2019).
3. Although the Betty Grable musical *Springtime in the Rockies* (Irving Cummings, 1942) also made over $3 million that year (Solomon 1988).
4. The advertisement can be viewed on YouTube at https://www.youtube.com/watch?v=inb5GRFoTck (accessed 4 January 2020).

Chapter 7

Power off-screen

Powerful publicity

Power was a cinematic star whose looks remained a vital component of his image throughout his career and a primary reason why he became a star so quickly; therefore, the dominant texts for exploring his star persona have, of course, been his films. As John Ellis points out, the cinematic work of film stars is the main reason for their stardom (1982: 91), while Richard de Cordova notes the principal importance of actors' screen performances results in their being known as 'movie stars' rather than, for example, 'magazine stars' (1990: ii). Bruce Babington declares that performers are 'ultimately dependent' on their films but proposes that stardom has extratextual dimensions (2001: 2), echoing Dyer's suggestion that studying a star image must undoubtedly include the performer's on- and off-screen presence (1979).

Having examined Power's on-screen career in the preceding chapters, this chapter uses extra-filmic texts to explore the construction and development of his off-screen image. The careful manufacture of star images was a device used by studios to attract audiences to films, and ultimately sell tickets. In the words of Maltby, at its height, the publicity machine almost had 'the status of a peripheral industry in its own right' with publicity generated around stars' off-screen lives designed to complement and play upon their screen images (1995: 89). This was certainly true of Power, who received extensive publicity from very early in his career, with fan magazines depicting his off-screen life in ways that often resonated with his on-screen persona, particularly in the 1930s. Additionally, while his professional acting career began in the theatre in 1933, he returned to regular stage work in the 1950s in a move that was mostly well received by critics. Given the instability of Hollywood's studio and star systems, it is noteworthy that Power remained under contract to Twentieth Century-Fox for almost two decades, a longevity reflected in the volume of publicity and promotion he received.

Power in the press

While not a common method of film analysis, the study of fan magazines emerged as an important area of star scholarship at the turn of the century, aiding in demonstrating how stars were presented to fans in different timeframes (see McLean 2004; Slide 2010; Jeffers McDonald 2013; Vincendeau 2013; Higashi 2014; Kelly 2019). As I have noted elsewhere, while in recent decades VHS, DVD, Blu-ray and, most recently, internet streaming sites supply instant access to film texts, historical audiences lacked the ability to view films outside movie theatres. Thus during Power's lifetime, magazines were a common and inexpensive way fans could 'gain access to, and engage with, stars outside of their screen work', providing a source they could keep returning to (Kelly 2019: 15).

Fan magazines comprised of a selection of articles, photographs and features. These included film stills, which provided a tie-in with a performer's screen work, professional studio portraits to be hung on walls or framed and 'candid' shots of stars depicting their off-screen lives. The number of times a star appeared on a magazine cover, received a full-page portrait or had an article dedicated to them usually reflected their popularity at the time, while showcasing performers for whom studios wanted to generate exposure. Likewise, since publishers wanted to sell their magazines, creating alluring front covers would encourage regular readers to stay faithful to their publication while attracting potential buyers scanning newsstands or shelves. Power appeared as a cover star from as early as 1937, continuing to regularly grace the cover of international publications in countries like the US, UK, Italy, France, Belgium and Brazil throughout his career and even after his death.

Bachelor days

In terms of constructing stardom, Sumiko Higashi sees fan magazines being as important as films (2014: 17). In the US in the 1930s there were around twenty fan magazines published, which boasted a circulation of between 200,000 and one million. The most popular were *Photoplay*, *Motion Picture* and *Modern Screen*, which all featured Power as the cover star more than once as well as in numerous articles inside. As he was often depicted on-screen, *Photoplay*'s December 1938 cover image presents a smiling Power dressed in a tuxedo. Exactly eight years later, the December 1946 issue carried an almost identical cover, only this time Power's bowtie was black instead of white. A more serious and sultry Power in a modern suit graced the April 1940 cover. He was *Motion Picture's* cover star alongside Sonja Henie in October 1937 and Alice Faye in July 1939, and alone in January 1938 and October 1946, when he was also the cover star for rival publication *Modern Screen*. He further appeared on the cover of *Modern Screen* alone in December 1947, with Loretta Young in August 1937 and with Henie in March 1938. Although the latter shows the pair in costume for *Thin Ice*, the cover's tagline relates to Power's off-screen life by asking 'Whom will Tyrone Power marry?' (Lewi 1938). Given the accompanying image, the reader is to assume that it is Henie and, indeed, the article of the same name inside mentions her throughout as a rival to Janet Gaynor for Power's affection. Two months earlier, *Photoplay* had explored this love triangle from the other side in 'How Tyrone Power stole the lonely heart of Janet Gaynor' (Hayes 1938). Thus, just as Power's on-screen characters regularly had at least two women vying for his attention, according to the fan magazines, this was also true in his private life and publications incessantly wrote about his love life and marital status.

As early as June 1937, *Movie Mirror* published 'The real truth about the Sonja Henie–Tyrone Power–Loretta Young triangle' (Madden 1937), while the following month *Modern Screen's* 'Not too many kisses' explored Power's on- and off-screen romances with these women, pondering whether he would marry Henie imminently (Maddox 1937). The same month, *Hollywood's* 'They carry a torch for Tyrone' added Faye to the mix by suggesting that she too was in love with Power (Lang 1937). The three women are mentioned as potential love partners in *Hollywood's* October 1937 issue, only here Power's mother (apparently) tells readers what she thinks of them in 'Tyrone Power's mother sizes up his girls' (Camp 1937). Coincidently, Power's regular on-screen pairings with Young, Henie and Faye throughout the decade would benefit from this on-screen/off-screen nexus. Although Power and Gaynor both starred in *Ladies in Love*, their characters did not interact, nor did they ever co-star as romantic partners. *Radio Guide's* 'Evolution of an idol' dedicates a section to Power's 'girls', including Henie, Young and Gaynor but also several old girlfriends from back home whom, it suggests, he often calls for dates (Reeves 1937), thus suggesting that Power may end up with an ordinary girl just like the readers.

From 1937 to 1939, marriage, or its lack, became the most prevalent aspect of articles on Power before he married Annabella. His lack of a committed relationship, but the thrill of romantic pairings, allowed Power to continue appealing to (female) readers as a bachelor not yet ready for marriage, and therefore still 'on the market'. This is exhibited in *Movie Mirror*'s 'Tyrone Power's bachelor guide to Hollywood', which explores where he buys his clothes, his favourite eateries and 'his girls'. As well as the four aforementioned actresses, this article adds Phyllis Brooks to Power's list of frequent dates (Spensley 1937). Likewise, in November 1937 *Radio Stars*' 'Tyrone power would like to marry, but—' quotes the actor as saying he wants to wait five years before marriage (Rogers 1937), while in August 1938 *Modern Screen* published the similarly titled 'Why should I marry?', in which Power defends his bachelor status. Opening with author Gladys Hall stating that Power answered 'no' when asked if he was going to marry, she hyperbolically calls this a 'revelation' and *the* 'good news of 1938 [which] burst upon a waiting world' (Hall 1938). His desire to wait five years was repeated in *Movie Mirror*'s 'The woman Tyrone Power will marry' from October 1938 (Lee 1938) and, although claiming she is a hypothetical woman at this stage, the article suggests that Power will marry within a year and that it will probably be to an actress. Accompanying the article is a still from *Suez*, the film Power was making at the time and where he met Annabella. According to the article, Power's main reason for getting married would be to have a son who could carry on his theatrical legacy, stories of his family heritage coming second only to his love life in fan magazines.

Annabella and war

One of the first articles to romantically link Power and Annabella was *Picture Play*'s 'Is Ty Power on a new love quest?', also from October 1938, which includes a photograph of the couple at dinner and calls her the '"last lady" in his life' (Fitch 1938). In April 1939, *Movie Mirror*'s 'Tyrone loves 'em and leaves 'em' considers 'all those lovely girls he has NOT married' while flitting 'from Sonja to Loretta to Janet to Alice to Annabella', the latter labelled as his 'newest crush', therefore suggesting that the relationship is not serious. Writer Wilson Brown links Power to four other women who are mentioned by first name only, although the 'Jane' is later revealed to be Jane Wyman, before declaring Power 'the love-'em and leave-'em-est guy in Hollywood today!' and speculating who will be next on his list of conquests (1939). That same month, *Movie Mirror* ran a rather bizarre article titled 'If Tyrone Power were married to Hedy Lamarr', which presented the fictional marriage of these two stars, who never worked together, as an 'utterly mad, imaginary romance' (Zeitlin 1939). Two months later, in *Modern Screen*'s 'Tyrone Power plans marriage' (Lee 1939), author Sonia Lee refers to her earlier article 'The woman Tyrone Power will marry', which stressed Power's promise that he would marry an actress, Annabella now having become that actress. In July 1939, the month he married Annabella, *Movie Mirror* ran an article closely resembling the publicity Power's Steve Layton received in *Love is News*, as discussed in Chapter 2. Displaying various headlines about his off-screen romances with Henie and Gaynor, it concludes by stating that he married Annabella that morning and includes a photograph of them cutting their wedding cake (Anon 1939a).

The marriage caused mixed reactions in the press and with fans, and two months after the event *Picture Play*'s 'Do you forgive Tyrone?' begins by suggesting that, although fans had been happy when Gable had married Carole Lombard and Taylor married Barbara Stanwyck, when Power married Annabella 'nothing short of fire and brimstone' broke loose (Manners 1939). This resonates with Annabella's words from several decades later when she told Romina Power that she had received bad press and become 'the monster undermining the career of the "poor young Adonis"!' (Power 2014: 62). That same month, however, *Screenland*'s two-page spread 'The Tyrone Powers at home' featured several 'candid' (but clearly staged) photographs of the couple sitting by their pool, walking arm in arm around the grounds and eating outdoors while dressed in casual attire. By announcing that the 'happy honeymooners' were letting readers 'be their first guests in their new home', the publication attempts to create an intimacy between the couple and fans (Anon 1939b). Likewise, in the magazine's subsequent issue, author Elizabeth Wilson claims to be 'the first writer to get invited to the Tyrone Powers for an intimate look-see at their new home'. Her article was accompanied by several photographs of the interior of their home, including the bedroom, thus it is a very intimate look indeed and almost turns the reader into a voyeur (1939).

Following his marriage, the overarching theme of articles on Power obviously had to change to reflect his new status since he was no longer one of Hollywood's most eligible bachelors. At the turn of the decade, *Movies*' 'Is Tyrone just a tyro?' suggests that Power's 'new responsibilities undoubtedly will have their effect upon his acting', and that since his marriage and becoming stepfather to Annabella's daughter, he had already displayed 'a new poise, an added depth, for he takes his new estate seriously', which 'unquestionably will enhance and elevate him to new levels' (Foye 1940). The following year, the magazine marked the couple's third wedding anniversary with 'A sailin' with Annie and Ty', the nicknames suggesting that Annabella had finally been accepted as Power's wife and was now being presented as an old friend to readers (Anon 1941a).

With his marriage presented in fan magazines as stable, at least at this point, after America joined the war, articles on Power shifted their focus to his military position. This is overtly shown through the titles of articles changing from the likes of 'The private life of the Tyrone Powers' (Anon 1942) to 'The private life of Private Power' (Arnold 1943) within a few months. The latter includes a full-page image of Power looking serious, dressed in uniform and holding up a rifle, as it notes that he is 'well aware that he was tackling the hardest role of his career . . . work[ing] over-time on that role with no assistance from a Hollywood director' (Arnold 1943). Similar is *Screen Guide*'s 'Marines – here comes Ty Power!', which states that 'he doesn't need a stand in to play his new role' (Anon 1942). In 'Why I'm glad to leave Hollywood', apparently written by Power for *Screen Guide*, the actor explains why he should not be given any privileges after enlisting, saying he dislikes 'being referred to as the self-sacrificing Mr. Power, the movie star who gave up a lucrative career to volunteer', since many men made the same, if not more, sacrifices. Comparing himself to others leaving behind wives, and perhaps children, Power presents himself as just another soldier fighting for his country, a gesture that may have helped enlistment numbers (1941).

While in service, and therefore off-screen for the duration, Power continued to appear regularly in fan magazines, only now it was his military life that was being written about. *Movieland*'s 'Tyrone Power's experiences in marine boot camp' (Alderson 1943) and *Motion Picture*'s 'A day with Marine Tyrone Power' (Anon 1943a) includes images of Power conducting tasks like shining boots, cleaning a rifle, giving blood, getting inoculated, doing washing and standing to attention for inspection. By September 1943 he had worked his way up from Private to Second Lieutenant, and while *Movies*' 'High-flying Ty' declared 'Leatherneck Power proves he's got plenty of what it takes' (Vaughan 1944), *Modern Screen* published an article simply called 'Shave tail', a pejorative name for the title. It notes that 'the day they pinned the gold bars to his shoulders, he wouldn't have traded places with a king', and ends by stating that 'Till the war is won – heart, body and mind, Ty's a

Marine' (Zeitlin 1943). The article is accompanied by a portrait of Power in uniform standing behind Annabella, his medals on show, alongside candid photographs of Power cleaning a rifle and visiting Annabella on a film set. Moreover, *Screen Guide*'s December 1943 cover image was a close-up of the smiling Power in uniform.

Power went from *A Yank in the RAF* on-screen to 'Pride of the Yanks' off-screen, the title of a *Modern Screen* article that begins by quoting Annabella as saying 'he's a private in the marines . . . I think I am prouder to say that than if he were a general or an admiral'. It calls their story 'interesting, not because they're movie stars, but because their experience is representative' (Anon 1943b). Indeed, Annabella became the fan magazines' face of the women left at home, with articles such as *Modern Screen*'s 'Her heart wears khaki', which depicted her as 'just like a million other soldiers' sweethearts' (Kerr 1943), and *Screen Guide*'s 'No tears for Tyrone!' noting that, although she awaits Power's return, 'she can sew better than most women and is an expert cook', thus presenting her as courageous, resourceful and self-sufficient (Anon 1943d). Likewise, *Modern Screen*'s 'Always goodbye' (Kinkead 1945) explores their brief few days together during his leave, another story many couples could relate to.

The couple divorced two years after Power returned from the war, and fan magazines also carried this news. *Photoplay* attempted to explain the breakdown of the marriage as a result of the war, since 'like many other service men and their wives, they just didn't make it' (St John 1948). British publication *Picturegoer* discussed the settlement that would provide Annabella with £12,000 a year (equal to £550,763 in 2020), alongside a mention of Power's affair with Lana Turner, the highest profile of his career (Mooring 1948).

Christian and children

After considerable publicity surrounding his romance with Turner, in *Movieland*'s 'Why Lana and Ty agreed to disagree', writer Monica MacKenzie speculates that, although many expected Power and Turner to marry, she believed the romance was over (1948). Referring to Turner's daughter Cheryl Crane, MacKenzie declares that 'Power is marrying no woman with growing children on hand to look after', although he had previously become stepfather to Annabella's daughter. The article proves that Power's newly acquired bachelor status was again making news, suggesting that he 'will continue to make the Hollywood rounds with such girls as Linda Christian, Cyd Charisse, and the other[s]' (1948). While *Photoplay's* 'Take-off' again connects Power with several women, not least Turner and Christian (St John 1948), marriage speculations appeared the following month in *Modern Screen's* 'If this isn't love ...', which claims that Power bought Christian a ring inscribed 'All my love – Ty' (Smith 1948). Later that year, Hymie Fink wrote in *Photoplay's* 'I was there' (Fink 1948) that although every Hollywood photographer had tried for months to capture an image of Power and Christian together, he finally got one after making 'the rounds of those cafes' they would most likely go to; the photograph accompanies the article. Exactly a year earlier, Fink had published another article in the magazine called 'I was there – Horseshoe Hymie has the luck to catch Lana Turner and Ty Power out on their first public date night' (1947). *Screenland's* December 1948 issue then carried the article 'The next Mrs. Ty Power?' featuring a full-length shot of Christian alongside smaller images of the pair playing cards and one of a shirtless Power (Anon 1948).

Their wedding attracted the international press, with photographs taken during the ceremony gracing the covers of publications such as France's *Noir et Blanc* (2 February 1949) and Italy's *Tua* (3 February 1949). Less than three weeks later *Noir et Blanc* featured the couple on its cover again, this time on their honeymoon (23 February 1949) and an almost identical photograph appeared on the front of the Italian publication *Cine Illustrato* (6 March 1949). Both publications also carried similar photographs inside, showing the couple skiing in Austria. In May 1949, several US publications carried the story of their honeymoon, including *Movieland's* 'Alone at last' (Anon), *Motion Picture's* 'Wedding in Rome' (Muir) and *Screenland's* 'Cobina Wright's Party gossip' (Wright), the latter also featuring them as cover stars. *Silver Screen's* 'Truly a love story' includes images from the ceremony, the couple cutting the cake and a shot from outside the church where it reports that mounted police held back eight thousand people from trying to get into the small church that holds only four hundred (MacDonald 1949).

In 1950, Christian (apparently) wrote the article 'So it is with Ty and me' for *Silver Screen*, for which she is credited as 'Mrs. Tyrone Power'. The article explores her two recent miscarriages, the couple's desire to start a family and Power's wish for a son to carry on the family name. She notes that Power was engaged in the stage production of *Mister Roberts*, calling it his 'first important starring role on stage' and stating the importance of it being on the London stage since this is where his great-grandfather and father famously played. Within a couple of months, rumours that the marriage was starting to dissolve began to emerge. The *Modern Screen* article, 'They're talking about the Powers', hints at Christian's infidelity, since she had been seen around town with several men, none of whom was her husband, while Power worked on the stage six nights a week (La Falaise 1951). These rumours were quashed, however, when their first daughter Romina was born in October 1951; *Hollywood Family Album* carried the story 'Ty's Romina: The thrill that comes once in a lifetime' alongside photographs of the beautiful, beaming couple and their baby. Although the article ends on a rather melancholy note by stating, 'For Ty, it's only the beginning of a dream come true. He wants a son, and Linda has promised him one. Next year, maybe there'll be a Ty, Jr.!' (Anon 1951).

Even after the birth of a second daughter, Taryn, rumours of a break-up never ceased. Elizabeth MacDonald, who had written 'Truly a love story' before their marriage, wrote 'Exploding those Ty–Linda rumors' for *Silver Screen* in August 1953. MacDonald declares that, while people always wonder about the durability of a rebound romance, for Power it was a double rebound when he went from Annabella to Turner to Christian, thus perhaps it was not 'truly a love story' after all. December's issue explores these rumours further, with author Earl Wilson stating, 'they can't break up – they CAN'T – it wouldn't be fair to Italy!' and that, 'I've heard all the rumors about the marriage not working. And everytime I've checked; well, it IS working' (1953). The following year they were again presented as the perfect family in *Hollywood Family Album*'s 'Ty Power: It's easy to spoil a miracle' (Anon 1954). But in 1955, it was announced that the pair would divorce, with Sheilah Graham calling it 'a marriage that had had rumors swimming around it almost from its inception. The first year . . . you could get odds that the whole thing was doomed' (1955), while the *Movie Stars Parade*'s article 'Never meant to last' suggests that the couple took their marriage vows too lightly, which is why they were easily broken (Anon 1955).

In March 1955, the pioneering scandal and gossip magazine *Hollywood Confidential* published the article 'Why Linda Christian and Ty Power went phffft!' It blames their break-up on Christian's wandering eye, and specifically her affair with Edmund Purdom, whom she later married and quickly divorced. Although the article discusses Christian's infidelities, it makes no mention of Power's, of which there were rumoured to be many. It indicates that she was playing around with Purdom while Power was 'slaving under the Kleig lights', but that his manners were nothing but impeccable when his wife flirted under his nose (Wright 1955). While *Silver Screen's* cover carries the tagline 'The inside story of the Ty Powers' break-up!', in similar terms to *Hollywood Confidential,* an accompanying article declares that 'after five years of a stormy marriage, the Powers have phffft' (Johns 1955). Power was back in *Hollywood Confidential* in September when his affair with Anita Ekberg made the news. The article, 'Why Tyrone Power caught a chill from Ekberg the iceberg', suggests that even this great screen lover could not thaw out the iceberg actress (Peters 1955). Thus, it seems that although both the press and film fans were shocked when Power divorced Annabella, with Christian it was not unexpected.

The final years

A new chapter seemed to be beginning in Power's life once he entered his forties. Becoming an independent agent for the first time after being signed with Twentieth Century-Fox for almost two decades, he was able to choose his own roles which showed a new diversity and range to his acting skills. As well as founding his own production company, he returned to the stage where he worked extensively throughout the 1950s in the UK and US. However, just months after marrying for the third time and with a baby on the way, on 15 November 1958 Power died of a heart attack at the age of forty-four in Madrid, Spain while filming *Solomon and Sheba.* Magazines and newspapers worldwide carried the news, it made front page headlines worldwide and many publications carried features on the event for months afterwards. Since his wife, Debbie, was due to give birth just a few months later, and because Power had always wanted a boy to carry on the family name, articles like 'Letter to an unborn child' (Anon 1959b) and 'Will Tyrone Power's last prayer be answered?' (Dinter 1959) appeared alongside more traditional tributes 'Goodnight sweet prince' (Anon 1959a), 'The death of Tyrone Power' (Canfield 1959) and 'The scene that killed Tyrone Power' (Anon 1959c). The last article discusses Power's early life and family legacy, his three marriages, his many romances, his screen and stage work and concludes with his promise of the future since his child was due the following month. Echoing the sentiment of most tributes to Power, the article fittingly ends: 'he was a great gentleman, and a great star; we say farewell to him with sadness. The End.'

Power on stage

Coming before and during his film career, when discussing Power's off-screen image his stage work also merits attention. In order to work on the London stage, where his namesake father had become famous, Power turned down the lead role in *The Robe*. Although it is impossible to analyse historical, live and lost performances, there does exist a 1953 recording of Power's excellent rendition of Stephen Vincent Benét's epic poem *John Brown's Body* alongside Judith Anderson and Raymond Massey, the oral element being the most important here, since the performers either stood or sat reciting the poem on a mostly bare stage.

An obvious difference between stage and screen actors is that the former stands in front of a live audience as a corporeal presence, whereas the latter has already performed, and been recorded by, a camera before audiences see their work. Walter Benjamin suggests that the screen actor's performance has a 'twofold consequence', in that he or she does not have the chance to adjust to the audience during their performance the way a stage actor does (2007: 25). Therefore, he continues, the audience can become a critic without any personal contact with the actor. 'The audience's identification with the actor is really an identification with the camera. Consequently, the audience takes the position of the camera' (2007: 25). However, if we are in the balcony of a large auditorium filled to capacity, are we really experiencing 'personal contact with the actor', as Benjamin claims? It is true that, unlike with a screen actor, we could alter a stage actor's performance by shouting out or doing something equally as distracting, but if we are merely watching a performance on stage how much personal contact do we really have with the actor? True, we are in the same room at the same time, but so are hundreds if not thousands of others, whereas we can watch a film alone. There are no close-ups and we decide where we are looking, thus we could look at the same performer throughout or scan the cast, whereas with film that choice is taken away from us.

In his study of contemporary American actor George Clooney, who possesses a similar star image to Power's, Paul McDonald notes that while Clooney achieved his initial fame and recognition in *ER* (NBC, 1994–2009), this also gave him a strong association with the 'inferior' medium of television, thus making it challenging for him to be taken seriously as a film performer (2019: 45). In Power's case, having started his career on the 'legitimate' stage, as the theatre was known at the time, he moved into what was deemed inferior, or lowbrow, cinematic work. However, despite his name and the legacy attached to it, Power did not achieve fame on the stage like his ancestors did (although perhaps he may have had he dedicated more years to it).

Power appeared regularly on stage in bit parts alongside his father before his minor roles in the films *Tom Brown of Culver*, *Flirtation Walk* and *Northern Frontier*. Returning to the stage, Power progressed to supporting roles in *Romeo and Juliet* (1935) and *St Joan* (1936), both starring Katharine Cornell, before being discovered by a Hollywood talent scout while performing in the latter. As Romina Power notes, her father longed to return to the stage and wanted it written into his contract with Twentieth Century-Fox that he be allowed to appear on stage for part of every year, but this never materialised (2014).

Power's return to the stage in the final years of his life almost went full circle when he starred opposite Cornell in the 1955 production of Christopher Fry's *The Dark is Light Enough*. Given that Power's stage work was a series of historical performances given to a live audience and were not recorded, it cannot be analysed in the same way that his films can. Nevertheless, the fact that ephemeral items such as programmes and playbills still exist allows us to see when and where performances occurred, while reviews show what theatre critics observing performances felt at the time. Referring to Cornell's performance as 'wonderful', Thomas K. Schwabacher, in *The Harvard Crimson* (Harvard University's daily student newspaper run entirely by undergraduates), calls her stage presence 'so overwhelming' that other actors often 'succumb to the temptation to shout in order to make an equal impact on the audience' before concluding that 'this defect is most noticeable in the performance of Tyrone Power . . . He projects the surface brashness of his character, but most of the other possible shadings of characterization are lost in verbal athletics', and that the play only works when Cornell is on stage (3 May 1955). However, John Chapman of *The New York Herald Tribune* suggests that when Power is 'doing the talking' the play comes 'alive, for he is a handsome vigorous actor with one of the best and clearest voices on the stage today'; the article includes a headshot of Power dressed in a tuxedo (24 February 1955). Likewise, John McClain of the *New York American Journal* praises Power as 'certainly in our top cadre of young actors', delivering his lines with strength and assurance and brilliantly projecting his character (24 February 1955), while Richard Watts Jr of the *New York Post* calls Power 'an excellent actor' and 'impressively forthright in the curiously unsatisfactory and equivocal role of the deserter' (24 February 1955).

The recording of *John Brown's Body*, directed by Charles Laughton, confirms the words of these reviews since Power's impressive performance, for which he relied on his oral skills, vocal control and voice projection, proves that he did not need Hollywood lights or close-ups in order to be viewed as a great actor – if anything he needed to move away from them in order to prove his worth as an actor on the same level as his father, since his physical appearance was such a consuming part of his star image for so long and took away from his actorly skills, which are reinforced here.

Conclusion

Star image

This book has presented the first substantial academic study of Tyrone Power, an important but considerably overlooked actor of Hollywood cinema's classical era. Exploring the construction and subsequent developments of Power's star image across his oeuvre, it has discussed each of his films, to a greater or lesser degree, using a genre studies approach to help organise his almost fifty films. Grounded in star studies, performance theory and textual analysis have also been used to explore Power's acting skills and visual presence within his films, while the book has placed them within their socio-historical, geographical and industrial frameworks, since stars are historically, culturally and socially significant.

Given that Power was consistently presented to audiences as a highly desirable object of the erotic gaze across his career and the genres he worked in, a central focus of the book has been the exploration of male beauty as a social construction, evaluating ways in which Power's star image was created and developed within the Hollywood film industry of mid-twentieth century America. Female characters often acted as surrogates for the audience in their appreciation of his good looks, which were reinforced by cinematic techniques such as bright lighting, extreme close-ups and costuming. Given this strong focus on his beauty, it is unusual perhaps that Power's face and body were frequently concealed and disguised on-screen; although this may have been done knowingly by filmmakers, leading to their eventual reveal having a greater impact on audiences.

Despite his early death, Power's career spanned the three decades of Hollywood's studio era from the 1930s to the 1950s, during which time he was one of the industry's most important leading stars; thus an exploration of his star image clarifies how both his home studio and the film industry in general functioned at this time. This brief conclusion explores the tension between individual stars and Hollywood's industrial approach to developing stars, and highlights Power's importance to both

Hollywood and film history in general, while suggesting why he is a significant star in need of reappraisal. According to McDonald, by focusing on singular personalities, Hollywood stardom 'celebrates exceptional individualism. What this approach obscures, however, is how stardom is a system, a set of industrially coordinated collective inputs for producing performers as exceptional individuals' (2019: 3). This tension remains poorly examined, however, as film studies has long neglected discussions that focus on individual performers or performances (Pomerance and Stevens 2019).

As my discussion of his career demonstrates, Power often portrayed cocky youths in his early films, being highly animated in comedies and musicals of the 1930s, before becoming more solemn as he matured and acquired a more staid, masculine presence that was both a natural biological process and part of the studio's adjusting of his persona as he aged. This is perhaps most overtly shown through the comparison of Power's 1941 role in *Blood and Sand*, in which his Juan Gallardo is an active young bullfighter determined to prove himself the best matador in history, with his 1957 character Jake Barnes in *The Sun Also Rises*, a jaded spectator of the sport, with echoes of Power's earlier filmic self now being presented in the bullring by more youthful players as Jake observes them from the stands, resulting in both Power and audiences becoming spectators to the ghost of his previous self.

Apollo incarnate

Predicated on the success of art critic Dave Hickey's *The Invisible Dragon: Four Essays on Beauty* (1993), Peg Zeglin Brand suggested at the turn of the century that beauty, 'once deemed timeless, unchanging, and universal by the ancient Greek philosopher Plato, is currently back in fashion' (2000: 6). Indeed, although much has been written about beauty over the last two decades, as noted in the introduction, this has mostly occurred within the discipline of fine art.

In 1896, George Santayana explored the manifestations of beauty, suggesting that its more familiar elements of matter, form and expression are 'least likely to lead us into needless artificiality', but that there must always be artificiality in 'the discursive description of anything given in consciousness' ([1896] 1955: 260). Artificially and the social construction of beauty is intrinsic to Hollywood cinema and the creation of star images, both female and male. Lighting, framing, make-up, costume and post-production all contribute to artificiality in order to create the illusion of spectacular, and unattainable, on-screen beauty. Indeed, the many extreme close-ups of Power are truly remarkable, and his brightly lit face in films such as *Marie Antoinette* is still impactful over eighty years later.

Power's face and body combine to create his beauty, and therefore his recognisable star image, individually (such as his eyes or torso) or as a composite whole. Just as Santayana suggests that 'the world of nature and fancy, which are the objects of aesthetic feeling, can be divided into parts in space and time' ([1896] 1955: 261), the progression of Power's career trajectory can be explored across different genres and decades, consideration being made for his appearance and age within each, perhaps most obvious when examining his first and final dramas at either side of his career, or comparing his performances in *Love is News* and its remake, *That Wonderful Urge*, eleven years apart. Moreover, unlike historical audiences we can watch Power's films in chronological order or out of sequence, resulting in gradual or subtle changes in his looks and developments of his performance skills with the former or more striking differences through the latter.

Since he is an actor, we know that when Power portrays either fictional characters, like Stanton Carlisle and Leonard Vole, or actual people, such as Eddy Duchin and Martin Maher, he is essentially still Power, just as his constructed off-screen image is a form of the constructed star persona 'Tyrone Power'. Power's many characterisations demonstrate Santayana's discussion of 'the earlier and the alter impressions made by the same object', and his suggestion that 'we can ascertain the coexistence of one impression with another' ([1896] 1955: 261). Thus, by applying a genre approach, this book explores, for example, Power's wartime characters side by side, demonstrating that they are all Power, just different versions of him; extra-filmic material adds yet another layer since he undertook active war duty off-screen. These impressions can also come from 'the memory of others' (Santayana [1896] 1955: 261), thus historical reviews, articles, fan letters, interviews with co-stars and interviews with fans who were alive during Power's career can be useful sources. Recent memory can provide further context with new or younger audiences discussing historical stars, sharing stories of films they have seen, the first film they saw a star in, their favourite performance, what they consider the star's best performance or when they looked their most beautiful on-screen, for example. In the digital age, this is much easier to achieve since fans worldwide are no longer restricted by geographical locations and limited film screenings but are able to communicate with other fans globally.

Santayana concludes that beauty, as we feel it, is 'indescribable: what it is or what it means can never be said'. Calling this feeling 'an affection of the soul . . . a pang, a dream, a pure pleasure', he declares that beauty exists for the same reason that an object which is beautiful exists. Thus, it is an experience that appears to be the 'clearest manifestation of perfection, and the best evidence of its possibility' ([1896] 1955: 262). Indeed, Power's breathtaking beauty embodies perfection of the male form, presenting audiences with a modern version of ancient Greek sculpture, of a twentieth-century Apollo incarnate.

Daniel S. Hamermesh enquires as to what human beauty is, and how it varies by gender, race and age (2011: 11). With a film star, beauty can vary in relation to the age or appearance of the same individual on-screen over several years and sometimes decades. Perhaps the most important question to ask, according to Hamermesh, is whether 'observers have at least somewhat consistent views of what makes a person beautiful' (2011: 11). This concept is particularly interesting when applied to Hollywood stars and their ability to create believable performances. For example, it would be less convincing if Power's and Welles's roles were reversed in *Prince of Foxes* or if Charles Laughton had played Leonard Vole in *Witness for the Prosecution*. However, in order to consider this point, we must first attempt to define beauty. Hamermesh offers an online dictionary definition: 'the quality or aggregate of qualities in a person or thing that gives pleasure to the senses or pleasurably exalts the mind or spirit' (2011: 11). Calling economics the study of scarcity and the behaviour that scarcity creates, Hamermesh suggests that 'a prerequisite for studying beauty as an economic issue must be that beauty is scarce' (2011: 6). This is certainly true of the Hollywood film industry, where performers like Power become financially viable stars because their rare beauty appeals to audiences.

Exploring how the scarcity of beauty arises from the genetic difference in physical appearance, Hamermesh suggests that some people are viewed as better looking than others through 'some socially determined criteria'. Thus the term '"scarce beauty" is redundant – by its nature beauty is scarce' (2011: 6). Hence, while the relationship between beauty and nature or beauty and art has been habitually explored, in anthropological studies beauty still tends to be reserved for discussions of women and viewed as detrimental to men's masculinity. However, both women and increasingly more men are investing copious amounts of money in the beauty industry in attempts to achieve unattainable beauty through Botox, face lifts, lip injections and so on. Even the use of cosmetics, the act of painting the face, is done professionally by make-up artists attempting to create beauty. This may also be a reason why male beauty is the least discussed form of beauty, thus perhaps it is the most natural and scarcest beauty there is (although male stars are also, to a degree, 'made up'). We might then wonder what it tells us about an individual's masculinity if beauty has been and remains an industry predominantly aimed at women, with unattainable beauty still the endpoint.

Hamermesh enquires as to whether beauty is the result of hair or hair colour, weight, height, physiognomy, internal beauty, facial expression, dress or a combination of these (2011: 12). If we consider these attributes in relation to Power, it is obvious that he typifies Western society's ongoing notion of tall, dark-haired males as the most attractive, their physical dominance being essential to their appeal. Power was significantly taller than most of his female co-stars and many of his male co-stars, thus making him a dominant presence on-screen, although he was also not too tall. His dark hair was usually worn short and slicked back in films set in modern times or slightly longer and wavy in historical films, sometimes with a carefully placed strand or two out of place adding to his visual appeal. Although Power looked rather thin at the start of his career, he soon bulked up and his broad shoulders and muscular arms were particularly highlighted in *The Black Swan*'s shirtless scenes and through the tight white t-shirt he wears in *Nightmare Alley*. Thus, once he had passed the adolescent stage, Power was neither too thin nor was he flabby or fat; instead he was toned, athletic and strong, befitting the increased number of action-adventure films he was cast in.

Despite Joan Fontaine's ironic critique of his face in *This Above All*, the composition of Power's face was extremely symmetrical and reflected the almost ideal beauty that had been contemplated since the original musings on the subject by ancient Greek philosophers. Power had an extremely pleasant face that looked good from any angle and from either side, whether in full face or profile, which is certainly not true of all stars. Additionally, his strong jawline connoting extreme masculinity was juxtaposed with a well-formed, slightly upturned nose, dark eyes, exceedingly long eyelashes and heavy eyebrows that combined to present a striking face. Filmmakers repeatedly focused on Power's face, especially in prolonged close-ups, such as the final scene in *Lloyds of London* and when Tim wakes up in a hospital in *A Yank in the RAF*; these scenes also relied on Power's acting skills, since there is no dialogue to express meaning.

Although off-screen, in posed photographs in magazines and paparazzi images, Power often wore tailored suits or casual attire such as polo shirts and slacks, his on-screen costumes varied greatly in order to suit the roles, although he was most often seen in a tuxedo, which emphasised his good looks, along with historical costumes that displayed his muscular frame. A lack of clothing also highlighted Power's beauty, no more so than in *Son of Fury*. Thus for Power it was the combination of the components put forward by Hamermesh when attempting to reach a definition for the widely used but complex and almost undefinable term 'beauty'. As a quintessentially tall, dark and handsome leading man, Power's status as a leading heartthrob surely proves this point. However, we might consider whether we view Power, or other beautiful stars, as more attractive in roles where their character is more pleasant or sympathetic.

As Hamermesh notes, standards of facial beauty differ across societies and change over time; however, 'most people even today would agree that [Rudolph] Valentino was quite beautiful – presumably this was a major underpinning of his success as a movie actor' (2011: 13). As Power's foremost predecessor in looks and audience appeal, it seems a fitting quote with which to end this book. Power's beauty was also enduring and timeless, still able to make an impression over sixty years after his death. But it has also detracted from his performance skills for far too long, and this book has aimed to readdress and reconfigure Power's status and prove that he was a great star, a great beauty and a great actor.

Power's filmography

Abandon Ship! (AKA *Seven Waves Away*) (Richard Sale, 1957)
Alexander's Ragtime Band (Henry King, 1938)
Ali Baba Goes to Town (David Butler, 1937)
American Guerrilla in the Philippines (Fritz Lang, 1950)
Black Rose, The (Henry Hathaway, 1950)
Black Swan, The (Henry King, 1942)
Blood and Sand (Rouben Mamoulian, 1941)
Brigham Young: Frontiersman (Henry Hathaway, 1940)
Café Metropole (Edward H. Griffith, 1937)
Captain from Castile (Henry King, 1947)
Crash Dive (Archie Mayo, 1943)
Day-Time Wife (Gregory Ratoff, 1939)
Diplomatic Courier (Henry Hathaway, 1952)
Eddy Duchin Story, The (George Sidney, 1956)
Flirtation Walk (Frank Borzage, 1934)
Girls' Dormitory (Irving Cummings, 1936)
House in the Square, The (AKA *I'll Never Forget You*) (Roy Ward Baker, 1952)
In Old Chicago (Henry King, 1938)
Jesse James (Henry King, 1939)
Johnny Apollo (Henry Hathaway, 1940)
King of the Khyber Rifles (Henry King, 1953)
Ladies in Love (Edward H. Griffith, 1936)
Lloyds of London (Henry King, 1936)
Long Gray Line, The (John Ford, 1955)
Love is News (Tay Garnett, 1937)
Luck of the Irish, The (Henry Koster, 1948)
Marie Antoinette (W. S. Van Dyke, 1938)
Mark of Zorro, The (Rouben Mamoulian, 1940)
Mississippi Gambler, The (Rudolph Maté, 1953)
Nightmare Alley (Edmund Goulding, 1947)
Northern Frontier (Sam Newfield, 1935)

Pony Soldier (AKA *MacDonald of the Canadian Mounties*) (Joseph M. Newman, 1952)
Prince of Foxes (Henry King, 1949)
Rains Came, The (Clarence Brown, 1939)
Rawhide (Henry Hathaway, 1951)
Razor's Edge, The (Edmund Goulding, 1946)
Rising of the Moon, The (John Ford, 1957)
Rose of Washington Square (Gregory Ratoff, 1939)
Second Fiddle (Sidney Lanfield, 1939)
Second Honeymoon (Walter Lang, 1937)
Solomon and Sheba (King Vidor, 1959)
Son of Fury: The Story of Benjamin Blake (John Cromwell, 1942)
Suez (Allan Dwan, 1938)
Sun Also Rises, The (Henry King, 1957)
That Wonderful Urge (Robert B. Sinclair, 1948)
Thin Ice (AKA *Lovely to Look At*) (Sidney Lanfield, 1937)
This Above All (Anatole Litvak, 1942)
Tom Brown of Culver (William Wyler, 1932)
Untamed (Henry King, 1955)
Witness for the Prosecution (Billy Wilder, 1957)
Yank in the RAF, A (Henry King, 1941)

Bibliography

Alderson, John (1943), 'Tyrone Power's experiences in marine boot camp', *Movieland* (April).

Altman, Rick (1999), *Film/Genre*, London: BFI.

Anderson, Janice (1985), *History of the Movie Comedy*, New York: Exeter Books.

Anon (1939a) 'The headline romances of Tyrone Power', *Movie Mirror* (July).

Anon (1939b) 'The Tyrone Powers at home', *Screenland* (September).

Anon (1939c), 'Marie Antoinette', *Film Weekly*, 4 February.

Anon (1941a) 'A sailin' with Annie and Ty', *Movies* (June).

Anon (1941b), '*Blood and Sand* tops Film Week at the theatres', *Roanoke Rapids Herald*, 5 June.

Anon (1942) 'The private life of the Tyrone Powers', *Movies* (October).

Anon (1943a) 'A day with Marine Tyrone Power', *Motion Picture* (June).

Anon (1943b) 'Pride of the Yanks', *Modern Screen* (February).

Anon (1943c), '"The Black Swan" is theater bill of week at theaters in city', *Roanoke Rapids Herald*, 28 January.

Anon (1943d), 'No tears for Tyrone!', *Screen Guide* (January).

Anon (1948), 'The next Mrs. Ty Power?' *Screenland* (December).

Anon (1949), 'Alone at last!', *Movieland* (May).

Anon (1951), 'Ty's Romina: The thrill that comes once in a lifetime', *Hollywood Family Album* (October).

Anon (1954), 'Ty Power: It's easy to spoil a miracle', *Hollywood Family Album* (February–April).

Anon (1955), 'Never meant to last', *Movie Stars Parade* (January).

Anon (1959a) 'Goodnight sweet prince', *Life Stories* (no. 9).

Anon (1959b), 'Letter to an unborn child', *Movie Stars TV-Closeup* (February).

Anon (1959c), 'The scene that killed Tyrone Power', *Screen Stories* (March).

Arce, Hector (1979), *The Secret Life of Tyrone Power*, New York: William Morrow and Company.

Aristotle ([4 BCE] (1964), 'Rhetoric, Book I', in Alfred Hofstadter and Richard Kuhns (eds), *Philosophies of Art and Beauty: Selected Readings in Aesthetics from Plato to Heidegger*, New York: Random House.

Arnheim, Rudolph (1994), 'A god's perfection', in Laurence Goldstein (ed.), *The Male Body: Features, Destinies, Exposures*, Ann Arbor, MI: University of Michigan Press, pp. 151–2.

Arnold, Maxine (1943), 'The private life of Private Power', *Stardom* (June).

Astor, Mary (1967), *Mary Astor: A Life on Film*, New York: Delacorte Press.

Babington, Bruce (2001), *British Stars and Stardom: From Alma Taylor to Sean Connery*, Manchester and New York: Manchester University Press.

Balio, Tino (1993), *Grand Design: Hollywood as a Modern Business Enterprise, 1930–1939*, New York: Charles Scribner's Sons.

Barnes, Jennifer (2017), *Shakespearean Star: Laurence Olivier and National Cinema*, Cambridge: Cambridge University Press.

Baron, Cynthia (2015), *Denzel Washington*, London: BFI.

Barthes, Roland, translated by Andy Stafford (2004), 'Dandyism and fashion', in Andy Stafford and Michael Carter (eds), *The Language of Fashion*, Berg: Oxford and New York, pp. 65–9.

Basinger, Jeanine (1986), *The World War II Combat Film: Anatomy of a Genre*, New York: Columbia University Press.

Belafonte, Dennis (1979), *The Films of Tyrone Power*, Secaucus, NJ: Citadel Press.

Benezra, Neal and Olga M. Viso (1999), *Regarding Beauty: A View of the Late Twentieth Century*, Washington, DC: Smithsonian Institution.

Benjamin, Walter (2007), 'The work of art in the mechanical reproduction', in Sean Redmond and Su Holmes (eds), *Stardom and Celebrity: A Reader*. Sage Publications: Los Angeles, London, New Delhi and Singapore, pp. 17–24.

Bolton, Lucy and Julie Lobalzo Wright (eds) (2016), *Lasting Screen Stars: Personas that Endure and Images that Fade*, London: Palgrave Macmillan.

Bordo, Susan (1999), *The Male Body: A New Look at Men in Public and in Private*, New York: Farrar, Straus and Giroux.

Bordo, Susan (2000), 'Beauty (re)discovers the male body', in Peg Zeglin Brand (ed.), *Beauty Matters*, Bloomington and Indianapolis, IN: Indiana University Press, pp. 112–54.

Bradley, Larry C. (1980), *Jesse James: The Making of a Legend*, Nevada, MO: Larren Publishers.

Brand, Peg Zeglin (2000), 'Introduction: How beauty matters', in Peg Zeglin Brand (ed.), *Beauty Matters*, Bloomington and Indianapolis: Indiana University Press, pp. 1–23.

Brown, Wilson (1939), 'Tyrone loves 'em and leaves 'em', *Motion Picture* (April).

Bruzzi, Stella (1997), *Undressing Cinema: Clothing and Identity in the Movies*, London and New York: Routledge.

Bruzzi, Stella (2005), *Bringing Up Daddy: Fatherhood and Masculinity in Postwar Hollywood*, London: BFI.

Burgoyne, Robert (2008), *The Hollywood Historical Film*, Oxford: Blackwell Publishing.

Burke, Doreen Bolger (1987), 'Painters and sculptors in a decorative age', in Metropolitan Museum of Art (ed.), *In Pursuit of Beauty: Americans and the Aesthetic Movement* (exhibition catalogue), New York, pp. 295–339.

Butler, Judith (1990), *Gender Trouble: Feminism and the Subversion of Identity*, New York: Routledge.

Byars, Jackie (1991), *All That Hollywood Allows: Re-Reading Gender in 1950s Melodrama*, Chapel Hill, NC and London: University of North Carolina Press.

Cameron, Deborah (2011), 'Performing gender identity: Young men's talk and the construction of heterosexual masculinity', in Jennifer Coates and Pia Pichler (eds), *Language and Gender: A Reader* (2nd edition), West Sussex: Wiley-Blackwell, pp. 250–62.

Camp, Dan (1937), 'Tyrone's mother sizes up his girls', *Motion Picture* (October).

Campbell, Andrew and Nathan Griffith (1994), 'The male body and contemporary art', in Laurence Goldstein (ed.), *The Male Body: Features, Destinies, Exposures*, Ann Arbor, MI: University of Michigan Press, pp. 153–76.

Canfield, Alice (1959), 'The death of Tyrone Power', *Motion Picture* (March).

Casper, Drew (2007), *Postwar Hollywood 1946–1962*, MA, Oxford and Victoria: Blackwell Publishing.

Chopra-Gant, Mike (2006), *Hollywood Genres and Postwar America: Masculinity, Family and Nation in Popular Movies and Film Noir*, London and New York: I. B. Tauris.

Christian, Linda (1950), 'So it is with Ty and me', *Silver Screen* (November).

Coates, Jennifer (2011), 'Pushing at the boundaries: The expression of alternative masculinities', in Jennifer Coates and Pia Pichler (eds), *Language and Gender: A Reader* (2nd edition), West Sussex: Wiley-Blackwell, pp. 263–74.

Cohan, Steven (1997), *Masked Men: Masculinity and the Movies in the Fifties*, Bloomington and Indianapolis, IN: Indiana University Press.

Coyne, Michael (1997), *The Crowded Prairie: American National Identity in the Hollywood Western*, London and New York: I. B. Tauris.

Custen, George F. (1992), *Bio/Pics: How Hollywood Constructed Public History*, New Brunswick, NJ: Rutgers University Press.

Davis, Ronald L. (1993), *The Glamour Factory: Inside Hollywood's Big Studio System*, University Park, TX: Southern Methodist University Press.

Davis, Ronald L. (1995), *John Ford: Hollywood's Old Master*, Norman, OK and London: University of Oklahoma Press.

Davis, Steven L. (2008), 'New Deal Masculinities: Working Class, Readers, Male Beauty, and Pulp Magazines in the 1930s', in Steven L. Davis and Maglina Lubovich (eds), *Hunks, Hotties and Pretty Boys: Twentieth-Century Representations of Male Beauty*. Newcastle upon Tyne: Cambridge Scholars Publishing, pp. 49–82.

De Cordova, Richard (2001), *Picture Personalities: The Emergence of the Star System in America*, Champaign, IL: University of Illinois Press.

Deleyto, Celestino (2009), *The Secret Life of Romantic Comedy*, Manchester and New York: Manchester University Press.

Dennis, Jeffery P. (2008), 'The teen idol: "Youthful muscles" from *Andy Hardy* to *High School Musical*', in Steven L. Davis and Maglina Lubovich (eds), *Hunks, Hotties and Pretty Boys: Twentieth-Century Representations of Male Beauty*. Newcastle upon Tyne: Cambridge Scholars Publishing, pp. 83–111.

Derrida, Jacques, translated by Avital Ronell (1980), 'The law of genre', *Critical Inquiry*, 7(1), 55–81.

Dinter, Charlotte (1959), 'Will Tyrone Power's last prayer be answered?' *Photoplay* (February).

Dixon, Wheeler Winston (2006), *American Cinema of the 1940s: Themes and Variations*, Oxford: Berg.

Doherty, Thomas (1993), *Projections of War: Hollywood, American Culture, and World War II*, New York and Chichester, West Sussex: Columbia University Press.

Dyer, Richard (1979), *Stars*, London: BFI.

Dyer, Richard (1982), 'Don't look now: The male pin-up', *Screen*, 23(3–4), 61–73.

Dyer, Richard (1997), *White: Essays on Race and Culture*, Oxon: Routledge.

Eberwein, Robert (2005), *The War Film*, New Brunswick, NJ and London: Rutgers University Press.

Ellis, John (1982), *Visible Fictions*, London: Routledge & Kegan Paul.

Epstein, Barbara (1994), 'Masculinity and the culture of anxiety in the postwar United States', *Rethinking Marxism: A Journal of Economics, Culture & Society*, 7 (2), 28–37.

Evans, Delight (1937), 'An open letter to Robert Taylor', *Screenland* (March).

Farber, Stephen (2001), 'A cynic ahead of his time', in Robert Horton (ed.), *Billy Wilder: Interviews*, Jackson, MS: University Press of Mississippi, pp. 161–5.

Fink, Hymie (1947), 'I was there – Horseshoe Hymie has the luck to catch Lana Turner and Ty Power out on their first public date night', *Photoplay* (August).

Fink, Hymie (1948), 'I was there', *Photoplay* (August).

Finler, Joel W. (1984), 'Tyrone Power', in Robyn Karney (ed.), *The Movie Stars Story*, London: Octopus Books. p. 84.

Fitch, Laura Ellsworth (1938), 'Is Ty Power on a new love quest?' *Picture Play* (October).

Flugel, J. C. (1971), *The Psychology of Clothes*, London: Hogarth Press.

Foye, Thomas (1940), 'Is Tyrone just a tyro?' *Movies* (February).

Fyne, Robert (1994), *The Hollywood Propaganda of World War II*, New York and London: Scarecrow Press.

Gallagher, Mark (2016), *Tony Leung Chiu-Wai*, London: BFI.

Girelli, Elisabetta (2014), *Montgomery Clift, Queer Star*, Detroit, MI: Wayne State University Press.

Glancy, Mark (1999), *When Hollywood Loved Britain: The Hollywood 'British' Film 1939–45*, Manchester and New York: Manchester University Press.

Graham, Sheilah (1955), 'Who's gonna get the nude statue?' *Sheilah Graham's Hollywood Yearbook 1955*, New York: Dell.

Guiles, Fred Lawrence (1979), *Tyrone Power: The Last Idol*, London and New York: Granada.

Gussow, Mel (1971), *Zanuck: Don't Say Yes Until I Finish Talking*, New York: W. H. Allen.

Hackspiel-Mikosch, Elisabeth (2009), 'Uniforms and the creation of masculinity', in Peter McNeil and Vicki Karaminas (eds), *The Men's Fashion Reader*, Oxford and New York: Berg, pp. 117–29.

Hall, Gladys (1938), 'Why should I marry?' *Modern Screen* (August).

Hamermesh, Daniel S. (2011), *Beauty Pays: Why Attractive People Are More Successful*, Princeton, NJ and Oxford: Princeton University Press.

Harvey, James (1987), *Romantic Comedy in Hollywood, From Lubitsch to Sturges*, New York: Da Capo Press.

Hayes, Barbara (1938), 'How Tyrone Power stole the lonely heart of Janet Gaynor', *Photoplay* (January).

Higashi, Sumiko (2014), *Stars, Fans, and Consumption in the 1950s: Reading Photoplay*, Basingstoke, Hampshire: Palgrave Macmillan.

Higham, Charles and Joel Greenberg (1968), *Hollywood in the Forties*, New York: A. S. Barnes.

Holmes, Janet (2011), "Complimenting – A positive politeness strategy', in Jennifer Coates and Pia Pichler (eds), *Language and Gender: A Reader* (2nd edition), West Sussex: Wiley-Blackwell, pp. 71–88.

Humphries, Reynold (1989), *Fritz Lang: Genre and Representation on His American Films*, Baltimore, MD and London: John Hopkins University Press.

Jeffers McDonald, Tamar (2013), *Doris Day Confidential: Hollywood, Sex and Stardom*, London and New York: I. B. Tauris.

Jeffords, Susan (1989), *The Remasculinization of America: Gender and the Vietnam War*, New Brunswick, NJ: Rutgers University Press.

Jensen, Paul M. (1969), *The Cinema of Fritz Lang*, New York: A. S. Barnes.

Johns, Murray (1955), 'A little too continental', *Silver Screen* (April).

Kant, Immanuel (1964), 'Critique of judgment: Critique of the aesthetical judgment', in Albert Hofstadter and Richard Kuhns (eds), *Philosophies of Art and Beauty: Selected Readings in Aesthetics from Plato to Heidegger*, New York: Random House.

Karney, Robyn (ed.) (1984), *The Movie Stars Story*, London: Octopus Books.

Kelly, Gillian (2016), 'Robert Taylor: The "lost star" with the long career', in Lucy Bolton and Julie Lobalzo Wright (eds), *Lasting Screen Stars: Images that Fade and Personas that Endure*, London: Palgrave Macmillan, pp. 85–98.

Kelly, Gillian (2019), *Robert Taylor: Male Beauty, Masculinity and Stardom in Hollywood*, Jackson, MS: University Press of Mississippi.

Kerr, Jeanne (1943), 'Her heart wears khaki', *Modern Screen* (May).

Kinkead, Jean (1945), 'Always goodbye', *Modern Screen* (March).

Kinsey, Alfred A., Wardell B. Pomeroy and Clyde E. Martin (1948), *Sexual Behavior in the Human Male*, Philadelphia, PA: W. B. Saunders.

Kitses, Jim (1996), *Gun Crazy*, London: BFI.

Knight, George Wilson (1967), *Poets of Action: Incorporating Essays from the Burning Oracle*, London: Methuen.

Koppes, Clayton R. and Gregory D Black (1988), *Hollywood Goes to War: Patriotism, Movies and the Second World War from Ninotchka to Mrs Miniver*, London and New York: I. B. Tauris.

La Falaise, Giselle (1951), 'They're talking about the Powers', *Modern Screen* (February).

Lambert, Gavin (1990), *Norma Shearer: A Life*, London, Sydney, Auckland and Toronto: Hodder & Stoughton.

Lang, Harry (1937), 'They carry a torch for Tyrone', *Hollywood* (July).

Lawrence, Amy (2010), *The Passion of Montgomery Clift*, Berkeley, Los Angeles and London: University of California Press.

Lee, Sonia (1938), 'The woman Tyrone Power will marry', *Movie Mirror* (October).

Lee, Sonia (1939), 'Tyrone Power plans marriage', *Modern Screen* (June).

Lemon, Richard (2001), 'The message in Billy Wilder's Fortune Cookie: "Well, nobody's perfect...", in Robert Horton (ed.), *Billy Wilder: Interviews*, Jackson, MS: University Press of Mississippi, pp. 38–59.

Lev, Peter (2013), *Twentieth Century-Fox: The Zanuck-Skouras Years, 1935–1965*, Austin, TX: University of Texas Press.

Lewi, Grant (1938), 'Whom will Tyrone Power marry?' *Modern Screen* (March).

MacDonald, Elizabeth (1949), 'Truly a love story', *Silver Screen* (May).

MacDonald, Elizabeth (1953), 'Exploding those Ty–Linda rumors' (August).

MacKenzie, Monica (1948), 'Why Lana and Ty agreed to disagree', *Movieland* (March).

Madden, George (1937), 'The real truth about the Sonja Henie–Tyrone Power–Loretta Young triangle', *Movie Mirror* (June).

Maddox, Ben (1937), 'Not too many kisses', *Modern Screen* (July).

Maltby, Richard (1995), *Hollywood Cinema: An Introduction*, Oxford: Blackwell.

Manners, Dorothy (1939), 'Do you forgive Tyrone?' *Picture Play* (September).

Manvell, Roger (1974), *Films and the Second World War*, London: J. M. Dent and Sons.

Mason, Fran (2002), *American Gangster Cinema: From Little Caesar to Pulp Fiction*, Hampshire and New York: Palgrave Macmillan.

Mayer, Geoff and Brian McDonnell (2007), *Encyclopedia of Film Noir*, Westport, CT and London: Greenwood Press.

McDonald, Paul (2019), *George Clooney*, London: BFI.

McDowell, Colin (1997), *The Man of Fashion: Peacock Males and Perfect Gentlemen*, London: Thames and Hudson.

McClain, John (1955), 'Fry Drama Lacks Action', *New York American Journal* (24 February).

McLean, Adrienne L. (2004), *Being Rita Hayworth: Labor, Identify and Hollywood*, New Brunswick, NJ: Rutgers University Press.

McNally, Karen (2008), *When Frankie Went to Hollywood: Frank Sinatra and American Male Identity*, Champaign, IL: University of Illinois Press.

McNeil, Peter and Vicki Karaminas (2009), 'Introduction: The field of men's fashion', in Peter McNeil and Vicki Karaminas, *The Men's Fashion Reader*, Oxford and New York: Berg, pp. 1–9.

McVeigh, Stephen (2007), *The American Western*, Edinburgh: Edinburgh University Press.

Mercer, John (2015), *Rock Hudson*, London: BFI.

Milne, Tom (1969), *Rouben Mamoulian*, London: Thames and Hudson.

Mirsky, Seth (1996), 'Three arguments for the elimination of masculinity', in Björn Krondorfer (ed.), *Men's Bodies, Men's Gods: Male Identities in a (Post-) Christian Culture*, New York and London: New York University Press, pp. 27–39.

Moore, Terry (2008), *How Do You Stay So Young?* Bloomington, IN: Xlibris.

Mooring, W. H. (1948), 'Hollywood once-over', *Picturegoer* (28 February).

Morgan, David, H. J. (2006), 'Theatre of war: Combat, the military, and masculinities', in Stephen M. Whitehead (ed.), *Men and Masculinities: Critical Concepts in Sociology, Volume 2: Materialising Masculinity*, New York and London: Routledge, pp. 444–52.

Morin, Edgar (1961), *The Stars: An Account of the Star System in Motion Pictures*, New York: Grove Press.

Moses, Montrose Jonas (1906), *Famous Actor-Families in America*, New York: Trow Press.

Muir, Florabel (1949), 'Wedding in Rome', *Motion Picture* (May).

Naremore, James (1988), *Acting in the Cinema*, Berkley, Los Angeles, CA and London: University of California Press.

Neale, Steve (2000), *Genre and Hollywood*, Oxon: Routledge.

Newton, Eric (1950), *The Meaning of Beauty*, London, New York and Toronto: Longmans, Green & Co.

Paglia, Camille (1990), *Sexual Personae: Art and Decadence from Nefertiti to Emily Dickinson*, Yale. CT: Yale University Press.

Palmer, R. Barton (2014), 'Cold War noir', in Homer B. Petty and R. Barton Palmer (eds), *Film Noir*, Edinburgh: Edinburgh University Press, pp. 80–102.

Parker, Mark and Deborah Parker (2011), *The DVD and the Study of Film: The Attainable Text*, Basingstoke, Hampshire: Palgrave Macmillan.

Peberdy, Donna (2011), *Masculinity and Film Performance: Male Angst in Contemporary American Cinema*, Basingstoke, Hampshire: Palgrave Macmillan.

Peters, Grant (1955), 'Why Ty Power caught a chill from Ekberg the iceberg', *Hollywood Confidential* (September).

Philips, Gene D. (1980), *Hemingway and Film*, New York: Frederick Ungar.

Plain, Gill (2006), *John Mills and British Cinema: Masculinity, Identity and Nation*, Edinburgh: Edinburgh University Press.

Pollock, Dale M. (2011), 'An unconventional war film: Death, disguise and deception in *Five Graves to Cairo*', in Karen McNally (ed.), *Billy Wilder, Movie-Maker: Critical Essays on the Films*, Jefferson, NC: McFarland and Company.

Pomerance, Murray (2016), *Moment of Action: Riddles of Cinematic Performance*, New Brunswick, NJ and London: Rutgers University Press.

Pomerance, Murray (2019), *Virtuoso: Film Performance and the Actor's Magic*, New York and London: Bloomsbury Academic.

Pomerance, Murray and Kyle Stevens (2019), 'Close-up: Great American performances', in Murray Pomerance and Kyle Stevens (eds), *Close-Up: Great Cinematic Performances Volume 1: America*, Edinburgh: Edinburgh University Press, pp. 1–12.

Power, Romina (2014), *Searching for my Father, Tyrone Power*, place not specified: Prime Concepts.

Power, Tyrone (1941), 'Why I'm glad to leave Hollywood', *Screen Guide* (August).

Power, Tyrone (1946), 'This is what I believe', *Screenland* (August).

Prettejohn, Elizabeth (2005), *Beauty and Art 1750–2000*, Oxford and New York: Oxford University Press.

Pulleine, Tim (1993), 'Tyrone Power', in Edward Buscombe (ed.), *The BFI Companion to the Western*, London: BFI, p. 377.

Reeves, Mary Watkins (1937) 'Evolution of an idol', *Radio Guide*, 9 October.

Rogers, Miriam (1937), 'Tyrone Power would like to marry, but—', *Radio Stars* (November).

Rollyson, Carl (2012), *Hollywood Enigma: Dana Andrews*, Jackson, MS: University Press of Mississippi.

Roper, Michael and John Tosh (2006), 'Histories and the politics of masculinity', in Stephen M. Whitehead (ed.), *Men and Masculinities: Critical Concepts in Sociology. Volume I: Politics and Power*, London and New York: Routledge, pp. 79–99.

Sanders, George (1960), *Memoirs of a Professional Cad*, Palm Springs, CA: Dean Street Press.

Santayana, George ([1896] 1955), *The Sense of Beauty: Being the Outlines of Aesthetic Theory*, New York, Random House.

Schatz, Thomas (1981), *Hollywood Genres: Formulas, Filmmaking and the Studio System*, New York and London: McGraw-Hill.

Schatz, Thomas (1988), *The Genius of the System: Hollywood Filmmaking in the Studio Era*, New York: Pantheon Books.

Schatz, Thomas (1997), *Boom and Bust: American Cinema in the 1940s*, New York: Charles Scribner's Sons.

Schwabacher, Thomas K. (1955), 'The dark is light enough at the Colonial Theatre', *Harvard Crimson* (3 May), available at: https://www.thecrimson.com/article/1955/5/3/the-dark-is-light-enough-pa/ (accessed 13 December 2019).

Shindler, Colin (1979), *Hollywood Goes to War: Films and American Society, 1939–1952*, Oxon: Routledge.

Silver, Alain and Elizabeth Ward (1980), *Film Noir*, London: Secker and Warburg.

Singh, Sunny (2017), *Amitabh Bachchan*, London: BFI.

Slide, Anthony (2010), *Inside the Hollywood Fan Magazine: A History of Star Makers, Fabricators and Gossip Mongers*, Jackson, MS: University Press of Mississippi.

Smith, Gary A. (2018), *Read the Book! See the Movie! From Novel to Film Via 20th Century-Fox*, Albany, GA: BearManor Media.

Smith, Maxine (1948), 'If this isn't love . . .', *Modern Screen* (April).

Solomon, Aubrey (1988), *Twentieth Century-Fox: A Corporate and Financial History*, Metuchen, NJ and London: Scarecrow Press.

Spensley, Dorothy (1937), 'Tyrone Power's bachelor guide to Hollywood', *Movie Mirror* (November).

St John, Elaine (1948), 'Take-off', *Photoplay* (March).

Steinhart, Daniel (2019), *Runaway Hollywood: Internationalizing Postwar Production and Location Shooting*, Berkeley, CA: University of California Press.

Stephens, Michael L. (1995), *Film Noir*, Jefferson, NC and London: McFarland.

Street, Sarah (2001), *Costume and Cinema: Dress Codes in Popular Film*, London and New York: Wallflower.

Thomas, Sarah (2012), *Peter Lorre: Face Maker, Constructing Stardom and Performance in Hollywood and Europe*, New York and Oxford: Berghahn Books.

Thomas, Sarah (2018), *James Mason*, London: BFI.

Thomson, David (1994), *A Biographical History of Film*, London: Andre Deutsch.

Vahimagi, Tise (1993), 'The Mark of Zorro', in Edward Buscombe (ed.), *The BFI Companion to the Western* (new edition), London: BFI, p. 285.

Vaughan, Carolyn (1944), 'High-flying Ty', *Movies* (May).

Vincendeau, Ginette (2013), *Brigitte Bardot*, London: Palgrave Macmillan.

Walsh, Keri (2014), *Mickey Rourke*, London: BFI.

Watts Jr, Richard (1955), 'Christopher Fry thinks it over', *New York Post* (24 February).

Wiethaus, Ulrike (1996), 'Christian piety and the legacy of medieval masculinity', in Stephen B. Boyd, W. Merle Longwood and Mark W. Muesse (eds), *Redeeming Men: Religion and Masculinities*, Louisville, KY: Westminster John Knox Press, pp. 48–61.

Williams, Michael (2013), *Film Stardom, Myth and Classicism: The Rise of Hollywood's Gods*, Basingstoke, Hampshire: Palgrave Macmillan.

Wilson, Earl (1953), 'Once more for Linda', *Silver Screen* (December).

Wilson, Elizabeth (1939), 'How Tyrone Power and Annabella stay romantic though married', *Screenland* (October).

Winter, Walter ([1913] 2018), *Tyrone Power*, place not specified: Franklin Classics.

Wright, Charles A. (1955), 'Why Linda Christian and Ty Power went phffft!', *Hollywood Confidential* (March).

Wright, Cobina (1949), 'Cobina Wright's party gossip', *Screenland* (May).

Young, Gwenda (2018), *Clarence Brown: Hollywood's Forgotten Master*, Lexington, KY: University of Kentucky Press.

Yu, Sabrina and Guy Austin (eds) (2017), *Revisiting Star Studies: Cultures, Themes and Methods*, Edinburgh: Edinburgh University Press.

Zanuck, Darryl F. ([1948] 1993), 'Everybody does it' (memo to Nunnally Johnson), in Rudy Behlmer (ed.), *Memo from Darryl F. Zanuck: The Golden Years at Twentieth Century-Fox*, New York: Grove Press.

Zeitlin, Ida (1939), 'If Tyrone Power were married to Hedy Lamarr', *Movie Mirror* (April).

Zeitlin, Ida (1943), 'Shave tail', *Modern Screen* (September).

Index

Printed in the USA
CPSIA information can be obtained
at www.ICGtesting.com
JSHW011534140823
46514JS00003B/109

9 781474 452953